The Origins of the Modern World

WORLD SOCIAL CHANGE
Series Editor: Mark Selden

Perilous Passage: Mankind and the Global Ascendance of Capital
  Amiya Kumar Bagchi

Water Frontier: Commerce and the Chinese in the Lower Mekong Region, 1750–1880
  Edited by Nola Cooke and Li Tana

First Globalization: The Eurasian Exchange, 1500–1800
  Geoffrey C. Gunn

Istanbul: Between the Global and the Local
  Edited by Caglar Keyder

Origins of the Modern World: A Global and Ecological Narrative
  Robert B. Marks

Leaving China: Media, Mobility, and Transnational Imagination
  Wanning Sun

Masters of Terror: Indonesia's Military and Violence in East Timor
  Edited by Richard Tanter, Desmond Ball, and Gerry van Klinken

Through the Prism of Slavery: Labor, Capital, and World Economy
  Dale W. Tomich

Politics and the Past: On Repairing Historical Injustices
  Edited by John Torpey

The Origins of the Modern World

*A Global and Ecological Narrative from the
Fifteenth to the Twenty-first Century*

Second Edition

ROBERT B. MARKS

ROWMAN & LITTLEFIELD PUBLISHERS, INC.
Lanham • Boulder • New York • Toronto • Oxford

ROWMAN & LITTLEFIELD PUBLISHERS, INC.

Published in the United States of America
by Rowman & Littlefield Publishers, Inc.
A wholly owned subsidary of The Rowman & Littlefield Publishing Group, Inc.
4501 Forbes Boulevard, Suite 200, Lanham, Maryland 20706
www.rowmanlittlefield.com

P.O. Box 317, Oxford OX2 9RU, UK

Map 1.1 reprinted from Janet L. Abu-Lughod, *Before European Hegemony: The World System A.D. 1250–1350* (New York: Oxford University Press, 1989), 34.

Figure 3.1 reprinted from Charles Tilly, *Coercion, Capital, and European States, A.D. 990–1990* (Oxford: Basil Blackwell, 1990), 176–177.

British Library Cataloguing in Publication Information Available

Library of Congress Cataloging-in-Publication Data

Marks, Robert, 1949–
   The origins of the modern world : a global and ecological narrative from the fifteenth to the twenty-first century / Robert B. Marks. — 2nd ed.
      p. cm.
   Includes bibliographical references and index.
   ISBN-13: 978-0-7425-5419-1 (pbk. : alk. paper)
   ISBN-10: 0-7425-5419-8 (pbk. : alk. paper)
   1. History, Modern. 2. Europe—History—1492– 3. Civilization, Modern—History.
4. Economic history. 5. Industrial revolution. I. Title.
D203.M37 2007
940.2—dc22

2006046223

Printed in the United States of America

∞™ The paper used in this publication meets the minimum requirements of American National Standard for Information Sciences—Permanence of Paper for Printed Library Materials, ANSI/NISO Z39.48-1992.

Contents

	List of Figures and Maps	vii
	Preface	ix
	Preface to the Second Edition	xiii
Introduction	The Rise of the West?	1
Chapter 1	The Material and Trading Worlds, circa 1400	21
Chapter 2	Starting with China	43
Chapter 3	Empires, States, and the New World, 1500–1775	67
Chapter 4	The Industrial Revolution and Its Consequences, 1750–1850	95
Chapter 5	The Gap	123
Chapter 6	The Great Departure	155
Conclusion	Changes and Continuities	199
	Index	209
	About the Author	221

Figures and Maps

Figure 3.1   Joint Involvement of European States in
              Great Power Wars, 1496–1514 and 1656–1674   85

Figure 5.1   Share of World GDP, 1700–1890   124

Figure 5.2   Share of World Manufacturing Output, 1750–1900   125

Figure 5.3   Population of India, China, and Europe, 1400–2000 126

Map 1.1   The Eight Circuits of the Thirteenth-Century
              World System   34

Map 2.1   The World circa 1400–1500   44–45

Map 3.1   The World circa 1760   90–91

Map 5.1   The World circa 1900   146–147

Map 6.1   The World's Poorest Countries by Region   182–183

Preface

September 11, 2001. Although the details of how and why nineteen hijackers of four U.S. domestic flights slammed them into the World Trade Center in New York and the Pentagon in Washington, D.C., may never be known, the events raise profound issues about the nature of the world we live in. Americans are searching not just for answers to who is responsible for killing nearly 3,000 people, but for how and why they could hate the United States that much. Osama bin Laden, leader of al Qaeda, the organization that stands accused of masterminding and financing those acts, has evinced a deep hatred for the modern world and a desire to resurrect a Muslim empire reminiscent of its eighth-century glory.

Is this the beginning of the "clash of civilizations" that some have been predicting? As this book will make clear, I think not. The reason is that the basic elements of the modern world are not "civilizations," but rather nation–states and global capitalism. To be sure, the modern West (the United States included) has benefited immensely from a world organized along the lines of nation–state and industrial capitalism, while others (including many in the Islamic world) have not. How and why that particular way of organizing the world came to be is the subject of this book, although it was written before the events of September 11. Thus, I do not specifically address the attacks in the body of the text, but I do believe my arguments are highly relevant to helping us place those events into a broader historical context. At the end of the conclusion I have appended an afterword where I reflect more on the events of September 11 and how the material in this book helps to frame an interpretation of what they might mean.

Like the modern world, this book has its origins. At the 1998 Pacific Centuries conference at the University of the Pacific in Stockton, California, several of us were discussing over lunch issues that had been raised at the various panels. Among those at the table were Andre Gunder Frank and Kenneth Pomeranz, two scholars whose new work has profoundly influenced me and this book. Gunder lamented the fact that it often takes decades for the results of new research to get transmitted from scholars to students, and thought that it would be a great idea for someone to make these new ideas accessible to a wider audience, college students and the educated public alike. I concurred, but quickly put the project out of mind because I already had another research project on my agenda.

However, I also teach an introduction to world history with colleagues at Whittier College, and we have been working to incorporate this new scholarship into our course. When my sabbatical began in the summer of 2000, I was still thinking about the questions we had faced in teaching that course and decided to spend a few months composing a brief narrative of the origins of the modern world for use in that class. Those months became a year, and that project became this book.

When college students take an introductory U.S. or European history course, most already know the broad outlines of the story. Not so with students taking an introduction to modern world history. If they come to class with any background knowledge at all about "the history of the world," it usually includes a variant of what Europeans had done in the past five hundred years. The problem is that the result of work by scholars like Frank and Pomeranz demands a wholly new approach—a new narrative—one that is not centered on Europeans. Additionally, I have found in over two decades of teaching Asian history that it is a good idea to provide students with a brief overview in the first two weeks of class so they have a framework within which to place all the new material they are learning. That is what I thought our students in world history needed too, and that is what I started to write: a narrative of the making of the modern world incorporating the results of new (and somewhat iconoclastic) scholarship.

The resulting book is brief. But that does not mean that it is easy or simplistic. In fact, this book covers some very contested terrain: virtually every sentence here can be debated (and probably will be). I have no intention of providing a "balanced" story, one that spends an equal amount of time (or ink) on anything and everything. Rather, this book offers to readers the narrative of the origins of the modern world that I have put together for myself and that I present to my students.

That does not mean that I do not owe immense debts of gratitude to other people from whom I have learned, and continue to learn. I have already mentioned Gunder Frank and Ken Pomeranz; without their scholarship, this book would be inconceivable. Gunder also criticized the last draft, but ("alas," he might exclaim) production of the book had progressed too far for me to do much with his comments. Team-teaching with José Orozco led us to explore the connections between Latin America and Asia by following the silver trail. My colleague Dick Archer read and critiqued the entire manuscript, for which I am grateful, as did two anonymous readers for Rowman & Littlefield. Mark Selden, editor for the World Social Change series at Rowman & Littlefield, offered encouragement, advice, and criticism; he read the manuscript more than once. Steve Davidson too graciously read and commented on an earlier draft. Students in my fall 2001 capstone seminar (Sarah Alvarado, Roy Contreras, Jhalister Corona, Daniel Diaz, Aaron Ellis, Josh Fields, Andres Gorbea, Evan Gramly, Rocky Holman, and Andrea Ybarra) read and critiqued the manuscript and developed materials that will become the basis for Web-based learning aids. At the press, executive editor Susan McEachern not only read and critiqued the manuscript, but pushed me to deal with details on cover art and layout, and Erin McKindley oversaw copyediting and production. Phil Schwartzberg drew three historical maps, without continually asking me questions like "Where was Samarkand?" Last but certainly not least, Joyce Kaufman offered me companionship and criticism as we both worked on books for Rowman & Littlefield. Time to write the book was made possible by a sabbatical leave from Whittier College and a grant (FB-36592) from the National Endowment for the Humanities; their support is gratefully acknowledged.

My colleagues and students thus offered me helpful comments and suggestions, all of which I take very seriously, much of which I accepted, and some of which actually got incorporated into the final draft. Determined to keep the narrative brief and as sharply drawn as possible, I resisted the temptations to explore additional topics, or to address the ones I do consider in greater detail. Because this book draws so heavily on the ideas of others, I cannot absolve them of all responsibility for the interpretation of the origins of the modern world history offered here. However, the synthesis of others' work into the narrative told here is mine, and for that I alone am responsible.

Preface to the Second Edition

In response to requests from colleagues and teachers of world history, this edition contains a new chapter that takes the narrative of the modern world through the twentieth century and into the early twenty-first century. The first five chapters remain much the same as the original edition, but for minor grammatical and factual corrections and the addition of a few footnotes. The conclusion to the first edition continues to be available at the book's website: http://www.rowman.com/isbn/0742554198.

The first edition ended in 1900 both because I felt that the main features of the modern world had come into being by then, and because of the difficulties and challenges of doing contemporary history. The closer to the present we get, the less sure we can be of the narrative because the story is not yet over—we do not yet have the historical perspective to know what is really important and how the story ends. Indeed, that makes the task of composing a brief narrative of the twentieth century exceedingly difficult, for themes and events that seem important to some observers necessarily had to be left out.

Nonetheless, there are questions that students are curious about and that were not completely obvious from a storyline that ended in 1900. American students, in particular, were interested in understanding the history of how and why the United States emerged as a world power in the twentieth century, and how it came to be the sole superpower by the end of twentieth century. This edition addresses that question by arguing that the rise of the United States as global hegemon was contingent upon other developments—it was not inevitable.

But that is not the whole, or perhaps even most important, part of the story of the twentieth century, for the resurgence of Asia toward the end of the twentieth century cautions us against assuming the permanence or even longevity of U.S. dominance. More importantly, though, those political and economic markers of the significance of the twentieth century may well recede into insignificance when compared with the vastly changed relationship of humans to the environment that was wrought in the twentieth century—what I call the "Great Departure"—and that is part of this expanded narrative as well.

Helping me think through the twentieth century were my students in Whittier College's history department senior seminar. The issue they wrestled with in the spring of 2005 was whether or not the twentieth century represented a major continuity with, or a significant change from, past patterns. Joyce Kaufman once again offered companionship, support, and love, in addition to reading and critiquing chapter 6 and the conclusion. At Rowman & Littlefield, Susan McEachern and series editor Mark Selden both helped me shape and sharpen my thinking about the twentieth century. Finally, at Whittier College support form the Richard and Billie Deihl Endowed Professorship gave me time to write and to travel to China. As always, the interpretations and whatever errors of fact or omission remain mine.

INTRODUCTION

The Rise of the West?

hegemony = control

Mirrors development of the world up until the 1970s/80s

July 20–22, 2001; Genoa, Italy. Leaders of the major industrial countries in the world—known as the Group of Seven, or G7—met in July 2001 in this Mediterranean seaport city to discuss the world economy. The G7 stated that "sustained economic growth worldwide requires a renewed commitment to [global] free trade. . . . Opening markets globally and strengthening the World Trade Organization (WTO) as the bedrock of multilateral trading is . . . an economic imperative."[1] The G7 meeting, like the 1999 WTO meeting in Seattle, attracted thousands of people opposed to both the meeting and its objectives. Indeed, during those three days in July, 100,000 protestors against "globalization" came to Genoa, most to hold countermeetings to point out inequities in the global economy, but thousands also marched, considerable numbers trashed stores and sparred with police, hundreds were arrested, and one was killed.

We start this brief history of the origins of the modern world with a recent event because the G7 meetings—which have been going on for the past twenty-five years and will continue into the foreseeable future—reveal much about the nature of the world we live in and raise some very interesting historical questions about how our globalized world came to be the way it is. Let us take first the description of the G7 as "major industrialized countries." This statement points to the fact that the world today is composed of sovereign political units called "countries," and that those G7 countries are industrialized. Indeed, the G7 countries account for two-thirds of all the world's economic output and wealth. By implication, the rest of the world is poorer and less, if at all, industrialized. The world is thus divided between those parts that are industrialized and those that are not or are trying to become industrialized.

When placed in a broad historical context, this G7 fact is exceptionally

Finds it surprising that these countries have come to power so recently

interesting and raises profound questions. Just 200 years ago, two other countries—India and China—accounted for two-thirds of the world's economic output, and they are not European. In the space of just 200 years, the world has seen a great reversal of fortune: where once Asians held most of the economic cards, today it is primarily Western countries and Japan. The first question centers around how this happened. How did industry and European-style countries called nation–states—rather than highly developed agrarian empires like China and India—come to define our world?

Second, among the issues on the G7 agenda was what, if anything, to do about the growing gap between the richest and the poorest parts of the world, the latter located mostly in Asia, Africa, and Latin America. Like industry, nation–states, and Western dominance, this gap, too, has appeared within the past 200 years. How and why large parts of the world and its people have been condemned to increasing poverty is also an important question addressed here, as is the question of whether some parts of the world got rich only at the expense of others becoming poorer.

Third, industry has conferred great power on the G7 countries, so great that their leaders can meet to set the rules for how the world economy works. Of course, this is one of the prime causes of the protests against the G7, the WTO, and other financial institutions (such as the International Monetary Fund [IMF]). Protestors are in effect asking, "How come you get to decide the rules?" and demanding that other global arrangements be made.[2] Nonetheless, the leaders of the industrial world do make the rules, a power that is exercised in part to ensure the continuing wealth and power of the industrialized world. Although this power is exercised mostly through global trade and financial institutions such as the WTO and the IMF, it is backed by substantial military power, sometimes wielded unilaterally by G7 nations (such as the United States) but also by alliances such as the North Atlantic Treaty Organization (NATO). When placed in a global historical perspective, this power is exceptionally interesting, for Westerners have not had this power for very long.

Thus, to understand our world we have to understand not just how nation–states ("countries" in the G7 statement) and industry came to shape the modern world, but how and why those European ways of organizing the world came to dominate the globe. Explanations abound, but for most of the past two centuries, the predominant explanation in the West, the United States included, has been "the rise of the West." As we will see, recent research has shown that that explanation is no longer persuasive, but because it is probably the one most readers may be familiar with, I will take some time exploring it and pointing out its flaws.

The Rise of the West

The concept of the rise of the West provides both a rationale and a storyline that purports to explain not just the modern world, but why it is defined by primarily European features. The idea behind it is fairly simple and began to emerge shortly after the Spanish conquest of the Americas, during the Italian Renaissance of the sixteenth century. Europeans were quite astounded to see hundreds of Spanish conquistadors vanquish huge and very wealthy American civilizations, in particular the Aztecs and the Incas. Being ignorant of the germ theory of diseases and the cause of the "Great Dying" in Mexico, where nearly 90 percent of the central Mexican population of thirty million succumbed to European diseases such as smallpox and influenza, Europeans first attributed their superiority to their Christian religion. Later, during the Enlightenment of the seventeenth and eighteenth centuries, they attributed their superiority to a Greek heritage of secular, rationalistic, and scientific thought.

In the late 1700s this storyline continues: both the Industrial Revolution and the French Revolution of 1789 reinforced the awareness in European minds not just that Europeans were different from the rest of the world, but also that Europeans were "progressing" rapidly while the rest of the world appeared to be stagnating, that Europeans were somehow exceptional—better, even—than the rest. Nineteenth-century European historians, impressed with what many considered to be the universal appeal of the ideals of the French Revolution—*egalité, liberté, fraternité* (equality, liberty, and brotherhood)—looked back to the ancient Greeks, their institutions of democracy and republics, and their rationalistic bent toward understanding the natural world in scientific, not religious, terms. In this early telling of the "rise of the West," the story is somewhat like a relay race, with the ideas of democracy that arose in Greece passed off to the Romans, who dropped the baton (the fall of the Roman Empire followed by the so-called Dark Ages), but Christianity was then on the scene to pick it up and run with it, creating a distinctive European culture during feudal times. The ancient Greek heritage was rediscovered in the Renaissance ("renewal"), elaborated during the Enlightenment, and ultimately fulfilled in the French and American revolutions and "the rise of the West."

If the West was "rising" during the eighteenth century, during the nineteenth its ascent was completed. As the Industrial Revolution of the late eighteenth and early nineteenth centuries was just beginning, the classical British political economists—Adam Smith, Thomas Malthus, and David Ricardo—developed another strand to be woven into the story of the rise of the West: the ideas of capitalist development as "progress," the West as "progressive," and Asia (and by implication, Africa and Latin America, too) as "backward" and "despotic." To be sure, contrasts between the virtues of the West and the flaws of the East—the Orient—may have dated back to the Greeks, but eighteenth-century Europeans had been impressed with the wealth and governance of Asian countries, especially China. As the pace of economic change accelerated in nineteenth-century Europe, while much of Asia was in internal decline, analysts like Smith and Malthus began to revert to a view of the West as dynamic, forward looking, progressive, and free, and Asia as stagnating, backward, and despotic.

Even Karl Marx and Friedrich Engels, the most powerful critics of the new capitalist world order, believed that nineteenth-century European expansionism was bringing "progress" to the rest of the world. As they wrote in *The Communist Manifesto*, published in 1848:

> The [European] bourgeoisie, by the rapid improvement of all instruments of production, by the immensely facilitated means of communication, draws all, even the most backward, nations into civilization. The cheap prices of its commodities are the heavy artillery with which it batters down all Chinese walls, with which it forces the underdeveloped nations' intensely obstinate hatred of foreigners to capitulate. It compels all nations, on pain of extinction, to adopt the bourgeois mode of production; it compels them to introduce what it calls civilization into their midst, i.e., to become bourgeois themselves. In one word, it creates a world in its own image.[3]

Of more importance for Western conceptualizations of their own history, though, has been Max Weber, a German sociologist who wrote around the turn of the twentieth century. Where Weber shared with Marx a fascination with explaining how and why capitalism developed in Europe—and only Europe—Weber parted with Marx in his explanation. Instead of focusing as Marx had on "materialist" explanations, Weber looked to those aspects of Western values and culture, in particular the rationalism and work ethic that he associated with Protestantism, as being crucial to the rise of capitalism. But rather than basing his ideas about the rise of the West solely on studies of the West, Weber actually investigated Chinese and Indian societies, compared them with Europe, and concluded that those two societies at least, and by implication all other non-European societies, lacked the cultural values necessary for capitalism. Nonetheless, they too could "modernize," Weber thought, but only by going through a painful process of cultural change, getting rid of their cultural "obstacles" to capitalist development.

"The Gap" and Its Explanations

Since the mid-nineteenth century, then, European social theorists have been aware of a growing gap between the industrialized countries and the rest of the world. Believing both that western Europeans—and they alone—had un-locked the secret of modernization,[4] and that others too could learn, twentieth-century followers of Smith, Marx, and Weber have propounded a "diffusionist" theory of how world history has unfolded. Europeans found out how to get rich first by industrializing, Japan and a few other places learned from the Euro-peans and have caught up, and eventually every other place on the globe will too, as long as they identify and eliminate the local institutions and cultural traits that prevent them from becoming modern.

Viewed now from the beginning of the twenty-first century, these ideas ap-pear to be quite unconvincing, particularly in light of the fact that the gap be-tween the wealthiest and poorest parts of the world continues to grow, not shrink, as "diffusionist" theory would have us believe. However, the fact that these eighteenth- and nineteenth-century European theorists—Smith, Malthus, Ricardo, Marx, and Weber—all accepted the idea of European ex-ceptionalism and sought, as one of their primary intellectual goals, to explain it, is important. These men were the founders of modern social science the-ory, and in the twentieth century virtually all of the social sciences, in partic-ular sociology and economics, have incorporated the idea of European exceptionalism into their basic assumptions. As historians sought to become more "scientific" in the twentieth century by adopting and adapting the in-sights of this social science to historical inquiry, they too became captivated by the search for the origins and causes of European exceptionalism. But as we will see, Europeans were not exceptional, and one of the most important points about the history of the world until about 1800 is the general compa-rability of Asia with Europe. Nevertheless, the search for answers to "why" Europeans were perceived as exceptional and hence ultimately superior con-tinues among historians today, even though many now think it is the wrong question to be asking.

In the post–World War II era, this search has produced an impressive body of scholarship looking for the key to what one economic historian has called "the European miracle."[5] These scholars begin with what they see as the fact of the rise of the West, but propose differing solutions to the questions of when and why the "rise" or the "miracle" began. The question of "when" will be discussed first, since in many ways it is relevant to considerations of "why."

Adam Smith saw 1492 and 1498 (the voyages of Columbus to the Americas and of Vasco da Gama around Africa to India respectively) as the most signifi-cant events in history. As Smith wrote in *The Wealth of Nations* (1776): "The discovery of America, and that of the passage to the East Indies by the Cape of Good Hope, are the two greatest events recorded in the history of mankind." Marx, too, saw these two dates as crucial, as have several twentieth-century scholars working in a Marxist tradition who have pointed to the subsequent European colonialism, slavery, and exploitation of colonies in the Americas and Asia as the primary explanations for the rise of the West. Many non-Marxists have contested the idea that Europe's rise was a result of the exploitation of others,[6] an inconvenient and awkward fact if true, and instead have turned their attention to those aspects of European culture that predate European colonialism, beginning with the Spanish conquest of the New World.

To avoid the possible embarrassment of attributing the rise of the West to its colonial ventures, and not its inherent virtues, much post–World War II scholarship on the origins of the rise of the West has looked farther back in European history, in some cases as far back as the Middle Ages in the eleventh and twelfth centuries, or yet earlier to the ancient Greeks, for factors that could only be attributed to Europe's own exceptional development. Factors that have been identified, in addition to the cultural values discussed by Weber, include environmental ones (temperate climates promote hard work, or poor soils stimulate agricultural innovation), technological ones (plows, stirrups, or reading glasses), political–military ones (feudalism leading to absolute monarchs and then nation–states and the evolving technology of war), demographic ones (small families promote capital accumulation), and in the minds of several historians, combinations of all or some of these.[7]

The implication of this body of scholarship is that Europe possessed some unique characteristics that allowed it—and only it—to modernize first, and hence gave it the moral authority and the power to diffuse "modernity" around the globe where cultural, political, or economic "obstacles" prevented modern development from occurring indigenously. Hence, this storyline purports to explain, justify, and defend the rise of the West to global dominance. Just how wrongheaded this theory is will become clearer as the industrial superiority of much of Asia to that of Europe, at least prior to about 1750, is revealed in the course of this book.

Before turning to the question of why all this matters, let me first say a few words about geographic units used in this book. In the paragraph above, I mentioned a comparison between "Asia" and "Europe," implying both that these units are comparable, and that they have some kind of unity that distinguishes each one from the other. That assumption is problematic, mostly for Asia, because of the immense variety of societies it includes, ranging from China and Japan in East Asia, through the nomadic peoples of Central Asia, to India in the south, and the Muslim West Asia (Middle East). Even Europe has little coherence if it is taken to include everything from Portugal to Russia. Moreover, until very late in our story (at least until 1850 or so), Asia contained about two-thirds of the world's population and was larger than Europe in virtually every respect. To that extent, Europe and Asia were not comparable. Furthermore, one of the most important points I make in this book is that understanding the origins of the modern world requires taking a global view, first of how the vast continent of Eurasia, coupled with Africa, interrelated, and then after 1500, how the New World fit into the story. Finally, even the geographic terms "China," "India," and "England" or "France" conceal much variation within their borders—different peoples, many languages or dialects, and vast differences in wealth and power. Nevertheless, I will use these geographic terms to begin locating the story, but readers should be aware that generalizations based on large geographic units will not be true at all times and places within the places named, and that in reality what was truly comparable occurred in *parts* of China, *parts* of England or the Netherlands, and *parts* of India.

Readers may be wondering why the issue of the rise of the West matters. Indeed, why even study history? The brief response is because our understandings of the past—who we are, where we came from, why we are here—inform our definitions of who we are in the present and have real implications and applicability for actions taken by us or in our name to shape the future. The ideas developed by the story of the rise of the West to explain the nature of the world we live in, especially the values of marketplace capitalism and democratic institutions, are thought to have originated uniquely within Western civilization, yet to have universal applicability—to be "good," not just for the West, but for everybody. Following that assumption, the solution to virtually all problems in the world today, at least according to U.S. and European political leaders (e.g., the G7), is the adoption of free markets.[8] Thus, to Russia after the collapse of the Soviet Union, to the communist leaders of China, to the leaders of Mexico, Nigeria, and Indonesia, Western leaders have said that the answer to any and all problems they face is "More democracy and free markets." The idea is that the institutions and values that supposedly propelled the rise of the West are universal, and can—indeed, must—be adopted throughout the world. That is a political agenda.

But what if this way of looking at the making of the modern world—the rise of the West and the spread of its system on the basis of its supposed cultural superiority to the rest of the world—is wrong? That is the possibility raised by a new body of scholarship, especially over the past twenty years.

No longer do all historians picture the world as merely a continuation of universal and necessary trends that began centuries ago in Europe. What many are seeing instead is a world in which population, industry, and agricultural productivity were centered in Asia until 1750 or 1800. The European world of industrial capitalism and nation–states is thus both quite recent and a reversal—for how long, though, remains the big question—of long-standing historical trends favoring Asia. Europeans may have painted a picture of the rise of the West over this original one, but the patterns of Asian strength and economic vitality are beginning to show through once again. Artists call this concept of one painting showing through an original painting or parts of it *pentimento*. As this book intends to show, the more we look at the world and its past through a new light, the pictures painted in our minds by the rise of the West will reveal another, and rather different pattern, underlying. To see it, though, we will have to begin shedding our Eurocentric perspectives.[9]

Eurocentrism

One critic has said that the idea that "the West has some unique historical advantage, some special quality of race or culture or environment or mind or spirit, which gave this human community a permanent superiority over all other communities" is a myth—the myth of Eurocentrism.[10] Another has seen Eurocentrism as an ideology, or a distortion of the truth, used by the West to mask its global dominance,[11] and still another deems it a "theoretical model," one explanation among several for how the world works.[12] In this section, we will examine two aspects of what critics call Eurocentrism: first, what it is; and second, the extent to which it can be seen as wrong, a myth, an ideology, a theory, or a master narrative.

The essence of Eurocentrism, according to the critics, is not merely that it views history from a European point of view (the "centrism" part)—it is not just one of many ethnocentric views of the world. A merely ethnocentric perspective recognizes that there are many different peoples and cultures in the world, but that mine is better *because* it arises from my people and culture. They are mine, better, and not yours. Eurocentrism also emphasizes the superiority of Western culture—all that is good, progressive, and innovative starts only in Europe—but it also sees that package as having universal applicability: it is not peculiar and limited to Europe, but has spread to encompass the globe by the twentieth century.

Going a bit deeper, critics say, Eurocentric views of the world see Europe as being the only active shaper of world history, its "fountainhead" if you will. Europe acts; the rest of the world responds. Europe has "agency"; the rest of the world is passive. Europe makes history; the rest of the world has none until it is brought into contact with Europe. Europe is the center; the rest of the world is its periphery. Europeans alone are capable of initiating change or modernization; the rest of the world is not.

On a deeper level yet, according to critics, Eurocentrism is not just a belief in the past or present superiority of Europe, but is "a matter of . . . scholarship"[13] (i.e., of established "fact"). It is not a "bias," but a way of establishing what is true and what is false. To that extent, Eurocentrism is a way of knowing that establishes the criteria for what its practitioners deem to be "the facts." It is thus a *paradigm*, a set of assumptions about how the world works, that generates questions that can then be answered by ferreting out "the facts."[14]

Finally, Eurocentric ideas about the world and how it came to be the way it is are deeply held by Americans. Indeed, American history is often presented as the pinnacle, the purest and best expression, of Western civilization. European and even world history are most often presented from a Eurocentric point of view, whether or not students or faculty recognize it. Mostly, it is assumed to be "true." The situation is like that faced by Keanu Reeves in the movie *The Matrix*, or Jim Carrey in *The Truman Show*. Those on the inside really do not have an independent way of knowing whether they are inside a matrix or an encapsulated TV stage unless they can get a look at it from the outside. Collecting more facts would not suffice, since all the facts on the inside tend to confirm the reality, the truth, of the matrix one is in. Some facts that are collected might not fit, but mostly those are simply discarded or ignored as being anomalous—accidents, if you will. The same is true of Eurocentrism. If Eurocentric ideas, if the rise of the West, are wrong, how would we know it? The way to know is by getting outside of that way of explaining how the world came to be the way it is and thinking about other ways of understanding the big changes that have shaped our world.

Readers may sense a paradox here. On the one hand, I started by pointing out that key features of the modern world are European in origin, and that I think an historical approach can explain how and why industry, the nation-state, and the gap between the wealthy and the poor define our world. On the other hand, I have just rejected the usual Eurocentric explanations of the origins of the modern world. How can there be a non-Eurocentric explanation of a world that has European features? In short, we can do that by broadening the storyline to include parts of the world that have thus far been excluded or overlooked—we can begin and end the story elsewhere.[15] When we do that, we will see that only a new, global storyline—one not centered on Europe—will suffice to explain the origins of the modern world.

Stories and Historical Narratives

For historians, constructing a narrative—a story with a beginning, a middle, and an end—is central to how we know what we know, how we determine what is true about the past.[16] The rise of the West is a story—to be sure, a story at the core of Eurocentrism—that provides the criteria for selecting what is and what is not relevant to that story. But because the rise of the West informs all the other historical scholarship mentioned above, it is more than just another story or narrative; it is a "master narrative," "a grand schema for organizing the interpretation and writing of history," "sweeping stories about origins," as historians Appleby, Hunt, and Jacob put it.[17]

So the only way to determine if the rise of the West is wrong is to construct an alternative narrative of how the world came to be the way it is: we have to get outside of the rise-of-the-West matrix. Doing so will accomplish three things. First, it will provide an independent way to tell which parts, if any, of the rise-of-the-West paradigm can be kept and which need to be rejected. Second, it will help readers to critically examine their own assumptions about how the world works. And third, it will raise the more general issue of how we know what we know about the world and its history. That is the task of this brief history. In the remainder of this introduction, I want to sketch out the elements of that alternative narrative.

I need first to introduce three additional concepts: those of historical contingency, of accident, and of conjuncture. We start with the idea of *contingency*. One very powerful implication of the storyline of the rise of the West, though it is seldom made explicit, is that the way the world turned out was the only way possible. Because of the historical advantages enjoyed by Europeans, possibly since the fall of the Roman Empire or even as far back as the Greeks or to European genetics, this interpretation implies that the rise of the West was *inevitable*. It might have taken some twists and turns, had some fits and starts, but sooner or later the West would rise above all other parts of the world.

Although we will also have to deal with the political, economic, and military dominance of Europe and its offshoots (e.g., the United States) for the past 200 years, there is no reason to think that that dominance was inevitable or, for that matter, that its dominance will continue. Indeed, it appears inevitable only because that storyline was centered on Europe. But once a broader, global perspective is adopted, the dominance of the West not only happens later in time, probably as late as 1750–1800 and perhaps not until the early nineteenth century, but it also becomes clearer that it was *contingent* on other developments that happened independently elsewhere in the world.

Most important, the economic engine driving global trade—and with it exchanges of ideas, new food crops, and manufactured goods—was in Asia. Probably as early as 1000 c.e., China's economic and population growth stimulated the entire Eurasian continent; another surge came after about 1400 and lasted until 1800 or so. Asia was the source of a huge demand for silver to keep the economies of China and India growing and also the world's greatest source of manufactured goods (especially textiles and porcelain) and spices. Also very significant in our narrative will be the beginning of Islam and the expansion, from the seventh to the seventeenth centuries, of Islamic empires westward into the Mediterranean Sea and eastward into the Indian Ocean as far as Indonesia. Where Asia attracted the attention and interest of traders from all over Eurasia, the Islamic empire blocked direct European access to the riches of Asia, stimulating a desire among Europeans to find new sea routes to the Indian Ocean and China.

Even Columbus's "discovery" of the Americas and Vasco da Gama's sailing around Africa to get to the Indian Ocean would not have done much for European fortunes had they not found both vast quantities of silver in the New World with which to buy Asian goods and a supply of African slaves to work New World plantations after European diseases killed off most of the Native American population. As we will see, the creation of the institutions and sources of wealth and power in a few advanced parts of Europe, enabling these areas to establish dominance over the rest of the world, was *contingent* upon these, and other, developments.

As late as 1750, as parts of Europe approached the levels of development reached in key areas of Asia, all of these most developed parts of Eurasia—Europe as well as Asia—began butting up against environmental limits to further growth, except in England, where easily accessible coal deposits enabled the British to escape from these constraints by industrialization based on the new sources of steam power. In the early 1800s this new power source was put to military use, and then—and only then—did the scale tip against Asians, and did Europeans, led first by the British, move toward establishing clear global dominance. The point is that the rise of the West was not inevitable, but was highly contingent. The world we live in might have been different; there is nothing in the past—unless you adopt the rise-of-the-West construct—that indicates that the world had to become one dominated by Western institutions.

Moreover, if the rise of the West were not inevitable but instead contingent, that would mean that the future too is contingent, and that is why it matters what our view of the past is. If nothing anybody could have done would have changed the outcome of history, then nothing we can do *now* can shape our future: we are trapped in a further elaboration and extension of that which exists in the present, unless some huge accident of history pushes us in a different direction. On the one hand, if history—and our view of it—is contingent, then the actions that we take in the here and now do indeed have the possibility of changing the world. We are not trapped, but rather we (and I take that to mean all the peoples in the world, not just Americans or those in the West) can have agency. If the past could have been different, then so too can the future. Being "contingent," on the other hand, does not mean that European dominance of the world for the past 200 years was an accident, for there were causes for that development, as this book will make clear.[18]

That does not mean that historical *accidents* do not happen, for they do. Let me give two examples that will be discussed later in the book. In agricultural societies, which is what most of the world was until very recently, climate changes could have a major impact on the size of the harvest, not just in one year but over decades. More favorable conditions could produce larger harvests, lowering the price of food for everyone and stimulating the growth of the economy. Poor conditions, such as happened in large parts of the world during the seventeenth-century "Little Ice Age," could put whole economies under severe pressure. Although climate changes do indeed have causes, from the point of view human history, they are accidents in the dual sense of being unpredictable and beyond human control.

Another "accident" is important to the story of coal and its relationship to industrialization. Coal deposits were laid down hundreds of millions of years ago, and where they were in terms of where people lived is purely accidental. Some coal deposits turned out to be near to where people both needed and knew how to use them, and some were far away and hence unusable. Neither the Dutch nor the Chinese, for example, both of whom had the ability and the need to develop a coal industry to supply energy to sustain their economic growth, had coal deposits near the areas that needed them. This was one reason that their economic growth in the eighteenth century slowed while that of Britain, which just happened to be sitting on huge, close, easily worked coal deposits, accelerated. The distribution of coal deposits thus is accidental as far as human history is concerned, but it certainly had a dramatic impact on which countries industrialized and which did not.

Next is the idea of "*conjuncture.*" A conjuncture happens when several otherwise independent developments come together in ways that interact with one another, creating a unique historical moment. For our purposes, one way to think about this is to consider the world as having had several regions that were more or less independent of one another, thus having their own histories. In China, for example, the decision in the early 1400s by the government to use silver as the basis for their monetary system arose out of circumstances particular to Chinese history. But this Chinese decision had global impact in the sixteenth and seventeenth centuries when Europeans discovered both huge supplies of silver in the New World and an even larger Chinese demand for it. As a result, silver flowed into China (and India), and Asian silks, spices, and porcelains flowed into Europe and the New World, inaugurating the first age of globalization. That was a conjuncture: things happening in different parts of the world for reasons having to do with local circumstances that then became globally important.

Conjunctures can also occur within a given region when several otherwise independent developments reach critical points and interact with one another. For instance, the development of nation–states as the dominant form of political organization in Europe happened for reasons quite independent of those leading to industrialization. Nonetheless, when the two converged in the nineteenth century—came together to produce a conjuncture—a very powerful global force developed, particularly when the two provided the basis for military preeminence.

The attention we give to contingency, accident, and conjuncture means that our explanation of major developments in the making of the modern world will involve several causes, not just one. Monocausal explanations are too simple to take account of the complexity of people, societies, and historical change. We should thus not look for "the" cause of the Industrial Revolution, for it will not be there. Instead, we will find a complex of factors that go a long way toward explaining the Industrial Revolution. I say "a long way" because we have to leave open the possibility that as we learn more or as our perspective changes, we might see the shortcomings of the explanation offered here.

So the narrative in this book about how the modern world came to be— the world of industrial capitalism, a system of nation–states and interstate wars, and a growing gap between the richest and the poorest in our world— will be one that has contingency, accidents, and conjunctures. The world could have been a very different place. Until about 200 years ago, the most successful way people found to organize themselves and to promote the growth of their numbers was in large land-based empires in Asia, Africa, the Middle East, and the Americas. But if not for a series of contingencies, accidents, and conjunctures, we might still be living in a world of agrarian empires.

Besides a plot, or a storyline, though, a narrative has a beginning, a middle, and an end, the choices of which significantly affect the story that is told. We have chosen to begin our story with how the modern world came to be around 1400. The reason for beginning around 1400 is that it predates the circumnavigation of the globe in the mid-1500s and hence allows us to examine the world and its dynamics prior to the first time a truly globally connected world became possible. The middle of the story revolves around the beginning of the Industrial Revolution in 1750–1800 with an explanation of why the most decisive events happened first in Britain and not elsewhere in the world. In the first edition of this book, the story ended around 1900 because that is when industrial capitalism and nation-states became fully elaborated on a global scale. This edition continues the story through the twentieth century.

This narrative of world history also strives to be a *non-Eurocentric narrative*, that is, to provide an alternative to the storyline developed around the existing master narrative of the rise of the West. But does it matter? Why should we care about constructing a new, non-Eurocentric narrative of the making of the modern world? That question can be answered on a number of levels. First, the overall story of the rise of the West may be misleading or wrong in fundamental ways, even though parts of it may be correct. For example, one of the most powerful of recent answers to the question of what caused "the European miracle" concerns families and the number of children each family had. The argument goes something like this: After the Black Death of the mid-fourteenth century, various economic and environmental pressures prompted European families to marry late, thereby reducing family size. Fewer children meant farming families could begin to accumulate capital, thus sending Europe on its way to an "industrious revolution." "By delaying marriage," according to a recent history, "European peasants set a course that separated them from the rest of the world's inhabitants."[19]

Although it may be true that West European peasants did behave that way, thereby freeing themselves from "instinctive patterns of behavior" (i.e., unregulated childbearing) that supposedly condemned other peoples to overpopulation and poverty, it simply is not true that European peasants were unique in this behavior. A recent work on China shows that rural families there too—and probably for a lot longer—limited family size, although the methods used differed.[20] In this instance alone, one prop has been removed from underneath the claim of the uniqueness of Europeans and the reasons for their "rise." Indeed, scholars recently have shown that virtually every factor that its proponents have identified with the "European miracle" can be found in other parts of the world;[21] that is, they were *not* unique to Europe, and hence cannot be invoked to explain the rise of the West.

This narrative also is non-Eurocentric because much of it will be devoted to showing the ways in which other parts of the world were either more advanced or at least equivalent to the most developed parts of Europe, over many centuries, at least until about 1800. This book could not have been written without the vast amount of scholarship published in English on Asia, Africa, and Latin America, which provides the basis for a non-Eurocentric narrative. We are thus fortunate to no longer be dependent for our understanding of the world on the accident that most of what has been written in the past 200 years has been by and about Europeans exploring their own history. As one critic put it, until recently historians have been like the drunk under the streetlight trying to find his lost car keys: when asked by a police of-ficer why he was looking there, he said, "Because this is where the light is." Fortunately, scholars recently have begun to shine a lot of light on other parts of the world, so we do not have to fumble around in the dark. We now know enough about the rest of the world to question the master narrative of the rise of the West and to begin constructing another, non-Eurocentric narrative.

If the concept of the rise of the West cannot adequately explain why the West and its institutions became the dominant force in the world over the past 200 years, still less the sustained rise of East Asia over the past four decades,[22] then continued use of it does indeed perpetuate a mythology. Some mythologies may well be harmless, at least when they are recognized as such, as when we find Greek or Native American stories about the constellations charming. But when a mythology perpetuates the idea that one group of peo-ple is superior, has been for centuries if not millennia, and that all others are thus in various ways inferior, as the ideas inherent in the rise of the West do, then the mythology does violence to others and should be abandoned.

The Elements of a Non-Eurocentric Narrative

First, we have to take the entire world as our unit of analysis, rather than par-ticular countries or even regions (e.g., "Europe," "East Asia").[23] We will have the opportunity to discuss developments in particular nations and empires, but always in a global context. For instance, we will see that while the Indus-trial Revolution started in Britain (and even there, in just a part), it was not because of English pluck, inventiveness, or politics, but rather because of global developments that included India, China, and the New World colonies. In other words, the Industrial Revolution was historically contin-gent on global forces.

However, taking a global perspective does not imply that the world has al-ways been an interconnected one with a single center from which develop-ment and progress spread to less-developed regions. Instead, it makes much more sense to think of the world in 1400 as having been composed of several regional systems, or in other words to have been "polycentric,"[24] each with densely populated and industrially advanced cores supplied from their own peripheries. Although trade and cultural exchanges did mean that most of the world regions interacted, or overlapped, on the margins (with the excep-tion of the regional systems in the Americas, which interacted with one an-other, but not until 1492 with Eurasia-Africa), what happened in these regions was more a result of dynamics specific to that place.

The assumptions that the world in 1400 was polycentric and large parts of Eurasia were broadly comparable in terms of levels of development help us understand how a much more integrated world came about, and how and why Westerners ultimately came to dominate it. The implication of the Eurocentric model is that development and progress originated in Europe and spread outward from there to encompass the rest of the world: Europeans acted, and the rest of the world was passive or stagnant (until having to react to Europe).[25]

In this narrative, by contrast, we will see that China and India in particular play significant roles, and that we cannot understand how and why the world came to be the way it is without understanding developments in Asia. We will learn how and why China developed such a huge appetite for silver that it created a global demand, drawing silver from around the world to China and flooding the world market with Chinese manufactures. We will also investigate other commodities and their global supply and demand as well, especially for sugar, slaves (unfortunately human beings were commodities), and cotton textiles, all of which were first produced (and produced more efficiently) in parts of the world other than Europe.

This book will emphasize historical contingencies and conjunctures; China and India; and silver, sugar, slaves, and cotton as we develop a non-Eurocentric picture of how the world came to be the way it is.

Notes

1. "Statement of the Group of Seven Leaders," July 20, 2001 (www.usinfo.state.gov/admin/004/). The G7 countries are Canada, France, Germany, Italy, Japan, the United Kingdom, and the United States. Russia was invited to join the G7 in 1998, so now it is sometimes called the "G8," or the "G7 plus Russia."

2. Michael Hardt and Antonio Negri, "What the Protesters in Genoa Want," *New York Times*, sec. A, July 20, 2001. A free, full version of this article can be found at www.commondreams.org/views01/0720-01.htm.

3. Karl Marx and Friedrich Engels, *The Communist Manifesto* (New York: Washington Square Press, 1964), 64–65.

4. Philip D. Curtin has sensibly defined "modernization" as the drive to achieve high economic productivity and high consumption levels, regardless of cultural differences. *The World and the West: The European Challenge and the Overseas Response in the Age of Empire* (Cambridge: Cambridge University Press, 2000), 110. However, post–World War II "modernization" theorists of the 1950s and 1960s developed a list of what it meant to be "modern" that looked very much like the United States.

5. The term is taken from a book by E. L. Jones, *The European Miracle* (Cambridge: Cambridge University Press, 1981).

6. Especially the British economic historian Patrick O'Brien. See his article "European Economic Development: The Contribution of the Periphery," *Economic History Review*, 2d ser., 35 (1982): 1–18.

7. As examples of these various theses, see David S. Landes, *The Wealth and Poverty of Nations: Why Some Are So Rich and Some So Poor* (New York: W. W. Norton, 1998) and *The Unbound Prometheus: Technological Change and Industrial Development in Western Europe from 1750 to the Present* (Cambridge: Cambridge University Press, 1969); Lynn White, Jr., *Medieval Religion and Technology: Collected Essays* (Berkeley: University of California Press, 1978); Alfred Crosby, *The Measure of Reality: Quantification and Western Society, 1250–1600* (Cambridge: Cambridge University Press, 1997); Geoffrey Parker, *The Military Revolution: Military Innovation and the Rise of the West 1500–1800*, 2d ed. (Cambridge: Cambridge University Press, 1999).

8. As U.S. President George W. Bush put it, international free trade is "a moral imperative" that will "build freedom in the world, progress in our hemisphere and enduring prosperity in the United States." Quoted in the *New York Times*, May 8, 2001, national edition, p. A7.

9. For a review of three recent books on this topic see David D. Buck, "Was It Pluck or Luck that Made the West Grow Rich?" *Journal of World History* (Fall 2000): 413–430.

10. J. M. Blaut, *The Colonizer's Model of the World: Geographic Diffusionism and Eurocentric History* (New York: Guilford Press, 1993), 1.

11. Samir Amin, *Eurocentrism* (New York: Monthly Review Press, 1989), vii.

12. Andre Gunder Frank, *ReOrient: Global Economy in the Asian Age* (Berkeley: University of California Press, 1998), 32.

13. Blaut, *The Colonizer's Model of the World*, 8–9.

14. The idea of scientific paradigms and the exploration of the conditions under which they might change was first developed by Thomas Kuhn in a classic work, *The Structure of Scientific Revolutions*, 2d enlarged ed. (Chicago: University of Chicago Press, 1970). Kuhn's primary example was the Copernican revolution, that is, the change from a view of the solar system with the earth at the center (the view then supported by the Catholic Church), to one with the sun at the center. Although Kuhn discussed "paradigms" and paradigm shifts only with respect to science, the idea has been extended to the way social science works too.

15. Some might object that even this approach remains mired in Eurocentrism because of several unexamined assumptions about the very concepts being used, the objects being identified as in need of explanation, and even history as a method, all of which some claim are implicitly Eurocentric. For example, some have questioned whether states and industrial capitalism are really all that important to be explained, raising instead the possibility that other aspects of our world might be more important to explore, such as our very concepts of self, body, sexuality, place, causation, and story, and they have proposed new "postmodern" methodologies of "deconstruction" or "discourse communities" and their "privileged language," which confers "power," to explore them. This is an extremely complicated topic, but those wishing a sensible introduction might start with Joyce Appleby, Lynn Hunt, and Margaret Jacob, *Telling the Truth about History* (New York: W. W. Norton, 1994).

16. Not all stories are "true." Some are invented by the author: they are fiction (like Goldilocks and the Three Bears, or the Harry Potter books). While both history and fiction develop stories, what distinguishes history from fiction is that historical facts are true.

Historians have developed sophisticated tools and methods for writing historical narratives (i.e., stories that are "true"). As the following discussion of "master narrative" shows, though, the idea of historical truth is complex and cannot be reduced merely to what is true and false, but must include a consideration of how we determine the criteria for deciding what is true and what is not.

17. Appleby, Hunt, and Jacob, *Telling the Truth about History*, 232.

18. For a succinct discussion of determinism and chance in history, see E. H. Carr, *What Is History?* (New York: Vintage Books, 1961), chap. 4.

19. George Huppert, *After the Black Death: A Social History of Modern Europe*, 2d ed. (Bloomington: Indiana University Press, 1998), 13.

20. James Z. Lee and Wang Feng, *One Quarter of Humanity: Malthusian Myths and Chinese Realities* (Cambridge, Mass.: Harvard University Press, 1999).

21. See the works by Blaut, *The Colonizer's Model of the World*; Jack Goody, *The East in the West* (Cambridge: Cambridge University Press, 1996); Frank, *ReOrient*; R. Bin Wong, *China Transformed: Historical Change and the Limits of European Experience* (Ithaca, N.Y.: Cornell University Press, 1997); Kenneth Pomeranz, *The Great Divergence: China, Europe, and the Making of the Modern World Economy* (Princeton, N.J.: Princeton University Press, 2000).

22. See Giovanni Arrighi, Takeshi Hamashita, and Mark Selden, eds. *The Resurgence of East Asia: 500, 150, and 50 Year Perspectives* (New York: Routledge, 2003).

23. Fernand Braudel is the most important of recent historians to take a global approach in attempting to explain at least one part of the European miracle, capitalism. His three-volume *Civilization and Capitalism 15th–18th Century* (New York: Harper and Row, 1979–1984) is an intellectual tour de force in which he argues that while many parts of the world developed highly sophisticated market economies, few came close to developing real capitalism, and it only flourished in Europe. Braudel makes the interesting point that capitalists were not at all interested in free markets and open competition, but instead worked to obtain monopoly concessions from European monarchs: under those peculiar circumstances, capitalism grew rapidly in a European hothouse. We will have an opportunity in later chapters to examine Braudel's ideas in more detail.

24. See Pomeranz, *The Great Divergence*, chap. 1. The question of whether the world was a single, integrated system and, if so, when it first became a single system is an interesting one that will be taken up more in the chapters to follow. Suffice it to say here that there are at least three basic positions. Like Karl Marx and Adam Smith, Immanuel Wallerstein (*The Modern World-System*, 3 vols. [New York: Academic Press, 1974–1989]), and J. M. Blaut (*The Colonizer's Model of the World*) take 1492–1500 as the time of the creation of a single world system; Janet Abu-Lughod (*Before European Hegemony: The World System A.D. 1250–1350* [New York: Oxford University Press, 1989]) has put forward strong evidence for a world system circa 1250–1350, which fell apart prior to the establishment of the modern world system; and Andre Gunder Frank and Barry Gillis have argued for a 5,000-year history of a single world system ("The Five Thousand Year World System: An Introduction," *Humbolt Journal of Social Relations* 17, no. 1 [1992]: 1–79).

25. This model, it should be pointed out, is equally shared by Marxists and by champions of capitalism, so I am not proposing to develop a Marxist narrative of the making of the modern world as an alternative to a celebratory rise of the West; that has already been done, several times over. See, for example, Eric J. Hobsbawm, the four-volume set including *The Age of Revolution*, *The Age of Capital*, *The Age of Empire*, and *The Age of Extremes*, all recently republished (New York: Vintage, 1994–1996) and the Marxism-influenced work, Wallerstein's *The Modern World System*.

CHAPTER ONE

The Material and Trading Worlds, circa 1400

We are born and raised under circumstances neither of our own choosing nor of our own making. In fact, the world we confront is composed of social, economic, political, and cultural *structures*. These large structures change very slowly, seldom as a result of conscious action on the part of a single person, and mostly only as a result of huge processes that are hardly detectable, by large and sustained social movements, or, as we will see, during historical conjunctures.

To understand the vast changes that accompanied the origins of the modern world, we thus need to start with some of the structures into which people in 1400 were born, lived, and died. Of course, we cannot possibly examine every facet of human life at that time, so we must be quite selective (especially to keep this history "brief," as I promised). What I have chosen to emphasize are but two of the major structural aspects of the world in 1400: first, the material and natural conditions under which most people lived, an overwhelmingly agricultural world, or what can be called "the biological old regime," and second, the trading networks that connected most of the Old World together. This chapter thus introduces two kinds of worlds, the material one in which most people lived quite restricted lives, and the trading, or commercial world, which brought the parts of the world into increasingly greater contact. To show how these are interrelated, the chapter concludes with an examination of the causes and consequences of the mid-fourteenth-century Black Death—one of the great catastrophes to befall human society—in western Europe and East Asia.

This chapter also introduces key concepts that will be used throughout the book. Most of this chapter focuses on the material world, in particular the size of the human population and the economic, social, and environmental conditions under which most people lived. The concepts that will be introduced in this chapter include the rise of *civilization* and the *agricultural revolution*, the relationships between towns or *cities* and the countryside, between *ruling elites* and *peasants*, also called *agriculturalists* or *villagers*, between civilizations and *nomads*, and between *people* and the *environment*. Taken together, these relationships constitute the *biological old regime*, the working out of which is examined in the Black Death of the mid-fourteenth century.

We will also examine the *world system* as it existed around 1400. Today, there is much talk about—and demonstrations against—the benefits and dangers of *globalization*. In this context, many people apparently consider globalization to be a new phenomenon, whether or not they think its impact on the whole is beneficial or harmful. However, if there is anything I hope readers will take away from reading this book, it is that "globalization" is hardly new: it has been unfolding for a very long time. Key concepts in this chapter will include *polycentric* (to describe a world system with many centers), and *core* and *periphery*, whether applied to a single or a polycentric world system.

Another major point about the fifteenth-century world is that most of its people—regardless of where they lived, their civilization, or even their various folk customs—shared a basically similar material world. The reason is that people had to eat, and after the agricultural revolution 5,000–8,000 years ago, the way most people have obtained their living has been from agriculture. To be sure, whether the main crop was wheat, rye, or rice mattered, but all of the agriculturists faced similar challenges in dealing with nature, the ruling elites, and one another. For this reason, much of this chapter will deal with the social, economic, and political structures essential to understanding the world from about 1400 to 1800. The following chapters take up the story of what happened after 1400; in this chapter we establish a baseline in terms of material life against which changes in the world can be assessed.

The Biological Old Regime

The number of people on earth is an important indicator of the relative success humans have had in creating the material conditions under which the human population can either increase or decline. Of course, there are tremendous variations in time and place of population dynamics, and we will consider some of them here. As a first approximation, though, we can start with simple global totals.

The Weight of Numbers

Here we look at the weight of numbers[1] to get an overall picture. Today, there are just over 6 billion people on earth. Six hundred years ago, in 1400, humankind was just 6 percent of that, or about 350 million people, slightly more than the current population of the United States of 280 million. By 1800, the population had more than doubled to 720–750 million.[2] Moreover, in that 400-year period from 1400 to 1800, as much as 80 percent of that population were peasants, people who lived on the land and were the direct producers of food for themselves and the rest of the population. The world was overwhelmingly rural, and the availability of land to produce food was a constant constraint on the number of people alive at any given moment. For most of that period, the population rose and fell in great waves lasting for centuries, even if the very long-term trend was very slightly upward and the declines came sharply and swiftly. In very broad terms, we can see three great waves of population increase and decrease over the past one thousand years. Beginning about 900–1000 C.E. (probably simultaneously in China and Europe), the population rose until about 1300, crashing precipitously around 1350 as a result of the Black Death. Another period of increase began about 1400 and lasted until a mid-seventeenth century decline. The third advance, beginning around 1700, has yet to halt, although population experts expect it to by about 2100.   *pop. increase + decrease*

Climate Change

It now appears that climate change was a general cause of the premodern population increases around the world. Given the interest in the past twenty years in our current problem of global warming, historians and meteorologists have reconstructed past climates and have indeed found significant changes in temperatures and rainfall.[3] The connections between climate change and human population dynamics are complex, but the major linkage, (especially in a world where 80–90 percent of the population made their living from the land,) has to do with food production. Variations in temperature, radiation, and rainfall affect all growing things, trees as well as wheat or rice. Better climatic conditions improved harvests, while harvest failures could spell disaster. Long-term cooling trends could thus seriously shrink the food supply and hence the ability of the society to sustain a given population, leading to population declines. On the other hand, generally warming conditions could mean larger harvests and a growing human population.[4] As we will see, though, climatic changes count less for population growth in the period since 1700 when New World resources and industrialization began to ease prior constraints on population growth.

cold = ↓ food suply = ↓ ppl

Worm = ↑ food suply = ↑ ppl

Population Density and Civilization

The 350 million people living in 1400 were not uniformly distributed across the face of the earth, but rather clustered in a very few pockets of much higher density. Indeed, of the 60 million square miles of dry land on earth, most people lived on just 4.25 million square miles, or barely 7 percent of the dry land. The reason, of course, is that that land was the most suitable for agriculture, the rest being covered by swamp, steppe, desert, or ice.

Moreover, those densely populated regions of earth corresponded to just fifteen highly developed civilizations, the most notable being (from east to west) Japan, Korea, China, Indonesia, Indochina, India, the Islamic West Asia, Europe (both Mediterranean and West), Aztec, and Inca. Astoundingly, nearly all of the 350 million people alive in 1400 lived in a handful of civilizations occupying a very small proportion of the earth's surface. Even more astoundingly, that still holds true today: 70 percent of the world's six billion people live on those same 4.25 million square miles.[5]

The densest concentrations of human population were (and still are, for the most part) on the Eurasian continent: China in the east, Europe in the west, and India in the south, with the populations of China and Europe about equal over large periods of historical time. So large are those three populations relative to the rest of the world that China alone represented 25–40 percent of the world's population (the latter percentage attained in the 1700s), Europe was 25 percent, and India was perhaps 20 percent. In other words, those three centers alone accounted for about 70 percent of the population of the world in 1400, increasing to perhaps 80 percent by 1800. Those amazing figures go a long way toward explaining why what happened in China, India, and Europe plays such an important role in this book.

The fifteen densely populated and highly developed civilizations shared several features, the most important of which was the relationship between those who lived in the countryside producing the food supply and those living in the cities consuming surpluses from that food production, even though the elites in the cities may have devised different means by which to ensure that food produced in the countryside made its way to the cities. This extractive relationship between town and countryside has a long history, going back to the Neolithic, or agricultural, revolution of 5,000–8,000 B.C.E.

The Agricultural Revolution

About 10,000 years ago, first in the part of the world aptly called the "Fertile Crescent" (currently Iraq), people learned how to grow their own food and to raise their own animals, thereby increasing the amount of food available. This change, from a hunting-and-gathering society to a sedentary agricultural society, occurred over long periods and independently in at least four parts of the world: about 10,000 years ago in the Fertile Crescent along the Tigris and Euphrates rivers; in northern China about 9,500 years ago, around 5,500 years ago in what is now Mexico in Mesoamerica, and around 4,500 years ago in what is now the eastern United States. It may have happened independently in parts of Africa and New Guinea as well, although it did not happen everywhere: grasslands suitable for animal pasture retained that character until well into the twentieth century.[6]

Although some have objected to the term "revolution" because the development of agriculture took such a long time even in the areas where it began,[7] it was nonetheless a revolutionary change in the way people lived, socialized, and died, for what agricultural advances made possible was ever-greater amounts of food than the direct producers could consume in any given year, in other words an "agricultural surplus," giving rise to social groups who did not have to produce their own food: priests, rulers, warriors, and outside raiders, usually nomadic people. The existence of this agricultural surplus meant that others could take it, either by force if necessary or more regularly as taxes. In either case, a major schism opened in society between the agriculturists and the nonproducing ruling elite: the job of the agriculturists was to produce the food and the surplus, the role of the priests was to explain how and why the world had come to exist in the first place, and that of the rulers was to protect the surplus from invading outsiders.

The agricultural revolution also gave rise to two additional defining characteristics of "civilization," cities and writing. Since priests and rulers did not have to produce their own food, they could live separate from the villagers, in their own compounds as it were. Rulers also gathered around themselves artisans to produce needed clothing, weapons, and buildings, giving rise to the larger concentrations of people we have come to call "cities." From there, the elite could rule their lands while keeping track of the number of agriculturists, the amount of food they produced, and in particular the amount they owed the rulers in taxes, developing systems of accounting and writing. Besides keeping count of population and taxes, writing was also useful for priests to record their origin stories, to compute calendars for agricultural and ritual purposes, and to forecast the future.

A city and its surrounding agricultural area typically was not self-sufficient, so people traded with other cities or with nomads or other pastoralists for raw materials (e.g., metals such as copper and tin, the makings of bronze, or later iron ore) or animals (especially horses). If the required goods were also strategic, that is, related to military sources of power, ruling elites tended to distrust trade and wanted to secure the strategic materials by bringing the producing region under its control, through the use of force if necessary. This dynamic gave rise, over time, to *empires*: geographically large political units ruled and controlled by a single ruling elite in which the subject population offered up their agricultural surplus to the ruler and the landowning elite, usually in the form of taxes and rents.

Towns and Cities in 1400

Although most of the world's population lived in the countryside, towns and cities of various sizes and functions did exist, and we can use the number and sizes of towns and cities as a very rough indicator of the overall wealth of a society (or to put it differently, of the ability of the peasantry to produce a surplus large enough to support those who did not grow their own food). A list of the twenty-five largest cities in the world in 1400 produces few surprises, in that most remain large cities today, but the world's largest urban populations in 1400 amounted to little more than 1 percent of the world's population.[8] What may be surprising, however, is that nine of the world's largest cities, including the largest, Nanjing, were all in China. The second-largest city was in south India (Vijayanagar), and the third was Cairo. Only when we get to the fourth-ranked city (Paris) do we get to Europe, which did have five cities in the top twenty-five. Other large cities included Constantinople on the Mediterranean; Samarkand, the Central Asia link in east-west trade routes across Eurasia; Baghdad, likewise an important trading city; and Fez in Morocco, which played an important role in African trade routes.

Of course, these largest cities in 1400 (which ranged in size from 80,000 to nearly 500,000 at the top) represented but 1+ percent of the world population, while another 9 percent or so (or thirty million people) lived in towns and cities ranging from 5,000 to 75,000. Not surprisingly, most of those too were in Asia, with China, Japan, and India accounting for the most. In Europe, by contrast, the largest city in Germany was Cologne at just 20,000 people. The wealth of the world in 1400, as measured by the number and size of cities, thus was concentrated in Asia.

To villagers, these towns and cities were somewhat magical places where people with great wealth ate foods peasants could only dream of and wore clothing of such finery that it put their coarse cloth to shame, all without most of the elite doing any visible work. Of course, the taxes, tithes, and rents the peasants paid supported these towns and cities, and they knew it. So too did another group of people, the nomads, who eyed the civilizations with their cities and productive agriculture warily, but also with a certain envy, and who had the military ability to attack when necessary.

Nomads

The agriculturally based civilizations occupied the best land for agriculture throughout the Eurasian continent. The great grassland known as the steppe, stretching east to west across the continent, as well as the deserts and swamps, while not amenable to agriculture because of too little (or too much) water, were not uninhabited. On the steppe especially, groups of people obtained their living from the land by hunting and gathering and following their herds.[9] For these nomads, mobility on horses was a way of life, taking their herds of horse, sheep, cattle, and goats wherever the grass was green. Their way of life was not completely self-sufficient, for they needed things that the cities produced—salt, pots and pans, textiles, other manufactured goods— trading in return horses, meat, honey, or other products they could gather and that people in the cities prized. Civilizations and nomads across the Eurasian continent thus had a symbiotic relationship—they depended on each other.

The relations between the two groups were for the most part peaceful, but the nomads could constitute fearsome fighting forces. As hunters, they were expert horsemen and archers. And when climate changes desiccated their grazing lands and threatened their food supplies, they were not averse to raiding the food supplies stored by the civilizations, whether they were cities or empires. Of course, ruling elites of civilizations had armies—and a duty—to protect the food supplies from raiding nomads. To those within the centers of the civilization, these nomads appeared to be the opposite of civilized: they had no cities, were crude and illiterate, and probably superstitious as well. In short, they were "barbarians." And when the civilizations themselves weakened, for various reasons, they became susceptible not just to nomadic raids, but to invasion, destruction, or conquest, all of which happened. Notable examples include the fall of the Roman and Han Chinese empires (300–600 C.E.; not discussed in this book) and, as we will see shortly, the Mongol invasions of China and Europe in the thirteenth century. Of course, when the centers of "civilization" weakened, rulers sometimes incorporated nomadic warriors into their frontier armies, further weakening the civilization and opening it to conquest from within by partially acculturated nomads.

Nomads were not the only ones to challenge the civilizations. In the forests, swamps, brush, and mountains there were other groups, who, unlike the nomads, were often quite self-sufficient and could obtain everything they needed from their environment. They did come into contact with the forces of civilization though, especially during periods of population growth when peasant farmers or the empire sought new land to accommodate the larger population. The Chinese, for example, had a long history of contact with these kinds of peoples, and in fact had come to classify them into two groups: the "cooked," those willing to accept some of the trappings of Chinese civilization, and the "raw," those who were not.[10]

Wildlife

Even though most of the weight of the world's population lived in just a few highly developed islands of civilization, the intervening expanses were inhabited by differently organized people to be sure, but people nonetheless. Indeed, by 1400 humans had migrated through or to virtually every place on the globe. Of course the hunters and nomads who lived in the vast spaces outside the densely populated civilizations were very few and far between, leaving much room for wildlife of all kinds. Three examples will suffice.

Wolves roamed throughout most of Europe, as can be attested by *Grimm's Fairy Tales*. But even more grimly, when human populations declined or hard winters made food precious for both humans and wolves, packs of wolves could—and would—enter the cities, as they did in Paris in 1420 and 1438, and even as late as the 1700s when the French went on a campaign to annihilate the species there "as they did in England six hundred years ago," according to a contemporary writing about 1779.[11] In China, tigers at one time inhabited most of the region and periodically attacked Chinese villages and cities, carrying away piglets and babies alike when humans disrupted their ecosystem by cutting away the forests that provided them with their favored game, deer or wild boar. Tigers remained so plentiful in Manchuria that the emperor's hunting expedition could bag sixty in one day, in addition to a thousand stags, and reports of tiger attacks on south China villages continued until 1800.[12] The greatest natural bounty, though, was in the New World, particularly North America, where the first European visitors described "unbelievable" numbers and sizes of fish, birds, deer, bear, and trees.[13]

Thus from 1400 to 1750, when the human population increased from 350 to 720 million, there was still plenty of room for wildlife of all kinds. Nonetheless, the relationship between the two populations clearly was inverse: the more people, the less wildlife, especially as those in the "civilizations" developed a desire for wearing furs (in China, Europe, and North America) or eating exotic fish and fowl. Great hunting expeditions to kill whales, tigers, bison, beavers, homing pigeons, sharks, fox—the list goes on— for their hides, their meat, their various other body parts, started then and continue to this day, except for those species already extinct or, in some parts of the world, protected.

The expansion of the human population on earth thus meant less land and hence habitat available for other species. Although we depend on the environment for our survival, our species has been willing to sacrifice others for our *Lebensraum*.[14] Sometimes the end for other species has come like a rifle shot, with the species wiped out without altering the rest of the physical environment, as when the wolves were eliminated from England, France, or Wisconsin, or bison from the Great Plains, leaving the forest or the plains intact—impoverished, but intact. At other times, the end for a species comes as a holocaust, where expanding human populations have burned and slashed entire ecosystems to turn them into agricultural fields, as happened to the south China tiger. However, with each of the great human population declines in the mid-fourteenth and then in the mid-seventeenth centuries, wildlife populations reestablished themselves and once again expanded. But since the mid-1700s, the human population of the world has steadily increased, putting pressure on all remaining wildlife.

Population Growth and Land

Population growth and decline each brought certain benefits and difficulties to a society. On the one hand, and as with any living organism, an increase in human numbers is an indication of our success in obtaining greater food energy from the ecosystem. Higher populations and greater densities made possible civilizations, cities, education, and trade, as well as a growing awareness and understanding of the human and natural worlds. Population growth thus can accompany improving conditions and rising standards of living for most people, at least up to a certain point, where the limits of land availability and the ability to feed the growing population were reached. In those instances, the human population could overshoot the capacity of the land to feed them, leading to deteriorating living conditions and greater susceptibility to death from disease and famine. As the population fell back, a better balance between the numbers to be fed and the amount of land available to feed them was reestablished.

A growing human population requires additional food and energy supplies to support it, and given the agricultural technology available in 1400, those increases could come from but three sources: bringing more land under cultivation, increasing the labor inputs on a given plot of land (including selecting better seed), or increasing the amount of water or fertilizer. In China over the period from 1400 to 1800, for example, the population almost quadrupled from 85 to 320–350 million, the increase being sustained almost equally by increases in the land under cultivation and by more intensive tilling and fertilizing of the land already under the plow.[15]

Of course bringing new land under cultivation implied human migration to new lands, fighting and displacing the wildlife as necessary, and also battling the "uncivilized" people of the mountains, forests, and bush. Some migrations, though, were easier than others, especially if the new lands were sparsely populated and poorly defended or the migrating people had the military might of their empire backing them (as was the case in China). Some areas, though, were for all intents and purposes off limits; Europeans, for example, could not look too far east because the lands were already occupied by various strong nomadic peoples: Turks, Tartars, and Mongols all sent shivers of fear down the spines of most Europeans and Asians.

In summary, nearly all of the world's 350 million people living in 1400 were rural people producing food and raw materials for handicraft industries to sustain both themselves and a small ruling elite that took a portion of the harvest as taxes (to the state) and rent (to landowners). Peasant families often spun and wove textiles that they used both for themselves and traded in local markets for goods they themselves could not produce, and at times their textiles entered into some very long-distance trade circuits, as we will see shortly. With good climatic conditions and hence better harvests, peasant families might look to increase their size,[16] especially if additional land were available nearby, or if their government encouraged more distant migration and would protect them from the wolves or tigers and nomadic invaders. If the population grew too much or too fast, overshooting the ability of the land to support them, a couple of poor harvests could spell famine and increase susceptibility to epidemic disease, as happened in the early 1300s, and would happen once again in the late 1500s and early 1600s.

Epidemic disease, famine, war, and other disasters kept human life expectancy much shorter than it is today. In many of the richest and most advanced parts of the premodern world, from China and Japan in East Asia to England and Germany in Europe, life expectancies at birth were 30–40 years,[17] or half of what they are today for most of the developed world. Of course those life spans were short largely because infant and childhood mortality were high: women bore many children and were lucky if half survived to age fifteen. Once past the dangers of death from childhood disease, many people could expect to live into their sixties—under good agricultural conditions, that is.

Famine

Food shortages, dearth, and famine were an all-too-real part of life (and death) for most of the people living in 1400. It is of course all too easy to blame such disasters on "natural causes" alone. But in that time period 80–90 percent of the world was composed of one vast peasantry, rural people who produced the food and industrial raw materials for the society and who were obligated to give up a certain amount of their harvest each and every year to agents of the state in the form of taxes and, unless they were in the small minority lucky enough to own their land free and clear, in the form of rent and labor services to the landowner.[18] Throughout much of the most densely populated part of Eurasia (that is, in China, Europe, and India), peasant families gave up as much as half of their harvest to the state and landlords.[19]

In good or improving times, peasant families might be able to make ends meet, providing for their own subsistence needs and also meeting their obligations to the tax man and rent collector, and to produce a surplus that might be sold in the market. But what about those times when the harvest fell short? A "good" government or a "good" landowner might recognize that to take their regular share would push the peasant family below *subsistence levels*, and thus would lower or cancel taxes and rents for that year. But if the government or landowners either could not or would not—if they had debts to pay others, for instance—then the squeeze would be on. Indeed, Japanese landowners in the eighteenth century said of peasants that they were like sesame seeds: the more you squeezed, the more you got.

So famine in peasant societies was not so much a "natural" as a "social" phenomenon.[20] This is important to understand because it is in this context especially that peasants developed concepts of their own about what rights they had in society, and under what conditions they could press them. The agrarian world that we have been considering thus was not made by the ruling elites, but came about as a result of the interactions, understandings, and agreements (both explicit and implicit) among state agents, landowners, and peasant producers.[21]

Peasant Revolt

Whether peasants would stand for circumstances that might cause famine or revolt against them depended in large measure on two factors. First, no matter how enraged peasants might be at cruel or life-threatening treatment by the state or landlords, if the government or lord had sufficient military force and was ready to use it—and the peasants knew that was the case—they might conclude that they had little choice but to endure, or flee, if they could. The second factor relates to the cohesiveness of peasant communities themselves. Even if force did not prevent them from acting, if the peasant community itself did not have the capacity for collective action, then they might just suffer in silence, and maybe even die over a long winter.[22]

Both conditions were met in sufficient times and places for peasant revolts and other forms of resistance to the established order to have been a major part of the dynamics of the old regime. In Japan from 1590 to 1871, for instance, there were over three thousand instances of peasant revolt, ranging from burning barns to taking up arms. China had fewer but larger-scale peasant revolts, especially in the mid-1600s and in the massive Taiping Rebellion of the mid-1800s. Russia too experienced massive peasant revolts, among the most famous the great Pugachev uprising in the 1700s, and France in some ways is the classic setting for peasant revolts, in particular those accompanying the French Revolution of 1789. England, Germany, and Italy in Europe too had histories of peasant revolt. Wherever peasants were under the thumb of ruling elites, it seems, they found ways to resist or to rebel, even if those acts seldom if ever resulted in a major change in how the society itself functioned.

Epidemic Disease

The 80 to 90 percent of the world that comprised this peasantry—whether in China, India, the various parts of Europe, or even Mesoamerica—thus supported the elites who governed, warred, ministered, and traded. The peasantry, in the words of one historian, thus made it possible for various forms of human "*macroparasites*" to live off of them. Additionally, the entire human population was subject to epidemic disease carried by *microparasites* (e.g., the plague bacteria of the Black Death, the smallpox or influenza viruses, the bacteria causing dengue fever or dysentery, and all the other germs and pathogens that caused diseases we now cannot identify because they have since mutated or died away).[23]

To be sure, the wealthy in both town and countryside had more ways of avoiding death from epidemic disease than the peasants or the poor of the towns and villages, but epidemics could—and did—affect entire populations. Epidemic diseases also traveled the world, slowly at first because of the slowness of trade and contacts between the centers of civilization, as in the period just after the collapse of the Roman and Han Chinese empires, when smallpox and the measles spread from their point of origin in Europe to China. As the world became even more linked together in the thirteenth century by long-distance trade, a single epidemic disease could—and did—move much more rapidly from one end of the Eurasian continent to the other: the Black Death spread from China to Europe in a matter of years, and once in Europe it engulfed nearly the entire region within three years from late 1347 to 1350. To understand how and why the Black Death could move so rapidly from China to Europe, and then spread within Europe, we need to understand the trading networks that linked most parts of Eurasia and made it possible for goods, ideas, and germs to travel from one end of the continent to the other.

The World[24] and Its Trading System circa 1400

During the fourteenth century, the Old World—the Eurasian continent and Africa—had been connected by eight interlinking trading zones within three great subsystems.[25] The East Asia subsystem linked China and the Spice Islands in equatorial Southeast Asia to India; the Middle East–Mongolian subsystem linked the Eurasian continent from the eastern Mediterranean to Central Asia and India; and the European subsystem, centered on the fairs at Champagne in France and the trading routes of the Italian city–states of Genoa and Venice, linked Europe to the Middle East and the Indian Ocean. Moreover, these subsystems overlapped, with North and West Africa connected with the European and Middle East subsystems, and East Africa with the Indian Ocean subsystem. (See map 1.1.)

Three primary trade routes linked the subsystems, enabling us to talk about an integrated trading system: all terminated in the eastern Mediterranean. The northern route went up through the Black Sea, and then overland through the Mongol empire, with Mongol blessing and protection, all the way to China. It was via this route, for instance, that Marco Polo ventured to China in the late 1200s. A central trade route went through Baghdad (controlled after 1258 by the Mongols) and then via the Persian Gulf into the Indian Ocean, thereby giving traders access to the spices and products of East and Southeast Asia. A southern route went from Cairo, controlled by the Mamluk empire, overland south to the Red Sea, and from there into the Indian Ocean as well.

This trading system that linked most of Afro-Eurasia in the thirteenth century is remarkable for a number of reasons. First, that it existed at all is surprising to historians who have focused their attention upon one part or the other of the world—China, India, or France, for example. Until quite recently historians have practiced their craft taking current nation–states (and their historical development) as their unit of analysis, rather than adopting a more global approach. Even historians who pioneered a more global perspective on the period since 1500 and invented the term "world system" argued that the world system only came into being following the voyages of Columbus and da Gama; prior to that empires tended to dominate the global landscape with little, if any, contact among them.[26] Even if there were trade among these empires, they argue, it tended to be only for precious goods destined for a small ruling elite. That many historians now recognize the existence of this previous world system thus raises questions about the connection between it and the one that developed after 1500: Was the post-

Map 1.1. The Eight Circuits of the Thirteenth-Century World System

Source: Janet L. Abu-Lughod, *Before European Hegemony: The World System A.D. 1250–1350* (New York: Oxford University Press, 1989), 34.

1500 system a wholly new creation, or did it arise out of the elements of the preceding one? I tend toward the latter interpretation, as will become clearer in the next chapter.[27]

The other quite remarkable feature of the thirteenth-century world system is that it functioned without a central controlling or dominating force. To those who conceive of the modern world system as growing under the domination of a single state or group of states, the idea that a system could work without a controlling center is somewhat novel.[28] To be sure, each of the trade circuits did have a predominating group—the Italians in the European system, Arabs in the Middle Eastern circuit, and Chinese in the East Asian circuit—but no one of those controlled the whole system. Force thus was not used to keep goods flowing throughout the system, although rulers in various parts did offer protection to traders, caravans, or ships. Indeed, most of the rulers recognized that trade was valuable—especially when they could tax it—and hence encouraged and protected it, not wanting to kill the goose that was laying golden eggs by trying to seize by force the goods of traders from another part of the world.

The world in the fourteenth century thus was polycentric: it contained several regional systems, each with its own densely populated and wealthy "core," surrounded by a periphery that provided agricultural and industrial raw materials to the core, and most of which were loosely connected to one another through trade networks. Moreover, I will argue, the world remained polycentric until quite late in our story, around 1800, when Europeans put into place the elements necessary to colonize most of the globe, in the process creating a global system with a highly developed core and an underdeveloped periphery. Even then, some regions—especially parts of East Asia—remained highly resistant to being fully colonized. The importance of conceiving of the world as having been polycentric rather than dominated by a single center will become more evident as we proceed with this narrative. Suffice it to say here that a polycentric conception of the world will attune us to voices and actions coming from several parts of the world, and not just Europe. It is, in short, a crucial part of a non-Eurocentric narrative of world history.

Finally, the Afro-Eurasian system circa 1300 is called a "world system," not because it literally spanned the entire globe, but because it was greater than any one given part.[29] Indeed, for all practical purposes, it was a world system, for it involved all those parts of the world where people traded and thus did know something, no matter how little, about one another. Obviously not yet connected to the Afro-Eurasian trading system were the Americas and the empires arising independently there, or Australia and the Pacific Islands.

The method I have used to describe the world, focusing on the linkages among the various regional systems, emphasizes the role of trade and merchants in forging those links. To be sure, the role of merchants and trade in creating the world system was important. As I will show in more detail in the next chapter, not only did trade allow different parts of the world to sell what they could best produce or gather, but merchants also served as conduits for cultural and technological exchange as well, with ideas, books, and ways of doing things carried in the minds of the merchants while their camels or ships carried their goods. Additionally, epidemic disease and death, soldiers and war also followed trade routes, as we can see by examining the world's experience with the Black Death in the mid-1300s, after which most Eurasians shared a common disease pool.

The Black Death:
A Mid-Fourteenth Century Conjuncture

The mid- to late 1300s constituted a serious crisis in world history.[30] The collapse around 1350 of the Mongol empire, which had served as the glue holding much of Eurasia together, was part of that crisis, and so too were the ravages of the Black Death, a virulent epidemic disease also known as the bubonic plague, which killed tens of millions of people in the mid-1300s. The reasons why the Black Death occurred when and how it did are complex, as are its consequences. But we can begin to understand it by applying the conceptual tool of "conjuncture" discussed in the introduction.

The bubonic plague is a result of a bacillus, that is, a disease-producing bacterium (*Pasteurella pestis*), that was endemic among burrowing rodents in southwestern China. The bacteria can live within the rodent populations without being transmitted to humans, but if passed to humans through flea bites, within days it usually led to the death of the human host. People who lived near those infected rodent populations developed taboos to keep themselves at a safe distance from the flea- and bacteria-carrying rodents. Not so those ignorant strangers or newcomers to an infected region, for that is what happened in southwestern China in the 1330s. Mongol troops campaigning there apparently carried the fleas or an infected rodent into the more densely populated areas of China, setting off an epidemic in 1331 which, according to Chinese sources, in some places killed two-thirds of the population.

The plague would have remained a Chinese dilemma and not such an important part of world history if several other unrelated things had not happened. First, a rodent host population in Europe had to grow and live among humans: that happened when, for whatever reasons, the black rat (*Mus rat-*

tus) took up residence in the attics and rafters of people's houses. Second, the European population had increased substantially from about 1000 C.E. on, with shortages of land and forest for fuel being notable by 1300. Then, the climate worsened, with winters becoming longer and harder and the growing season shorter, putting the population under severe stress. Circumstances were ripe in Europe for some kind of disaster: if it wasn't the plague, it might have been something else, maybe not at the same time or place, but surely the kindling had been laid and all that was needed to set it afire was a single spark. That it was the plague, and that it spread rapidly, was occasioned by three additional factors.

First, the Mongol empire spanned almost the entire Eurasian continent, and their communications system took advantage of a northerly route across the vast, treeless steppe where their horses could transmit messages very rapidly. Moreover, that steppe ecosystem harbored a certain burrowing rodent that lived in vast underground "cities" and was susceptible to the plague bacillus. Soon after the plague broke out in 1331 in China, Mongol riders heading west probably transmitted the plague to the rodents on the steppe, spreading it across Eurasia.

Second, Europeans had developed a regional trading network linked by the activities of Italian merchants from the city–states of Genoa and Venice. Still, the plague might not have spread to Europe had it not been for the third circumstance. The trading city of Caffa, located on the Black Sea, was the link between the trans-Eurasian trade routes: it was the western terminus for caravan trade from China and the eastern terminus for trade carried on Venetian and Genoese ships, both of which apparently docked at Caffa in December 1346. At the time, Caffa was being besieged by the forces of a Mongol prince, and the city might have fallen had not the plague broken out among the Mongol troops, killing most and forcing the prince's withdrawal. The plague might have stopped there had not fleas, rodents, or infected Italians climbed aboard their ships bound for home. When they reached there in December 1346, the plague was let loose in Europe, and it spread rapidly to other towns via the trade routes that had been established, especially the shipping routes. Not only did the black rats now living in European houses spread the plague to people; infected humans too could spread it directly to others by coughing. The plague raged across Europe. By 1350 it had spread all the way to Sweden and then that winter on to Moscow.

Like famine, the plague was not a purely "natural" phenomenon either, but instead required a host of circumstances to come together for it to have such a major impact on the world and its history. The population of Europe plummeted from 80 to 60 million in just a few years, while in China, the plague coupled with civil war in the 1350s and 1360s saw the population tumble from 120 million in 1200 to 85 million by 1393. Although few records exist to confirm it, the plague probably also decimated the Islamic world, India, and the nomadic Mongol peoples of the steppe as well.[31]

The death toll was high and it etched a permanent memory in the minds of the living. But despite the horror of corpses piled high in village lanes, carted off for burial, or set afire on rafts pulled out to sea, those living fifty years later in 1400 did have more and better land, more fuel, and more resources of all kinds, even if the tempo of trade among the various regions of the global trading system had slowed considerably. The story of the fourteenth-century Black Death thus not only illustrates the impact of epidemic disease on human populations and the course of world history; it also demonstrates the very early connectedness of world regions, in this case Europe and East Asia. Not only did commodities, people, and ideas ride the trade routes, so too did horrifying disease.

Conclusion: The Biological Old Regime

This balancing act of people fending off or dying from both macro- and microparasites—elites living off peasants, civilizations fighting off or losing to nomadic invaders, and germs multiplying inside of and then killing nomads and city dwellers alike—has been called our "biological ancien regime," or biological "old regime."[32] In this world—the world not just of 1400 but the world for millennia before and then afterward until well into the nineteenth century (as we will see in chapter 5)—the human population lived very much in the environment and had to be very mindful of the opportunities and limits it placed on human activity. As a result, the human population did not increase so much or so fast as to threaten the environmental basis for society, except in a few cases,[33] or until later developments shattered the biological old regime and opened up new possibilities, but that is a story for later in this book.

Agriculture not only provided the food for the entire society, but most of the raw materials for whatever industry there was, especially textiles for clothing. In China, silk and cotton reigned supreme; in India, cotton and silk; and in northwestern Europe, wool: the raw materials all coming from farms. Fuel for processing these materials, as well as for keeping warm, also came from forests. To this extent, the biological ancien regime was organic; that is, it depended on solar energy to grow crops for food and trees for fuel. The biological old regime thus was one that limited the range of possibilities for people and their history because virtually all human activity drew upon *renewable* sources of energy supplied on an annual basis by the sun.

All living things need food for energy to live, and increasing amounts of both to sustain larger populations. What agriculture allowed people to do, in effect, was to capture natural processes and to channel that energy into the human population. In the biological old regime, agriculture was the primary means by which humans altered their environment, transforming one kind of ecosystem (say, forest or prairie) into another (say, rye or wheat farms, rice paddies, fish ponds, or eel weirs) that more efficiently channeled food energy to people. The size of human populations was thus limited by the amount of land available and the ability of people to use the energy from that land for their purposes.

Regardless of whether the Old World population was pushing environmental limits by about 1300, as some historians think, the Black Death drastically reduced the global population, in particular in China and Europe. Then, from about 1400 onward, the human population of the world began increasing again, and, as we will see, 350 years later once again was reaching some of the limits imposed by the biological old regime. To be sure, by 1750 the population of the world had reached some 750 million people, twice that of the medieval maximum of 360 million in the year 1300.

To support twice as many people as before, something had to change in terms of the relationship of people to the availability of land and their efficiency in working it. On the one hand, Europeans were to encounter a whole new world, the Americas, and to populate it. Although this New World was already quite populated in 1400 and the land already used by Native Americans, a massive biological exchange would radically alter those relationships, making the Americas a relatively depopulated world by the year 1600. We will examine that story in chapter 3. On the other hand, global trading relationships became reestablished, allowing a considerable increase in overall production and productivity as specialization allowed people in one part of a regional trading network to produce goods that their environment was especially suited to, and to trade via markets with countless others who were doing the same thing. Market specialization spread, thereby allowing economies throughout the world to produce more than they ever had in the past, yet without escaping the limits of the biological old regime. How those global networks became reestablished is in part the story of the next chapter.

Notes

1. The phrase is from Fernand Braudel, *Civilization and Capitalism 15th–18th Century*, vol. 1, *The Structures of Everyday Life*, Sian Reynolds, trans. (New York: Harper and Row, 1981), chap. 1.

2. Because no one actually took a census, these population figures are reconstructions by historical demographers, and there is much discussion and debate about all matters having to do with the size, distribution, and dynamics of human populations in the period covered by this book. Braudel's discussion in the chapter mentioned above is as good a place as any to enter into the uncertainties about the size of premodern populations. See also Colin McEvedy and Richard Jones, *Atlas of World Population History* (New York: Penguin Books, 1978).

3. Climatologists have identified several "forcing" factors, ranging from astronomical cycles to volcanic dust and cycles in the sun's activity. On how climate works and its impact on human society, see H. H. Lamb, *Climate History and the Modern World* (London: Methuen, 1982). For a detailed examination of how volcanic activity affected climate and human society, see William Atwell, "Volcanism and Short-term Climatic Change in East Asian and World History, c. 1200–1699," *Journal of World History* 12, no. 1 (Spring 2001): 29–98.

4. Until recently, research on the effect of climate change on harvests was limited to marginal areas such as Scandinavia. My own work on south China has shown that climate changes can in fact affect harvests in even semitropical areas. However, that climatic conditions affected human population dynamics does not imply a kind of geographical determinism, that is, that human societies are determined by the nature of the climate and geography in which they find themselves. Rather, people are amazingly adaptable and can create social institutions to compensate for the vagaries of climate or geography. Eighteenth-century China, for instance, had both government granaries, which dispensed grain in times of need, and markets, which moved grain from areas of surplus to those of deficit, both of which began to detach China's population dynamics from any simple response to climatic variations, but that began to happen only in the late 1700s. See Robert B. Marks, *Tigers, Rice, Silk and Silt: Environment and Economy in Late Imperial South China* (Cambridge: Cambridge University Press, 1998), chaps. 6–8.

5. Braudel, *Civilization and Capitalism*, vol. 1, 56–57. Braudel does not include the Aztecs and Incas in his list of civilizations because they did not have iron, the wheel, and plows or large draft animals. I include them because despite lacking these, they did create empires with cities, social classes, and, in the case of the Aztecs, writing, all of which I think are emblematic of civilization. See also Jared Diamond, *Guns, Germs, and Steel* (Cambridge: W. W. Norton, 1998), for additional discussion of why the Old World had domesticated draft animals and the New World had not.

6. For an interesting discussion of the dating and why food production emerged in these areas, see Jared Diamond, *Guns, Germs, and Steel*, esp. chaps. 4–10.

7. For an excellent discussion see Clive Ponting, *A Green History of the World: The Environment and the Collapse of Great Civilizations* (New York: Penguin Books, 1991), chap. 4. Ponting prefers the term "transition."

8. Estimating city size in 1400 is no more scientific than estimating the total population. Nonetheless, Tertius Chandler has complied lists of the largest cities in the world in his compendium, *Four Thousand Years of Urban Growth: An Historical Census*, 2d ed. (Lewiston, Me.: Edwin Mellen Press, 1987). Although one might take issue with his figures, what interests us more at this point is the relative ranking and geographic distribution of these cities.

9. Following G. W. Hewes, Braudel lists twenty-seven identifiable groups of hunter-gatherers, seventeen nomadic peoples, and an additional eighteen primitive agriculturists. *Civilization and Capitalism*, vol. 1, 56–60.

10. For a fascinating discussion of the "cooked" and the "raw" in the context of Chinese expansion into a frontier area, see John Shepherd, *Statecraft and Political Economy on the Taiwan Frontier 1600–1800* (Stanford, Calif.: Stanford University Press, 1993).

11. Cited in Braudel, *Civilization and Capitalism*, vol. 1, 66–67.

12. See Robert B. Marks, *Tigers, Rice, Silk, and Silt: Environment and Economy in Late Imperial South China* (Cambridge: Cambridge University Press, 1998), chap. 10.

13. William Cronon, *Changes in the Land: Indians, Colonists, and the Ecology of New England* (New York: Hill and Wang, 1983).

14. This German term was used by the Nazis after World War I to express their desire, fanned by a sense that the German population had expanded beyond the ability of the German territory to sustain it, to expand at their neighbors' expense. It seems an apt term to describe what humans in general have felt about expanding their territory at the expense of the natural world.

15. There is much scholarly debate on the size of China's population and its rate of growth from 1400 to 1850. The baseline was established by Ping-ti Ho in 1953 in *Studies on the Population of China* (Chicago: University of Chicago Press), followed by Dwight Perkins, *Agricultural Development in China* (Chicago: Aldine, 1968). Where G. William Skinner thinks the generally accepted figures for 1850 of about 420–450 million have to be reduced to about 380 million ("Sichuan's Population in the Nineteenth Century: Lessons from Disaggregated Data," *Late Imperial China* 8, no. 1 (1987): 1–80), F. W. Mote thinks the population in 1600–1650 and later was much larger than previously believed. See his *Imperial China 900–1800* (Cambridge, Mass.: Harvard University Press, 1999), 743–747, 903–907.

16. The question of whether and how peasant farming families in Europe and elsewhere decided to limit their size is an important question that will be discussed more when we discuss the Industrial Revolution in chapter 5.

17. See Kenneth Pomeranz, *The Great Divergence: China, Europe, and the Making of the Modern World Economy* (Princeton, N.J.: Princeton University Press, 2000), 36–40.

18. In much of Europe, the Church "tithed" the peasants too, expecting one-tenth of their produce. Monasteries could be large landowners as well.

19. This circumstance coincided with the very origins of civilization and persisted for many years into the twentieth century. For a brief and readable history, see Ponting, *A Green History of the World*, esp. chap. 6.

20. For a full development of this argument, see Amaryta Sen, *Poverty and Famines: An Essay on Entitlement and Deprivation* (Oxford: Clarendon Press, 1981). See also David Arnold, *Famine: Social Crisis and Historical Change* (New York: Basil Blackwell, 1988).

21. On the agency of peasants in the making of their own world, see James C. Scott, *Domination and the Arts of Resistance: Hidden Transcripts* (New Haven, Conn.: Yale University Press, 1990). A similarly interesting case was made about black slaves in North America by Eugene Genovese, *Roll, Jordan, Roll: The World the Slaves Made* (New York: Pantheon Books, 1974).

22. There is a wonderful literature on peasants and peasant rebellion in agrarian societies. See James C. Scott, *The Moral Economy of the Peasant* (New Haven, Conn.: Yale University Press); Eric Wolf, *Peasant Wars of the Twentieth Century* (New York: Harper and Row, 1969); and Barrington Moore, *The Social Origins of Dictatorship and Democracy: Lord and Peasant in the Making of the Modern World* (New York: Beacon Press, 1966).

23. The idea of macro- and microparasites is developed in William McNeill, *Plagues and Peoples* (New York: Anchor Books, 1976).

24. For the time being, this formulation excludes the Americas, southern Africa, and much of Oceania.

25. This description is based upon Janet Abu-Lughod, *Before European Hegemony: The World System A.D. 1250–1350* (New York: Oxford University Press, 1989). A summary is available from the American Historical Association as a pamphlet, *The World System in the Thirteenth Century: Dead-End or Precursor?* (Washington, D.C.: American Historical Association, 1994).

26. Immanuel Wallerstein, *The Modern World-System*, 3 vols. (New York: Academic Press, 1974–1989).

27. Abu-Lughod and Wallerstein see the post-1500 world system as being something new, created by Europeans, and not related to the previous one.

28. The example of the Internet, though, should sensitize us even more to the possibility that huge, complex organizations can develop without any central control. To create a Web page, for example, one need not seek the permission of anyone, other than registering a domain name.

29. Immanuel Wallerstein describes the capitalist "world-system," with a hyphen, in *The Modern World-System I: Capitalist Agriculture and the Origins of the European World-Economy in the Sixteenth Century* (New York: Academic Press, 1974), 15. His use of the term "world-system" means specifically the world-system that he argues emerged first in Europe and then was spread by Europeans across the globe from 1492 on. Others use the term "world system" without a hyphen to indicate something similar, yet different, such as the "polycentric" world system I have been describing (i.e., one that was a "world" but not created, diffused, or necessarily controlled by Europeans).

30. This section is based primarily on McNeill, *Plagues and Peoples*, chap. iv.

31. Michael Dols, *The Black Death in the Middle East* (Princeton, N.J.: Princeton University Press, 1977).

32. The term is used both by Braudel, *Civilization and Capitalism*, vol. 1, 70–72, and Ponting, *A Green History of the World*, chap. 12.

33. For examples, see Ponting, *A Green History of the World*, chaps. 1, 5, and 17.

CHAPTER TWO

Starting with China

"Why was the Indian Ocean so important?"

Historians agree that the voyages of Christopher Columbus across the Atlantic in 1492 and of Vasco da Gama around Africa's Cape of Good Hope into the Indian Ocean in 1498 constitute important developments in the emergence of the modern world. Indeed, they were. Where historians disagree is *how* important they were: Did they represent a new era? Did they really change all that much? Eurocentric interpretations tend to see them as major steps taken toward the inevitable rise of the West. Some, on the other hand (myself included), think it is important to place those voyages of discovery in a broader global context of the real structure of wealth and power in the world around 1500. From that perspective, the Indian Ocean can be seen as the most important crossroads for global exchanges of goods, ideas, and culture, with China, India, and the Islamic Near and Middle East meeting there as the major players, and Europe as a peripheral, marginal player trying desperately to gain access to the sources of wealth generated in Asia. Our story in this chapter thus starts in Asia, with China.

China

When the founding emperor of China's Ming dynasty (1368–1644) died in 1398, succeeding him to the throne was not one of his sons, but his grandson. The emperor had wanted his eldest son to succeed him, to establish a firm principle of primogeniture to be followed for the rest of the dynasty, but when that son died, the emperor anointed his eldest son's eldest son as heir to the throne. This decision did not sit well with the emperor's fifth son, the Prince of Yan, a man with impressive military credentials, who

Map 2.1.   The World circa 1400–1500

waited only eighteen months after his father's death to begin unseating his nephew, now the emperor. In a civil war that lasted from late 1399 to mid-1402, the Prince of Yan destroyed his nephew's forces and captured the throne, but not without some ambiguity, for rumors abounded that the nephew had escaped the inferno that had burned down his palace.

As the new emperor, the Prince of Yan sought to extend China's power and influence in all directions. He campaigned to the north and northwest against the Mongols, trying to push China's previous rulers so far into the steppe that they would never again threaten China. As part of this policy, he moved the capital from Nanjing ("Southern Capital") on the Yangzi River farther north to Beijing ("Northern Capital"), less than one hundred miles from the Great Wall and the last defense against Mongol invasions. He sent embassies far into Central Asia to secure the acknowledgment by those rulers of China's preeminence. He also intervened in affairs in Vietnam, hoping not just to put rulers favored by China on the throne, but actually to incorporate Annam, as northern Vietnam was then called, into the Chinese empire. In one of the greatest adventures in world history, he launched massive maritime expeditions into the Indian Ocean.

The Voyages of Zheng He, 1405–1433

In the autumn of 1405, the largest fleet of ships the world had ever seen—or would see for another 500 years—began assembling in the mouth of the Yangzi River on China's eastern coast.[1] Over 300 ships manned by 27,000 sailors waited for the reliable winter monsoon winds to begin blowing from the northwest to take them south toward Indonesia and then west through the Strait of Malacca into the Indian Ocean where they had set Calicut, a major trading city on India's west coast, as their destination.

Under the command of Admiral Zheng He, this armada had three primary objectives. First, the emperor ordered it to track down his nephew, the emperor he had deposed, who was rumored to have escaped. Second, the emperor was outward looking and wanted to "show the flag," impressing all of the foreign countries in that part of the world. Confident that China was the wealthiest, most powerful civilization in the world, he wanted to prove it. And finally, the emperor wanted to encourage overseas trade.

In this regard, the emperor was like the emperors of earlier dynasties, especially the Tang (618–907) and Song (960–1279), and even the hated Mongols who had ruled China under the Yuan (1279–1368), who had encouraged overseas trade, well aware of the wealth that could be generated both for society and the state. His father and nephew, though, had wanted a China that returned to and celebrated its agrarian roots with a staunchly conservative and inward-looking Confucian philosophy.[2]

But when the emperor took the throne (literally), China was experiencing some economic difficulties. To be sure, his father's policy of "agriculture is the foundation" had some success as farmers reclaimed land and set about growing food for themselves and to support the empire. But China's monetary system, based on paper money, had collapsed along with the Mongols. Initially, the Ming (as the new dynasty was called) government simply printed large amounts of paper money, resulting both in inflation and loss of public confidence in the currency. Soon, the government decided to abandon paper money altogether, leaving a huge unmet need for currency.

At first, copper coins from previous dynasties were used, but eventually the regime reopened silver mines and allowed unminted silver bullion to be used to settle private commercial transactions. China's domestic production of silver was insufficient for its uses, so it imported more from Japan. Eventually, sufficient amounts of silver were circulating in some parts of the empire that the government commuted taxes there from payment in kind (grain, silk, etc.) to silver, creating a huge demand within China for silver. We will return to this part of the story in the next chapter. Here, suffice it to say that the collapse of the Mongol empire in the mid-1300s led to the severing of overland trade routes linking east and west Eurasia and a recognition by the emperor that an aggressive foreign policy might bring some rewards to China, pushing back the Mongols in the north and exploring opportunities in what the Chinese called the "Western Ocean," that is, the Indian Ocean.

To prepare for these voyages, China had undergone "a frenzy of shipbuilding." Between 1404 and 1407, some 1,681 ships were built, the largest—the gigantic nine-masted "Treasure Ships" of Admiral Zheng He—were about 400 feet long and 160 feet wide, longer than a football field. Other ships of the fleet, ranging in size and function, carried horses, goods for trade, supplies, water tankers, and marines; some were warships bristling with cannons and rockets. So much wood was required to construct the fleet that much of the coast was deforested, and timbers had to be floated a thousand miles down the Yangzi River to the shipyards.

When the first armada assembled under Admiral Zheng He that fall day in 1405, it must have been an impressive sight: hundreds of colorfully painted, watertight ships unfurling bright red silk sails. Altogether, the Chinese mounted seven two-year voyages (they had to await favorable winds to return to China) between 1405 and 1433. During that period, Chinese ships sailed as far as Mozambique on the east coast of Africa, into the Persian Gulf, all around the Indian Ocean, and throughout the Spice Islands of Southeast Asia. They navigated their huge ships through unknown waters and into unfamiliar harbors, traded with local rulers, collected curiosities such as rare gems and even a giraffe, and in a few instances intervened in local affairs to install rulers more friendly to China. (See map 2.1.)

For the fourth voyage (1413–1415), planned for the Arabian port city of Hormuz and the Persian Gulf, the admiral took on board Ma Huan, a Chinese Muslim well versed in both Arabic and classical Chinese. Being Chinese and Muslim was not unusual: Admiral Zheng He himself was Muslim, and his father's given name, Hajji, suggested that he had made the pilgrimage to Mecca. Pilots speaking Arabic had been on all the previous voyages, since the language of commerce and shipping in the Indian Ocean from eastern Africa to the Spice Islands was Arabic, and the Chinese needed Arabic-speaking guides to get around. For the fourth voyage, which apparently had the express aim of establishing diplomatic relations with the Islamic world, Admiral Zheng He and his emperor brought their own interpreter, Ma Huan.[3] Indeed, as a result of the fourth voyage, ambassadors from a large number of Muslim lands, including those in East Africa, returned with the fleet to the Chinese capital, and on the seventh voyage (1431–1433), while in the Red Sea, Admiral Zheng He contacted the sultan of Egypt, who allowed him to call at the port of Jedda, just a few days from Mecca on the Arabian peninsula. On the return trip, China established formal relations with twenty more realms.

By 1435, it appeared that a powerful Chinese presence in the waters of the Indian Ocean was secure, opening a sea route linking the eastern and western parts of the Eurasian continent with trade circuits in India and in Africa, and placing much of the ocean-going trade in the world under Chinese eyes, if not control. Surprisingly, though, the seventh voyage was the last, and Chinese seaborne power declined so rapidly and thoroughly that by 1500 not only were there no Chinese warships in the Indian Ocean, but the Chinese navy had even ceased to exist in the waters off China's own shores.[4] Fortunately for Chinese merchants, the Indian Ocean was a mostly peaceful place to conduct trade, and they continued doing so, even after the withdrawal of the navy.

As we will see, China's withdrawal of the most powerful navy on earth from periodic patrols on and around the Indian Ocean turned out to be of immense importance for the course of world history. For now, though, we have to ask why the Chinese court abandoned the Indian Ocean. The short answer is that political struggles within China, struggles that had been going on for some time at the imperial court between those who wanted the voyages to continue and those who wanted China to apply its resources to the greater threat of the Mongols to the north, finally resolved themselves in favor of the latter when the emperor died in 1435. From that point forward, the Chinese state abandoned the seas, paid attention to how an agrarian economy could feed a growing population, and saw their main enemy as being the nomads roaming the steppe to the north. Rebuilding and lengthening the Great Wall became of greater importance to China's rulers than continuing the expensive voyages of the Treasure Ships.[5] The abandonment of a navy, though, did not mean that Chinese commercial voyages ended as well; quite the contrary, for the Indian Ocean was the world's most important crossroads of trade.

India and the Indian Ocean

The Mongols' overland trade route linking east and west on the Eurasian continent had not been the only, or even the most important, trade route. Where the collapse of the Mongol empire and the ravages of the Black Death may have been part of a wider mid-fourteenth-century crisis that affected much of Eurasia, there is little evidence of much of a slowdown in trading on the Indian Ocean. Indeed, the Indian Ocean had been, and would remain, not just a crucially important link in the global trading system, but a source of great wealth and access to luxuries, spices, and manufactured goods to any and all who could get their merchants, goods, or ships to the major trading cities on the Indian Ocean. The Chinese thus had not been wrong in seeing the importance of the Indian Ocean and wanting to send their ships there.

1776 - dec. of ind.

In fact, the Chinese excursion was but one episode in a longer history of the Indian Ocean, starting in about 650 with the expansion of the Islamic world and the establishment of the Tang dynasty in China, and ending around 1750 with the British colonization of India on the eve of the Industrial Revolution.[6] During those 1,100 years, the Indian Ocean arguably was the single most important crossroads of trade and generator of merchant wealth in the world, and for our purposes its history can be usefully subdivided into three periods.

From 650 to 1000, Arab traders and mariners carried goods and ideas all the way from the Islamic Near East to Southeast Asia and China, and back again. Arab traders spread their language and the Islamic religion throughout the region, from East Africa to Indonesia, providing a common language and culture for those who traveled there. In the ninth century, for instance, over 100,000 Arabs, Persians, and Jews had taken up residence in the south China city of Guangzhou, and the Islamic mosque built there served as a beacon for ships sailing into its port. In the second period, beginning around 1000 and lasting until 1500, Chinese merchants saw the profits to be made in the trade, and, with or without the support of their government, sailed into the Indian Ocean to compete with the Arabs.

The Chinese entrance into the Indian Ocean divided trade in the Indian Ocean into three overlapping trade circuits, determined largely by the pattern of monsoon winds and hence the opportunities for sailing. Arab traders were still important throughout the region, but they were not the only ones plying the waters of the Indian Ocean. In the western zone, from East Africa to the Red Sea, the Persian Gulf, and the west coast of India, Arab traders were most active, although Indian merchants also participated in that trade. The central circuit from Ceylon to the Bay of Bengal and to Southeast Asia was dominated by Indian merchants, although Arabs and other Muslims were very active there too. The Chinese dominated the South China Sea trade circuit from China to Indonesia and the Strait of Malacca.

Within and among these three zones, great trading cities arose to handle the trade. In the western circuit, the ports of Aden, Hormuz, Cambay, Calicut, Mogadishu, and Kilwa (the latter two on the east coast of Africa) were the most important. Linking the eastern and middle circuits was Malacca, a trading port that arose in a strategic strait where the monsoon winds shifted, thereby making a convenient layover place for traders waiting for the next leg of their journey.[7] Nothing else accounts for the rise of this city, but the economic and strategic importance of Malacca was not lost on either the Chinese in the early 1400s or, a century later, the Portuguese. (See map 2.1.)

During the first two periods (spanning 650 to 1500), trade in the Indian Ocean seemed to have been self-regulating. No one political power dominated, or tried to dominate, the trade linking those three zones; that was true even during the voyages of the Chinese Admiral Zheng He, for Arab and Indian merchants continued on with their activities unobstructed by the Chinese or shut out in favor of Chinese merchants. Another notable feature of the trade was that it was conducted largely without resort to force of arms. African dhows (traditional boats), Chinese junks, and Indian and Arab merchant ships all sailed without naval convoys from their native lands. None of the great ports of trade—Aden, Hormuz, Calicut, Puri, Acheh, or Malacca—were walled or fortified. The assumption in this wide-ranging trade seems to have been that force of arms was not needed to protect shipping or to enforce deals.

During the third period, from 1500 to 1750, all of this changed when first the Portuguese and then the Dutch, English, and French introduced "armed trading" into the Indian Ocean, forcing others already there to arm themselves in defense or to pay the intruders for protection (this topic will be taken up in more detail later in this chapter). Europeans literally tried to muscle in on the huge and profitable trade in the Indian Ocean, to control shipping lanes and port cities by force, and to monopolize, if they could, trade in commodities valued in Europe.[8] Despite the fact that Europeans introduced a new element into Indian Ocean trade, the trade was so great that they did not dominate it until the advent of steamships in the late 1800s enabled them to undercut trade carried by Arab, Indian, or Chinese ships.

Four great centers of civilization and economic power provided the impetus for the Indian Ocean trade: the Islamic Near and Middle East, Hindu India, China, and Indonesia, or the Spice Islands. To Malacca, the Chinese brought manufactured goods, in particular silk, porcelain, and iron- and copperwares, and in return took to China spices, other edibles, pearls, cotton goods, and silver. Indians brought cotton textiles and returned with spices. To the Middle East and East Africa, India exported cotton textiles, some of which found their way to West Africa, and other manufactured goods. From Africa and the Arabs, Indians received palm oil, cocoa, ground nuts, and precious metals. In general, agricultural and other raw or primary products of the ocean, forest, or mines, including silver and gold, flowed to China and India, while those two areas exported manufactured goods, especially textiles (cotton in India and silk in China).

The engines of this immense global trade were primarily China and India. In the fifteenth century, in the words of one historian:

China was still the greatest economic power on earth. It had a population probably in excess of 100 million, a prodigiously productive agricultural sector, a vast and sophisticated trading network, and handicraft industries superior in just about every way to anything known in other parts of Eurasia. After a visit to the great Central Asia political and commercial center of Samarkand early in the fifteenth century, for example, a European diplomat described the Chinese goods he found there as "the richest and most precious of all [imported into the city] . . . , for the craftsmen of [China] are reputed to be the most skillful by far beyond those of any other nation."[9]

As a great agrarian empire, China produced much of what it needed, although it did have to trade for horses, some raw materials, preciosities, and silver. Its rulers mostly saw foreign trade as useful if it could bring additional wealth to the state or satisfy consumer demand for black pepper (which had become an integral part of Chinese cuisine) or other exotic foods like edible bird's nests or sea slugs. The rulers of the Chinese empire found most of these imports to be nice, but saw the potential troubles caused by Chinese and foreign merchants to be large, so for most of the time China controlled foreign trade through its tribute trade system of official monopolies, in addition obtaining substantial revenues for the imperial treasury as a result. However, beginning in the early 1400s, China's new and growing demand for silver to keep the wheels of its domestic economy going could not be satisfied by domestic mines alone. Thus to obtain its silver, China had to engage in foreign trade, at first getting most of its silver from Japan, but then increasingly in the 1500s from Europeans, which we will explore in the next chapter.

India had three great textile manufacturing centers: Gujarat on the west coast, Madras in the south, and Bengal on the east. Cotton was spun and woven in artisan homes with material advanced to them by merchants who then collected the thread and cloth for dyeing and printing before being brought to market to sell. Most of this cotton cloth met internal Indian demand, but a considerable amount was produced for export. Some, as we have seen, was bound for Africa or China, but Indian textiles traded as far as Poland and the Mediterranean. To meet both domestic and foreign demand for their cotton textiles, Indians had created a whole manufacturing system from growing the cotton to finishing it. In turn, those Indians who participated in the textile industry had to look to the market to supply their food needs, further commercializing the Indian economy and increasing both production and productivity. Much like the Chinese economy, the Indian economy was highly developed and was the source of select but important manufactured goods for much of the Old World.

Unlike China, though, India at this time was not a unified empire and indeed had a history of both political disunity and unity imposed by outside conquerors. Although India looks like a "place" on a map because of its distinctive geography, it was never really politically unified until the mid-1500s, and then only tentatively because it broke apart again by the mid-1700s. The center of Indian civilization was in the north, in particular the Indus River valley, an agriculturally rich area open to conquest by invaders coming through the Kyber Pass. The Huns did so first in the sixth century, leaving in their wake numerous weak, warring states.

In the eighth century, Arabs spreading the Islamic faith invaded north India and did so again at the end of the tenth century. At the end of the twelfth century, north India was invaded yet again, this time by Turkish Muslims who established a new kingdom, which lasted for two hundred years, the Delhi sultanate. Islam thus gained a stronghold in northwest India where Pakistan now sits, and mosques were built wherever the sultan's power extended. The Delhi sultanate lasted until 1398 when Timur the Lame invaded, ravaged northern India, and sacked Delhi. South India was never easily conquered; it had its own language (Tamil) and political history. Despite the political disunity, Hindu religious ideas spread south in the seventh and eighth centuries, and political leaders soon found Hinduism useful in ruling there too. Thus, not only was India politically divided, but a major religious divide between Muslims and Hindus had opened as well.

Because the rulers of most Indian states supported trade, political and religious disunity did not hinder economic activity, for as we have seen, there was much to be traded when the Chinese Admiral Zheng He began visiting Indian ports in the early 1400s. Muslim merchants, speaking Arabic, could trade easily within a linguistic sphere that spread from East Africa, to the Red Sea and the Persian Gulf, all the way to Acheh and Malacca, both of which had rulers who had converted to Islam in the thirteenth century. Muslims have played an important part in our story so far, and it is now time to explore the question of how Islam originated and spread so far from its point of origin on the Arabian peninsula.

Dar al-Islam, "The Abode of Islam"

In 1325 at the age of twenty-one, a young Muslim man by the name of Ibn Battuta left his home in Tangiers on the North African coast for his pilgrimage (*hajj*) to the holy city of Mecca. Traveling overland to Cairo, he visited Damascus and Medina before reaching Mecca in October 1326. But rather than returning home, Ibn Battuta decided to see more of the world, setting out on a twenty-nine-year journey of 73,000 miles (almost three times the distance around the world). He traveled to Iraq, Persia, down the east coast of Africa, across Anatolia (Turkey) and Central Asia, across the Indian Ocean with stops at the islands of Ceylon and the Maldives, to northern and southern India, probably to south China, back to North Africa and across the

Strait of Gibraltar to the city of Granada, and then back across the Saharan desert to the West African kingdom of Mali.[10]

Amazing by almost any standard, what makes Ibn Battuta's travels significant for us is that virtually everywhere he traveled in the mid-1300s was *dar al-Islam*, "the abode of Islam," or places in the world where Islam was practiced and educated people spoke (or wrote) Arabic, the language of the Quran (Koran). Everywhere he went, Ibn Battuta encountered familiar cultural and linguistic signposts, much like a North American traveling to western Europe today. Although that part of dar al-Islam that he visited was vast, it was not all of it, for Islam had spread to parts of Indonesia and Southeast Asia as well. A fundamental fact of the fifteenth century, then, was the extent of the Islamic world and what that meant for how the world worked. (See map 2.1.)

Islam had burst upon the world in the early seventh century, and in the century following the death of the Prophet Mohammed (in 632 C.E.), Muslim (meaning "believer") armies had unified the Arabian peninsula, captured much of Persia, and took Mesopotamia, Palestine (including Jerusalem), and Egypt and North Africa. Although virtually all other political forces on the Eurasian continent had become seriously weakened prior to the arrival of the Muslims, Byzantium in the west (Eastern Orthodox Christianity with its capital at Constantinople) and China in the east still had sufficient force to check the Muslim advance. Nonetheless, Muslim cavalry consolidated control of North Africa and then took most of the Iberian peninsula within seven years before being turned back by the French, while simultaneously pushing into north India. By 750, a huge new Islamic empire had arisen in the middle of the Eurasian continent.

The significance of the spread of Islam for the course of world history was profound. First and foremost it created a realm of common language and custom covering much of the Old World within which trade, ideas, and culture could develop. Fortunately for the rest of the world, the Islamic world loved books and libraries; indeed, the largest libraries in the world during the eighth to the fifteenth centuries were in Islamic lands, the most famous perhaps being the library at Alexandria in Egypt. In these libraries were stored not just the treasures of the Islamic world, but the classics from ancient Greece and Rome as well. Second, the expansion of Islamic empires in the Mediterranean Sea cut Europe off for centuries from the Indian Ocean, the dynamic center of world trade. It was said that as long as Muslims dominated the Mediterranean, Europeans "couldn't even float a plank on it." To that extent, the flourishing of the Islamic world contributed to the withering of trade within Europe and to their self-described "Dark Ages."

Soon, however, central political control over the Islamic empire began breaking up, with numerous areas asserting effective independence, and a new, more stable Islamic dynasty, the Abbasid with its capital at Baghdad, effectively governing a core region and claiming to be the authoritative center for dar al-Islam. Those areas that had broken free of this central control, though, remained Muslim, as with the Emirate of Cordoba on the Iberian peninsula. In 1258, though, Mongol forces captured and destroyed Baghdad, killing the last Abbasid caliphs and severely disrupting the established Islamic world. Out of this disarray, three new Islamic empires arose: first the Ottoman, which inherited much of the western part of the Islamic world, and then in the early 1500s the Safavids established their rule over Persia, and the Mughals conquered most of India.

The Ottoman empire originated in the late thirteenth century when Turkish nomads, led by Osman Bey (from which the term "Ottoman" comes), began consolidating their power on the Anatolian peninsula (current Turkey), and then, in the 1300s, when Osman's successors constructed an impressive military machine built around the new technology of gunpowder weaponry and a slave-based army called the Janissaries, they ousted the Mamluks from Egypt. Fueled by a desire to be *ghazi* (Muslim religious warriors), the Ottomans pressed hard against the Balkan lands of Christendom held by the Byzantine empire, taking Serbia in 1389 and by 1400 reaching the Danube.

The real prize, though, was the city of Constantinople, the capital of the Byzantine empire and the eastern outpost of Christendom, albeit Eastern Orthodox, not Roman Catholic. Constantinople sat astride the Bosporous Strait and controlled trade in the eastern Mediterranean and on the Black Sea. For centuries, Eastern Orthodoxy and the Byzantine empire had checked the Western advances of the Ottomans and Islam. But Ottoman forces besieged Constantinople in the middle of the fifteenth century, and when it fell in 1453, the Ottomans made it their capital, renamed it Istanbul, and turned St. Sophia's cathedral into a mosque. From there the Ottomans completed their conquest of the Balkans, including Greece and Albania, took the island of Crete, captured Genoan ports in the Black Sea, and planned to take Rome.

The fall of Constantinople in 1453 was a huge blow to Christian Europe. The eastern outpost of Christianity in the Mediterranean, Constantinople had served as a launching pad for some of the crusades into the Levant and represented the hopes of many Christians for an ultimate recapture of Palestine and Jerusalem. But when Constantinople fell to Ottoman rule, it served as a stern reminder that the forces of Islam were not spent and that Europeans could become even more marginalized in the world than they already were.

The Ottomans blocked European access to the eastern Mediterranean and hence the trade circuits to China and the Indian Ocean, forcing Europeans to search for alternative routes to gain access to the riches of Asia.

Africa

Ibn Battuta's travels point out the extent and power of the Islamic empires in the early modern world, even into Africa. Indeed, North Africa, sub-Saharan Africa, and East Africa all were part of dar al-Islam. When Ibn Battuta traveled in Africa, he was visiting not just places in "the abode of Islam," but highly developed civilizations with all that that included: productive agriculture, cities, ruling and subject classes, regional trading systems, and advanced mining industrial activity, including an iron industry. By 500 c.e. the social, economic, and cultural complex characteristic of highly civilized people had spread throughout Africa, and great empires soon arose, the largest of which was Ghana in West Africa. Situated at the juncture of three different ecosystems—the savanna, the tropical rainforest, and the Sahara desert—and therefore able to take advantage of the products from all, Ghana was the most strategically located state at the time of the Muslim arrival in North Africa. After the explosion of Islam across the Mediterranean in the seventh century, all of the African empires that traded north across the Sahara converted to Islam between the tenth and twelfth centuries c.e.[11]

After the kings of Ghana converted to Islam, their kingdom continued to expand. The kingdom of Ghana produced some gold itself, but the Muslims' demand for it proved sufficiently strong and the goods they brought to trade in sufficient demand in West Africa (cloth from India, horses, beads, mirrors, and, most important, salt, which was not locally available) that gold flowed into the capital of Ghana, Koumbi-Saleh, fueling an already thriving trade.

Even more extensive than Ghana was the Mali empire that replaced it. From the 1200s to the early 1400s, Mali controlled and taxed almost all the trade in West Africa, which was indeed substantial. Huge caravans of up to 25,000 camels stretching for miles across the desert brought gold and slaves out of Africa and Indian cotton textiles (among other goods) into Mali. The cities of Mali prospered, and not just the capital city of Niani. Commerce turned Timbuktu into a great center, attracting scholars, architects, poets, and astronomers to its university, and Muslim theologians came there to the more than one hundred schools established to study the Quran.

The height of Mali wealth and influence came during the reign of Mansa Musa (1312–1337), a Muslim who made the pilgrimage to Mecca in 1324–1325 with such a huge procession and amount of gold it was said that when he sojourned in Cairo he gave away so much gold to all whom he met that its value plummeted 25 percent. Most of the gold from Africa found its way first to Cairo, the great trading port linking Asia with the Mediterranean and northern Europe, and from there via trade to India and to the Italian city–states of Venice and Genoa, who then took it farther north into western Europe. In the fourteenth and fifteenth centuries, access to African gold was crucial for Europeans: in the view of one scholar, it was "absolutely vital for the monetization of the Mediterranean economy and for the maintenance of its balance of payments with [India]."[12]

The other route Islam followed into Africa was along the maritime trade routes south from Cairo and the Red Sea along the east coast of Africa to the trading cities of Mogadishu, Malindi, Mombasa, Kilwa, and Sofala. Even during Greek and Roman times, ships had called at East African ports, so the arrival of Muslim traders was not a major change, except that in addition to goods, they brought Islam, and gradually the peoples of East Africa converted to Islam. These cities, though, were so cosmopolitan—traders coming from inland Africa, Arabs, Persians, South Asians, Malays from Indonesia, and even Chinese (some of whom may have stayed behind when Admiral Zheng He's ships departed)—that people intermarried, giving rise to a new coastal culture and language called Swahili, a dialect with strong Arabic influence. Like West Africa, East Africa was a great source of primary products for the world economy, in particular ivory, animal skins, gold, and slaves.

The existence of large empires in Africa, though, should not obscure the larger fact that political power throughout most of Africa was highly fragmented, with hundreds of "ministates"—territories with less than four hundred square miles and just 3,000–5,000 inhabitants—in West Africa alone. Medium-sized states may have been ten times as large, but there were fewer of them. Although there was much warfare between and among African states, there was not much pressure within African society for warring states to expand their territory at the expense of their neighbors. The reason, according to historian John Thornton, is that land was not considered private property, and land was not the basis of wealth in African society.[13] Rather, and in sharp contrast to China, India, or Europe, in Africa control of labor was the source of wealth. It is in this context that we must understand the institution of African slavery.

Slavery

Slaves were used in virtually every society discussed so far in this book: Europe, the Islamic empires, China, and India all had them. Mostly, slaves were used as domestic servants in the households of the wealthy and powerful, and slave status had nothing to do with skin color. Indeed, one of the major sources of slaves was eastern Europe, especially the areas around the Black Sea inhabited by people called Slavs, giving us our word for slave. One of the major "commodities" that Venetian merchants traded to the Mamluk empire in Egypt in fact were these "Slavs," sold for spices and gold in the markets of Cairo. In short, there was a world market for slaves, and European and Muslim traders were eager to supply it.

Africans too kept slaves. Because land was not owned privately and hence was not a source of wealth and power, elite Africans (political heads and merchants mostly) owned labor, that is, slaves. This absence of private property in land made slavery pervasive in Africa. Slaves were used as domestics in households, for agricultural labor, as the mainstays of the armies of several states, and in commerce. Slaves were not necessarily given the most degrading or demanding work in the society, and mostly they were considered as "permanent children," albeit ones who could be inherited by one's real children. There was thus a huge indigenous market for slaves within Africa, many of whom were acquired in the wars between states.[14] In the centuries from 750 c.e. to 1500 c.e., scholars have estimated that as many as 10,000 Africans annually were enslaved, and that the total over those 750 years may have reached 5–10 million.[15] Of course, a major part of the story of African slavery is connected to Europe's Atlantic slave trade to the Americas, and that will be taken up in the next chapter.

Although there is much that is interesting and significant to know about Africa, for our purposes two things stand out. First, African people had constructed large and successful empires, extensive internal trading networks, and productive agriculture and industry, especially mining and refining, long before Europeans arrived on the scene in the fifteenth century. Second, Africa already was an integral part of the world system, supplying gold and slaves and purchasing in return manufactured goods, many of which originated in Asia, such as brightly colored cotton textiles from India and porcelain from China. Although Africa was not an engine propelling the global economy, unlike India or China, neither was Europe.

Europe and the Gunpowder Epic

Although I have used the terms "Europe" and "China" as if they were similar units of comparison, politically they were not at all alike. For most of its long imperial history, China was a huge empire ruled by a single sovereign, as large as the United States today and in 1400 with 85–100 million people. "Europe," on the other hand, is just a convenient shorthand to name the western-most peninsula of the Eurasian continent. Though I have been using the term "Europe" as if there were some unity to it, the truth is that Europe in 1400 was divided among hundreds of political units, from city–states (like Venice or Genoa), to principalities, bishoprics, duchies, kingdoms, and even a Muslim caliphate on the Iberian peninsula, each suspicious of the others, most at war at one time or another with their neighbors, and all trying to build armies and navies for their own protection if not gain at the expense of another.

This system of fragmented sovereignty was a legacy of the breakup of the Roman Empire by the end of the sixth century and the spread of Islam in the eighth century. After the fall of Rome and the loss of access to Mediterranean trade, much of what we now call Europe had regressed into a rural protectionist mode, with a nobility resident in castles for protection against invaders and marauders, collecting dues from the peasantry tied to the land. Military force was used for protection against outsiders, against other untrustworthy nobles, against subordinates who wanted power, against serfs if they rebelled, and in the Crusades against the "Infidel," the Muslims who had taken the Holy Land. In this world, holding a piece of land (and the agricultural produce from its serfs) was the primary objective, and a castle was the main means of securing it.

With swords, knives, lances, pikes, and long- and crossbows being the most lethal weapons available to medieval Europeans, an area could be held by these stone-built castles high on hills overlooking fertile river valleys. By the eleventh century, the usefulness of these essentially defensive structures proved sufficiently effective that they proliferated throughout western Europe. For the next three centuries, defeat of an enemy meant capture of his castle, a feat that usually entailed lengthy sieges. What towns there were—and they were beginning to develop in various places—also built walls for protection, the most famous in northern and central Italy.

It was into this situation of almost constant warring, castles, and fortified towns that a new military technology was introduced in the late fourteenth century: cannons fired by gunpowder.[16] Exactly when cannons became available to Europeans for use in their wars is not clear, but the means by which they got there are. The Mongols not only transmitted the Black Death to Europe in 1347, but sometime in the preceding century Europeans learned about cannons from them too, for by 1327 we have pictorial evidence of an early European cannon.

Gunpowder and cannons had been invented by the Chinese in a process beginning around 1000 C.E. when Chinese sources describe "fire lances" and other weapons including bombs, rocket launchers, flame throwers, land mines, and poison smoke. Unfortunately for the Chinese, the Mongols gained access to this new technology, improved it with the development of early cannons called "bombards," and then used those bombards against Chinese cities in their final campaign of conquest in the late 1200s. The Mongols also used these devices in their attacks against Europeans in the 1200s as well, and some enterprising (or frightened) European stole or bought the technology from the Mongols.

Bombards were not particularly effective at hurling projectiles far or with much accuracy; indeed, they were used initially mostly to scare horses. But Europeans quickly improved them. First to be improved was the shot, at first made of rounded stones but then later of cast iron. Next, European rulers were fortunate to have within their realms craftsmen expert in casting huge church bells. The technology to make cannons was essentially the same, and soon bell casters were hard at work improving cannons, making them stronger, smaller, lighter, and hence more mobile.[17] In the context of nearly constant warfare among European rulers, this new military technology was to prove very useful.

From 1000 to 1500, the major activity of European states was warfare: preparing for war, paying for war, recovering from war. This circumstance, plus the fact that wars became even costlier with the introduction of cannons and other guns, drove European states toward a common form: a territorial state with sufficient wealth generated in towns and cities, and a population sufficiently large to sustain armies. For a while, states that were small but wealthy (such as the Dutch) could hire mercenaries, while those that were large but poor (such as Poland) could conscript serfs into their armies and force them to fight. But by and large the combination that was to prove most successful in the European system of warring states was those with both urban wealth to pay for wars and young men from the countryside to fight in them. Those who had these weapons could claim to be sovereign within their territories and then by force, if necessary, make others subject to them. In the fifteenth century, the consolidation of political power—not just by European rulers—proceeded apace as cannons blazed the way.

In 1453 the Ottoman Turks used cannons to capture Constantinople, and by the same year the king of France had used cannons to drive the English out of France by leveling their fortifications and pushing them back across the English Channel, thereby bringing the Hundred Years' War to an end. By 1453, cannons had proved their worth to the leaders of the hundreds of various-sized political entities spread across Europe. A few decades later in Spain, the "Catholic Kings" Ferdinand and Isabella used a siege train of 180 guns to drive the Muslims from Granada, their last stronghold on the Iberian peninsula.

Because Europe was so fragmented politically, no one leader could get or maintain a monopoly on these new weapons and use them to establish an empire in Europe, although there was a brief moment at the end of the 1400s when that might have been possible, had it not been for the defensive inventiveness of the Italians. The French kings used their new military power to consolidate their grip on Burgundy and then Brittany, before deciding in 1494 to expand their territory by invading Italy. Italian city–states had long been at war with one another, and when Florence attacked Pisa in 1500 with the new cannons, they discovered that behind the stone fortifications lay a new wall—a berm, actually—of soft dirt dug up from a trench. Cannonballs harmlessly hit the dirt, and the fortifications of Pisa held. Soon news of this new defensive maneuver spread throughout Europe, and once again sieges became a prime feature of European warfare.[18] Neither the French kings, the Holy Roman emperor, nor Ferdinand and Isabella of Spain now had the military power to sweep away all the small territories and successfully reunite Europe into an empire, although the attempt would be made again, as we will see, in the not-too-distant future.

Armed Trading on the Mediterranean

The reason for much of this warfare was the attainment, maintenance, and enhancement of wealth and power. Although the understandings of those two concepts meant different things in different times and places, the fact is that most rulers (and others) found the accumulation of wealth to be a good thing. The problem for fifteenth-century Europeans was that their part of the world was relatively poor. Sure, one ruler might be able to take the land of a neighbor by force, but that land and the people on it for the most part were as poor as their neighbors. The land was sparsely populated, with much of it given over to pasturage and raising horses used to pull the plows through the heavy soils. Among the various problems that European farmers had was that they just did not have enough feed to keep all their animals alive through the winter, so they usually slaughtered a fair number of their draft animals. But to prevent that meat from going to waste, Europeans had to find a way to preserve it, and for that salt and especially pepper were critical commodities. Salt could be obtained locally, but pepper came only from Asia, and it was exceptionally expensive. For the most part, Europeans had little to sell in exchange for the pepper.

But Europeans did fight constantly over who would have access to those spices from Asia, in particular the northern Italian city–states of Genoa and Venice, both seaports on the Mediterranean. For centuries, Venice and Genoa competed for access to Asian goods that could be traded within Europe. The competition was not only economic, but military as well. Preying on each other, and seeking protection from North African "pirates," each side began building warships to protect their merchant ships, and ships left port not singly but in convoys. The government of each city provided the protection, paid for by the creation of public debt. Furthermore, all the sailors were expected to be fighters as well. Trade on the Mediterranean thus was armed trade.

A series of events in the thirteen and fourteenth centuries enabled Venice to gain the upper hand, by 1400 securing for its merchants a virtual monopoly on access to Asian spices and textiles.[19] Besides the Genoans, the Venetian victory and use of military force also kept other Europeans out of the Mediterranean. Nonetheless, seafaring Europeans long had fantasized about a direct route to Asia, outflanking the Muslims who stood in the way and avoiding the Venetian monopoly on spices. The Mongols had made an overland route available for a while (which enabled Marco Polo to get to China), but that ended with the collapse of the Mongol empire in the late 1300s. By the 1400s, only one route to Asia existed for Europeans: the Venetian connection through Egypt.

Portuguese Explorations of the Atlantic

The Islamic world thus blocked European access to the spices and manufactured goods of Asia, except through the hands of Egypt's Venetian collaborators. To find a different sea route to Asia around these obstacles, Portuguese mariners on the Atlantic coast of Europe under the leadership of Henry of Avis, better known as "Henry the Navigator," began probing southward in the Atlantic, well aware that Muslim navies still patrolled the Strait of Gibraltar. He was also aware of the Arab belief that at the southern tip of Africa was a cape that could be rounded, leading directly to the Indian Ocean. He was determined to find that route, both to establish direct trade with Asia, thereby cutting out both the Venetians and the Egyptians, and to outflank the Muslims, thereby continuing the work of the crusaders in driving Muslims from the Mediterranean and the Holy Land.

In 1415 Henry the Navigator began his quest with an attack on Muslim positions, and every year thereafter sent ships to explore the African coast. By 1460, when Henry died, Portuguese ships had reached Sierra Leone, near the equator, and established trading relations with Africans. The Portuguese found both gold and slaves in Africa, which they obtained by trading cotton textiles and guns. But the big prize still was Asia via the Indian Ocean, and the Portuguese pressed farther south until 1488 when Bartholomeu Dias finally reached and rounded the Cape of Good Hope. The prize was nearly in

Portuguese hands, and so, when a Genoan sailor named Christopher Columbus approached the Portuguese crown with his idea to reach Asia by sailing west across the Atlantic, he was rejected. As we all know, the Spanish rulers Ferdinand and Isabella ultimately granted Columbus his commission. When news of Columbus's success reached Spain (and Portugal) in 1493, the Portuguese redoubled their efforts to get around the cape, in 1497 sending a new mission under the command of Vasco da Gama. (See map 2.1.)

By the time Henry the Navigator began his voyages in 1415, Admiral Zheng He had already established Chinese dominance throughout the Indian Ocean. Had the Chinese themselves decided to round the Cape of Good Hope and head north along the African coast—which they could have done, having the technology and the ability to learn the tricky winds off the West African coast—they would have encountered the Portuguese in the 1420s making their way down the coast of Africa, but it is hard to imagine that the Portuguese would have presented much of a threat to the Chinese fleet. Thus, it might have been the Chinese, not the Portuguese, who established a direct water route between Asia and Europe, reaping the profits from that trade and keeping the Europeans close to home. As it turned out, of course, the Chinese instead decided to call their navy home, leaving the Indian Ocean an open and peaceful place. Rather than encountering a formidable Chinese force that could have turned them back with little difficulty, the Portuguese in 1498 instead sailed into an Indian Ocean remarkably free from naval power or port cities protected by walls or bastions.

Armed Trading in the Indian Ocean

After rounding the Cape of Good Hope in 1498 and taking on an Arabic-speaking pilot, Vasco da Gama set sail for Calicut on India's west coast (the same destination, it might be remembered, of Admiral Zheng He) and on May 18 he dropped anchor. Upon his return to Lisbon, Portugal's capital, in 1499, the Portuguese crown knew he had pioneered the way to the riches of Asia and quickly sent another expedition, this time under the command of Alvares Cabral. Armed with cannons and instructions to expel the Muslims from Calicut, Cabral bombarded Calicut for two days, targeting Arab ships as well. Then in 1502–1503, according to Arab chroniclers, "the vessels of the [Portuguese] appeared at sea en route for India, Hormuz, and those parts. They took about seven vessels, killing those on board and making some prisoner. This was their first action, may God curse them."[20]

The Portuguese had introduced armed trading into the Indian Ocean, and, in the words of one historian, "abruptly ended the system of peaceful oceanic navigation that was such a marked feature of the region."[21] By 1515, the Portuguese had taken by force several trading cities, including Malacca and Hormuz. To consolidate their grip in the Indian Ocean, they had defeated a combined fleet of Egyptian and Indian ships trying to break the Portuguese blockade of the Red Sea. Even though their numbers were small and they could not possibly control much land, they could (and did) capture the sea lanes first by force and then by creating a protection racket, selling passes to Indian traders. The Portuguese used force to take up a prominent position in the Indian Ocean, although they were never able to control or monopolize trade there.

After taking Malacca, the Portuguese moved into the South China Sea, sparred with the Chinese in order to get rights to trade at Guangzhou, eventually obtaining from them a territorial concession at Macao on the southern edge of China. The Portuguese traded with Japan, and because Japanese trade with China had been banned, they profited handsomely by taking silver and gold from Japan to China and returning with silks. Bolstered by the pope's 1494 division of the world into Spanish and Portuguese halves, for most of the sixteenth century the Portuguese ruled the roost in the Indian Ocean, even though their objective of obtaining a monopoly on the spice trade to Europe remained elusive.[22]

Having felt the effects of the European style of armed trading, some Asian rulers of coastal trading cities responded by walling their territories and purchasing their own cannons and guns. This was especially true of the Islamic rulers in the Spice Islands, in particular Acheh on the northwestern tip of Sumatra. There the Islamic ruler in the early 1500s built a formidable navy for the dual purpose of running the Portuguese blockade and capturing their ships and arms. Later in the 1500s, through its contacts with the Ottoman empire, Acheh imported several large and well-made Ottoman guns, sufficient not just to defend themselves from the Portuguese, but to threaten Portuguese-controlled Malacca. Portuguese armed trading may have altered much in the Indian Ocean, but dar al-Islam continued to limit what Europeans could and could not do in the world.

Conclusion

With the exception of the Americas, southernmost Africa, and most of Oceania, the world's societies in the fifteenth century had extensive and systematic interactions and linkages forged by trade. This early modern system was made possible by three factors.[23] Some parts of the world, in particular China and India, had a *technological advantage* over the rest, and hence were able to produce industrial goods cheaper and better than anyone anywhere else, in particular silk and porcelain in China and cotton textiles in India. Second, *climatic and geographic constraints* limited some natural products to one or a few places on earth; examples include spices from the Indonesian archipelago, ivory from Africa, certain kinds of incense from the Middle East, or gold from Africa and silver from Japan. And third, *consumer tastes and social conventions* shaped demand for luxury items (e.g., silk, spices, pearls and raw gems, etc.), increasingly mass market items like cotton textiles, and for precious metals as the foundation for a monetary system (e.g., silver in China). The trade linkages among the various parts of the world emerged as an outcome of the complex interplay of these three factors.

Moreover, the linkages that did exist, especially in the Indian Ocean, were for the most part mutually agreeable and peaceful. No one part of the world attempted to seize or impose control over the whole system, even though the expansion of Islam in the seventh and eighth centuries did result in the conversion of huge numbers of people to that religion. The fifteenth-century voyages of Admiral Zheng He briefly extended Chinese influence over much of the Indian Ocean. The world was polycentric, with three major regions centered around China, India, and the Islamic world, and others connected to one or more of those powerhouses.

Most societies could participate in this world system by producing and trading something that others wanted. Europeans, however, were particularly handicapped by the fact that they had little to trade with the rest of the world, with the possible exceptions of wool and, with Africa, firearms. Mostly what Europeans possessed were peculiar forms of armed trading that allowed first the Portuguese and, as we will see in the next chapter, then the Dutch, English, and French to muscle in on the otherwise peaceful trading in the Indian Ocean. In finding a route around the Cape of Africa and across the Atlantic, Europeans had developed into true blue-water sailors; that is, they could sail out of sight of land, a capability that gave them significant advantages in the Indian Ocean. And, oh yes, Europeans were to stumble across huge stores and mines full of silver in the Americas, which allowed them, in the words of one analyst, "to buy a ticket on the Asian train."[24] How that happened is the story of the next chapter.

Notes

1. This section is based upon Louise Levathes, *When China Ruled the Seas: The Treasure Fleet of the Dragon Throne, 1405–1433* (New York: Simon and Schuster, 1994), and *The Cambridge History of China*, vol. 7, parts 1 and 2, *The Ming Dynasty, 1368–1644* (Cambridge: Cambridge University Press, 1988 and 1998). See also Robert Finlay, "The Trea-

sure Ships of Zheng He: Chinese Maritime Imperialism in the Age of Discovery," *Terrae Incognitae* 23 (1991): 1–12.

2. Confucius was a minor government official and teacher who lived in the sixth century B.C.E. His ideas, which posited the importance of the family and the role of good government, were developed by later philosophers and became the ideological basis of the Chinese state for 2,000 years.

3. Ma Huan wrote an account of this and later voyages, translated by J. V. G. Mills as *The Overall Survey of the Ocean's Shores* (Cambridge: Cambridge University Press, 1970).

4. Levathes, *When China Ruled the Seas*, is the best readable source.

5. In our own time, an analogy might be the U.S. decision both to send manned missions to the moon and to end them when the costs became too great to bear.

6. This periodization and much of the material in this section is based upon K. N. Chaudhuri, *Trade and Civilization in the Indian Ocean: An Economic History from the Rise of Islam to 1750* (Cambridge: Cambridge University Press, 1985).

7. For a discussion of Malacca and trading cities like it, see M. N. Pearson, "Merchants and States," in James D. Tracy, ed., *The Political Economy of Merchant Empires: State Power and World Trade 1350–1750* (Cambridge: Cambridge University Press, 1991).

8. For a detailed description of European trading in the Indian Ocean, see R. J. Barendse, *The Arabian Seas 1640–1700* (Leiden: Leiden University Press, 1998), and the North American edition of his book, *The Arabia Seas 1640–1700: The Western Indian Ocean of the Seventeenth Century* (New York: M. E. Sharpe, 2001). Barendse's point of view—assessing the role of European trading companies—is quite different from that of Chaudhuri, and so the picture he paints of the impact of Europeans is different too. An accessible summary of his argument can be found in "Trade and State in the Arabian Seas: A Survey from the Fifteenth to the Eighteenth Century," *Journal of World History* 11, no. 2 (Fall 2000): 173–226.

9. *The Cambridge History of China*, vol. 8, part 2, 378.

10. See Ross E. Dunn, *The Adventures of Ibn Battuta: A Muslim Trader of the 14th Century* (Berkeley: University of California Press, 1986).

11. See Herbert S. Klein, *The Atlantic Slave Trade* (Cambridge: Cambridge University Press, 1999), esp. chaps. 1, 3, and 5.

12. R. A. Austen, *Africa in Economic History* (London: James Currey/Heinemann, 1987), 36.

13. John Thornton, *Africa and Africans in the Making of the Atlantic World, 1400–1800*, 2d ed. (Cambridge: Cambridge University Press, 1998), 105.

14. Thornton, *Africa and Africans in the Making of the Atlantic World*, chap. 4.

15. R. A. Austen, "The Trans-Saharan Slave Trade: A Tentative Census," in H. A. Gemery and J. S. Hogendorn, eds., *The Uncommon Market: Essays in the Economic History of the Atlantic Slave Trade* (New York: Academic Press, 1979).

16. This section is based on Joseph Needham, "The Epic of Gunpowder and Firearms, Developing from Alchemy," in *Science in Traditional China: A Comparative Perspective* (Cambridge, Mass.: Harvard University Press, 1981), chap. 2.

17. Geoffrey Parker, *The Military Revolution: Military Innovation and the Rise of the West, 1500–1800*, 2d ed. (Cambridge: Cambridge University Press, 1996), chaps. 1–2.

18. For a discussion, see Parker, *The Military Revolution*, chap. 1.

19. For the details, see Janet Abu-Lughod, *Before European Hegemony: The World System A.D. 1250–1350* (New York: Oxford University Press, 1989), chap. 4.

20. Quoted in Chaudhuri, *Trade and Civilization*, 65.

21. Chaudhuri, *Trade and Civilization*, 63.

22. Although spices continued to seep into Europe via the Red Sea route, the establishment of a direct sea route connecting Asia and Europe all but doomed Venice as an economic power in Europe.

23. These are derived from Chaudhuri, *Trade and Civilization*, 17.

24. Andre Gunder Frank, *ReOrient: Global Economy in the Asian Age* (Berkeley: University of California Press, 1998).

CHAPTER THREE

Empires, States, and the New World, 1500–1775

In the period from 1500 to 1775, many of the ways in which the world was organized began to change. First and foremost, most parts of the world were drawn into regular, ongoing contact in ways that had never happened in the past. Where previously there had been several "worlds" in the world—the Chinese world, the Indian Ocean world, the Mediterranean world, and the Americas, as yet unknown to Europeans, Asians, or Africans—after 1500 two new links drew the entire globe into a single world for the first time. The voyage of Christopher Columbus in 1492 opened up the New World and established new relations among the Americas, Europe, and Africa. But there was also a less well-known Pacific route linking the New World to China after the Spanish established a colony in the Philippines in 1571. These new linkages led to the exchange around the world of commodities, ideas, germs, foods, and people, in the process creating a dynamic but also very peculiar kind of New World, quite different from the Old (that is, Afro-Eurasia). We can easily think of these sixteenth-century developments as the "first globalization."

A second large process was the continued growth and vitality of empires throughout Eurasia. In the sixteenth century, empires remained the most common political form for bringing large parts of the earth under human control. Of all the various kinds of political and economic systems that humans have devised to draw sustenance from the land and to increase our numbers, by far the most successful was an empire. Why we are not now living in empires instead of nation–states is worth pondering. We aren't because a new kind of state system developed in western Europe. To be sure, Spanish control of much of the New World initially gave them the resources to attempt to establish an empire, but that attempt also elicited fierce resistance among other European states, both killing the prospects for an empire in Europe and launching a new kind of international political order.

The third major process concerns the growth of a system of sovereign states in Europe and the linkage between that process and war. In comparison with Asian empires, the European states appear to be small and rather fragile constructs that could not possibly compete with the larger empires. Their rulers were so poor that they constantly had to seek loans to maintain their militaries. They were so small that they did not have within their borders all the resources necessary for their own defense, and, had the Spanish succeeded in establishing an empire in Europe and eliminating interstate war, independent European states might not have developed at all. As it was, the system of European interstate war favored a particular kind of state that developed in England and France in the sixteenth and seventeenth centuries, leading to conflict between those two for much of the eighteenth century.

By the late eighteenth century, England would emerge on top of the European state system. In Asia, the dynamics of empires in India and China would lead to the weakening of India and the strengthening of China. From a global perspective at the end of the eighteenth century, it is not too much to say that two very differently organized worlds would come to confront each other: a China-centered East Asian world system, and a British-centered Euro-American world system.[1] That the nineteenth century would see the balance of power tip in Britain's favor is part of the story that is told in chapters 4 and 5; here we need to examine the three processes introduced above.

Empire Builders and Conquerors

Across Eurasia, five empires expanded dramatically after 1500, remaking the political demarcations of the continent and all but ending the role of nomadic warriors there: China in the east, Russia in the center, Mughal India in the south, Safavid Iran in the southwest, and the Ottoman empire in the west. Although they did not all expand at the same time or rate, and one or the other experienced significant setbacks at one time or another, the expansive thrust of these empires was so great that by 1775 nearly all of Eurasia—except for the European far west—was under the control of one or the other of these empires.

Russia and China

The two most dramatic cases of empire expansion were Russia and China, the former more than quadrupling its size from 1500 to 1800 and the latter more than doubling its size. The Russian empire expanded from the principality of

Moscow, which in 1300 was little more than a stockade (called a "kremlin") surrounded by a few thousand square miles of forest interspersed with farms. Over the next 150 years, Muscovite rulers expanded their territory by conquering other Russian-speaking principalities. The most dramatic expansion came in the 1500s when the Muscovite ruler Ivan IV ("the Terrible," r. 1533–1584) pushed his empire east to the Ural Mountains, north to the Barents Sea, and south to the Caspian Sea. Following a "time of troubles" around 1600, the new Romanov dynasty (which ruled Russia until 1917) expanded the Russian empire east into Siberia and then all the way to the Pacific Ocean. Eighteenth-century rulers Peter the Great (r. 1682–1725) and Catherine the Great (r. 1762–1796) also extended Russian boundaries to the west, taking the Baltic nations, partitioning Poland, and crushing resistance to Russian rule in the Ukraine and Crimea.

China had the world's longest tradition of empire, a 2,000-year stretch beginning around 200 B.C.E. and lasting until the early twentieth century. Although experiencing significant periods of disintegration and conquest by non-Chinese forces, the traditions and techniques of imperial rule perdured. In 1500 China had been ruled by the Chinese Ming dynasty since 1368. Conquered in the mid-1600s by Manchus from the northeast, the new Qing dynasty soon set out on a series of military campaigns, especially under the leadership of the Qianlong emperor (r. 1736–1795). The Qianlong emperor campaigned in the northwest and west, defeating several non-Chinese peoples, in particular the Muslim Uigurs and the Tibetans, and incorporating them and their lands into the empire. By the time he was finished in the 1770s, the size of the Chinese empire had doubled with the incorporation of Tibetan, Mongol, and other peoples, although the new territories were sparsely populated steppe, semidesert, or mountainous regions.

China was the center of a "tribute trade system," which included most of East Asia, including neighboring areas that were not formally incorporated within its empire. To the north, west, and southwest, stateless peoples of various ethnicities paid tribute, both literally and figuratively, to China's emperor by sending periodic missions to the capital in Beijing. China's rulers also considered neighboring states, such as Vietnam, Korea, Java, and even Japan, to be tributary, and expected to receive tribute missions from them as well. The tribute missions not only recognized the dominant position of China within East Asia, but also provided lucrative official and private trade opportunities linking China and the tributary states. China thus exercised substantial direct and indirect influence over a territory much greater than that directly governed, incorporating most of Southeast Asia within the East Asian tribute trade system.[2]

Mughal, Safavid, and Ottoman Expansion

The Mughal, Safavid, and Ottoman empires, which together spanned the southern and southwestern portions of the Eurasian continent, shared many similarities. First, they all had Turkish ruling dynasties. Originally the Turks had been one of the nomadic peoples of Central Asia, developing sufficient military strength to conquer the more densely populated agricultural regions of north India, the Persian peninsula, and the Anatolian highlands. I have already discussed the origins of the Ottoman empire in the previous chapter. Here, suffice it to say that after conquering Constantinople in 1453, the Ottomans continued to expand their empire around the Mediterranean Sea, including Greece and the Balkans on the northern coast, Syria, Lebanon, and Palestine in the Levant, and the entire southern coast from Egypt to Algeria. Similarly, in the early 1500s leaders of Turkish bands conquered Persia, establishing the Safavid dynasty, and India, establishing the Mughal dynasty.

Second, these three dynasties all embraced one branch or another of Islam. The Ottomans were staunch Sunni believers, the Safavids were Shiite, and the Mughals (a Persian word for "Mongol"), initially at least, were quite tolerant not just of the various branches of Islam, but of Hindu practices and beliefs as well. These three empires, then, were all successor states of the first great Islamic empire that arose in the eighth century. Nonetheless, the doctrinal differences between Sunni Ottomans and the Shiite Safavids were so great that they clashed militarily, first in the Battle of Chaldiran in 1514, and then intermittently for the next two hundred years.

Third, these Islamic empires had similar political and economic structures. The conquering rulers established dynasties in which their sons ascended to the throne following their death in a way very similar to the Chinese system. Also like China, the Islamic successor states ruled their territories through a bureaucracy of officials posted throughout the realm and responsible to the emperor. These empires all rested on productive agricultural economies that produced a surplus the rulers could tap by taxing the peasant producers or larger landowners.

The Dynamics of Empire

Although all of these empires faced difficulties, especially arising from what historians call "the mid-seventeenth-century crisis,"[3] the fact is that, even with their ups and downs, they were expansive and successful forms of organizing political economies over vast territories in the period from 1500 to 1775. What they showed they could do was to mobilize resources within their control to augment and extend the power of the ruling dynasty into new areas. Indeed, by 1700 most of the Eurasian continent was under the control of an empire of one kind or another. Ironically, since all of these empires except the Russian had been established by conquerors from the steppe, these expansive empires ended any further nomadic threat to their existence by placing the remaining nomads under their control. To be sure, even into the nineteenth century these peoples and others could "revolt" and cause substantial disruption, but the power of the large central states was rolling over that of the nomads. One of the previous dynamics of empires—nomadic invasions causing collapse or strain—was thus extinguished.[4]

But other dynamics internal to particular empires continued to account for their rise and decline. In India, the peak of Mughal power was reached under the rule of Aurangzeb (d. 1707). Shortly after his death, various Indian princes challenged Mughal power and effectively asserted their independence, fragmenting political power and leaving openings, as we will see in the next chapter, for Europeans to establish footholds in India. China's power during the eighteenth century seemed to be quite well established, although in retrospect we now know that corruption at the highest levels was beginning to sap political will, and population growth coupled with economic difficulties fueled a large rebellion at the end of the century. The costs of suppressing the White Lotus Rebellion caused other problems to begin surfacing in the early nineteenth century.

Throughout most of the Eurasian continent, empires flourished over the centuries from 1500 to 1800. Although they each had their own particular histories and cultures, they did share commonalities. Mostly, empires were political systems encompassing large territories over whom a single person (usually called "emperor") claimed sovereignty. Empires tended to be so large and encompassed so many peoples speaking different languages that emperors ruled indirectly through intermediaries rather than through centrally appointed local officials (although the Chinese emperor did try to rule that way). Empires proved to be quite effective in ruling people, so it is not surprising that they developed and were used elsewhere in the world too, especially in western Africa and in the pre-Columbian Americas, and that even Europeans, as we will see, harbored dreams of a unified empire. In chapter 2, I discussed the West African empires; here I will bring the Americas and Europe into the story.

The Americas

North and South America prior to the arrival of the Europeans was populated with peoples who had constructed varying kinds of social and economic systems, ranging from hunting-and-gathering societies to highly developed agrarian societies, in the centuries after humans first migrated into the Americas around 15,000 B.C.E.[6] It thus should not be too surprising that these people could also create the highest form of political organization in the biological old regime, an empire. Two in particular are important to our story, the Aztecs in central Mexico and the Incas in the mountains of what is now Peru and Chile. (See map 2.1.)

The Aztecs

The valley of central Mexico had long sustained impressive civilizations, starting with the Olmecs about 1500 B.C.E. On the Yucatan peninsula, the Mayas had built a magnificent civilization with cities, large pyramids, and a highly productive agriculture that peaked around 600–900 C.E., after which the Mayan state dissolved into numerous smaller agglomerations. By 1100 C.E., the Valley of Mexico was dominated by the Toltecs, who had a capital at Tula at the northern end of the Valley. With rich soils and regular supplies of water from snow-fed rivers originating in the surrounding mountains, the Valley of Mexico was agriculturally rich and attracted peoples from all over North America.

Among those migrating into the Valley of Mexico around 1350 were a people called the Mexica, also known as the Aztecs.[7] As latecomers with dubious civilizational achievements and agricultural competence, the Mexica were shunted off into the worst land—swamps and a lake, to be precise—and were considered to be subordinates of others. After making the mistake of sacrificing the daughter of one of their superiors, the Mexica were exiled to some islands in Lake Texcoco. Dredging up fertile muck from the lake bed into small floating plots called *chinampa*, the Mexica gradually created an island in the middle of Lake Texcoco upon which their city, Tenochtitlán (the site of modern-day Mexico City), ultimately arose. Being interlopers and forced to defend themselves, the Mexica became excellent warriors, sometimes working for others but all the while building their own defenses and power.

By 1400, the Valley of Mexico was studded with numerous warring city–states. Three or four were major players, while the Mexica were mercenaries and minor players until 1428 when they established a Triple Alliance with two other groups. The Mexica then were powerful enough to begin conquering and subduing their neighbors and demanding that they send tribute to the capital at Tenochtitlán. Two Mexica rulers in the mid-1400s—Itzcoatl (1428–1440) and Moctezuma I (1440–1469)—led the alliance, which came to control all of the Valley of Mexico and beyond. At the peak of its power in the early 1500s, the empire ruled over some 489 subject territories totaling 25 million people, all of whom were expected to pay tribute to the Mexica at Tenochtitlán.

The Mexica rulers thus accumulated considerable wealth from their tributary states. Food, textiles, jewelry, furs, rubber balls, precious stones, gold, and silver flowed to Tenochtitlán, not because the conquered peoples wanted to send these items, but out of fear of retribution if they did not. The Mexica ruled their empire not through a bureaucracy or assimilation, but through terror, and used the least sign of resistance as a pretext for war and the taking of prisoners for sacrifice to their gods.[8] The Mexica thus constructed a large empire built upon the extraction of tribute from subject peoples, periodic wars, and the daily sacrifice of hundreds if not thousands of captives. Tenochtitlán may have been an exceptionally wealthy city, but the foundations of the empire itself were not strong, resting largely on the fear the Mexica instilled in their subjects.

The Inca

The same could not be said about the other empire being built in the Americas by the Inca. Unlike the Mexica (and the Maya), the Inca did not develop a written language, so most of what we know about them comes from accounts compiled in the early 1500s by European conquerors. Nevertheless, the story is impressive. Settling in the highlands of Peru around Lake Titicaca in the mid-1200s, the Inca (the name originally referred to the title of their emperor, but later European usage expanded it to refer to the people as well) launched military campaigns in the 1400s that created a huge empire, stretching some 2,500 miles from modern Quito in the north to Santiago in the south.

Unlike the Mexica, the Inca consciously incorporated the conquered peoples into their culture, forcing them to adopt a common language (Quechua) and directly governing them with professional administrators. Besides being exceptionally long, covering most of the Pacific highlands of South America, the Inca empire was also "vertical." The Peruvian mountains reached to 13,000 feet, some cities sat at 9,000 feet, and Incan villages were scattered all the way up and down the mountains and the valleys. Besides a challenge to governing, verticality was also a challenge to growing food; because of the vast changes in ecosystems arising from the different altitudes, different crops had to be grown in different locals. To ensure the unity of such an unusual empire, the Incas paved mountain roads with cut stone for imperial runners and armies.

Surprisingly, for such a large empire, the Inca did not have a true writing system, but instead developed an ingenious system of colored, knotted cords that allowed the rulers to keep track of vital information (population, taxes, labor services owed the government) to keep the empire together. Movement from one's village was prohibited, and the absence of money and private trade limited the development of private property and wealth. Nonetheless, the empire itself was wealthy, ruling over sixteen million people.

Like the Mexica empire, though, stresses had built within the Inca empire as it expanded. The Inca believed that their ruler was descended from the sun god, and to keep him happy (and the crops growing) after death, the ruler was mummified in order to be taken out for all important occasions or decisions, thereby maintaining the link to the sun god. Moreover, the mummified leader's direct descendants were given all his land and possessions in order to sustain this activity. A new Inca ruler thus came to the throne land poor and had to conquer new lands and peoples of his own, thereby giving a certain dynamic to Incan imperial expansion. When that expansion slowed, as all available lands were conquered or the Incan armies suffered defeat—as they did when they went down the east side of the Andes into the Amazon rain forest where they were then driven out—tensions within the royal family began to run high and soon exploded when an Incan emperor died in 1525, leading to a succession crisis and contest for the throne between two half brothers.

By 1500, both the Aztec and Inca empires were well established and quite powerful, although each had weaknesses. The Aztecs had constructed an empire based on forced extraction of surplus from subjugated people, while the Incas had a system that required expansion in order for the new ruler to obtain new lands to support his family. Then, the arrival of the Spanish, first Columbus in 1492 of course, but more importantly Hernan Cortéz in 1519 and Francisco Pizarro in 1531, changed everything.

The Conquest of the Americas and the Spanish Empire

In 1500, Tenochtitlán, the capital of the Aztec empire, had a population of 250,000, making it one of the largest cities in the world. The city boasted pyramids, botanical gardens, canals, zoos, a sewage system, and streets that were cleaned daily by about one thousand men. Tenochtitlán was an impressive place. Aztec warriors instilled fear in the people they conquered, ensuring the flow of food and goods into the capital. Yet this large, complex, and powerful empire was brought down by just six hundred Spanish "conquistadors" led by Hernan Cortéz; an even smaller "army" under Francisco Pizarro conquered the Incan empire in the 1530s. How did that happen?

In 1519, after Cortéz landed on the coast of Mexico near what would become the city of Vera Cruz, he heard stories of vast amounts of gold inland and that various people the Aztecs had conquered would help him by providing intelligence, food, canoes, and warriors. The Aztec emperor, Moctezuma II, at first believing that Cortéz was a returning god, sent gifts of gold to appease the Spaniards, hoping they would go away. But, according to Cortéz, "we have a disease of the heart that can only be cured with gold," and so began the expedition overland to Tenochtitlán.

Exploiting the feelings of hatred the conquered peoples had toward the Aztecs, Cortéz enrolled their help both in getting to Tenochtitlán and then in war against the Aztecs. Even though the Aztecs were fierce warriors who had developed many instruments of war that worked well in the Valley of Mexico, ultimately the Spaniards had a huge technological advantage. Where the Spaniards had steel swords and armor, the Aztecs had bronze weapons and cloth armor; where the Spaniards had cannons, the Aztecs had none; where the Spaniards had wheels, the Aztecs had none; where the Spaniards had horses, the Aztecs had none; where the Spaniards had "the dogs of war," the Aztecs had none; where the Spaniards fought to kill and to conquer territory, the Aztecs fought when equally matched and did not kill all their enemies. And finally, the Spaniards unwittingly brought the smallpox virus, which unleashed an epidemic in the summer of 1520, killing over half the residents of Tenochtitlán, demoralizing the Aztec warriors, and enabling the disciplined Spanish soldiers to take advantage of the moment to seize Tenochtitlán.

A similar combination of factors allowed Francisco Pizarro's small band of men to conquer the Incas.[9] In this case, though, the smallpox epidemic had already spread to Peru from Mexico in the 1520s, decimating Andean Indian populations long before Pizarro arrived. When he did, he exploited differences among Incan claimants to the throne, lured them into a trap, and then killed almost all, initially sparing the last Incan ruler until he delivered a sufficient amount of gold but then strangling and decapitating him.

Although we use the word "conquest" to describe what happened to the Aztecs and Incas in the sixteenth century, the fact is that Spanish victory was neither swift nor complete, for the native peoples of the Americas put up a long and valiant struggle against European invaders. The Incas resisted for another century, the Spanish in fact faced several defeats at the hands of the Seminoles in Florida, and as we know, the history of the United States is riddled with Indian wars. Indeed, in some ways Native American resistance has not yet ended, as the events in Chiapas, Mexico, in the 1990s serve to remind us. However, if not fully defeated and if continued resistance allowed Native Americans to negotiate or win concessions at the margins, the fact is that ultimately Europeans and Africans replaced the Native Americans as the most populous peoples in the Americas, as we will see in more detail below.

The Columbian Exchange

The conquest of the Americas led to a global exchange of natural products and foodstuffs, especially of New World foods to the Old World agrarian economies. Maize (corn), potatoes, tomatoes, chiles, and other foods spread rapidly throughout Eurasia, enriching the diets of commoners and elites alike. Sweet potatoes, for instance, reached China by the mid-1500s, making it possible for peasants there to sell their rice rather than eat it. Certainly the spread of New World crops into the Old World made it possible for populations there to increase above what would have been possible on the basis of the existing basket of foods.

But the Columbian exchange was a two-way exchange and it seems that the native peoples of the New World were the losers, for the encounter between Old and New Worlds brought two hitherto separate disease pools into contact. The Native American ancestors had migrated into the Americas during the last Ice Age when a land bridge linked Alaska to Siberia, thousands of years before the agricultural revolution in Eurasia brought people and domesticated animals together in a rich recipe for the transfer of animal pathogens to humans, leading to a whole range of diseases including smallpox, chicken pox, and influenza. Eurasians contracted these diseases and over time developed some immunities to them; New Worlders did not have a chance to do the same. When the Ice Age ended and the melting glaciers raised the ocean level above the Bering Strait land bridge, the peoples in the Americas were isolated from the diseases that then became an everyday part of the material world in Eurasia, rendering some of them "childhood" diseases from which most people easily recovered. The diseases for which Europeans had developed immunities over the centuries proved to be deadly to those in the Americas (and later the Pacific Islands too) without immunity.

The Great Dying

The smallpox epidemics that weakened both the Aztecs and Incas, paving the way for the Spanish conquest of both empires, were just the beginning of a century-long holocaust that almost wiped out Native American populations. From 1518 to 1600, seventeen major epidemics were recorded in the New World, spanning a territory from what is now Argentina in the south to what is now Texas and the Carolinas in the United States. Not just smallpox, but other killer diseases—measles, influenza, bubonic plague, cholera, chicken pox, whooping cough, diphtheria, and tropical malaria—ravaged American populations.[10] Disease was not the only cause of the depopulation of the Americas in the century after the Spanish Conquest. The Conquest itself, war among the American natives, oppression by the conquerors, the forced requisitioning of Indian labor, and lowered fertility among the surviving native population all contributed to the disaster.[11]

In Mexico alone, where there had been 25 million people in 1519, fifty years later there were 2.7 million, and a hundred years later there were but 750,000, or 3 percent of the original total. Similar fates befell the Incas, the inhabitants of the Caribbean Islands (starting with the Arawak on Española), and the Indians of (what is now) the southeastern United States, although at different rates. Whether or not European-introduced diseases ravaged the Indians of the American Northeast, the upper Mississippi, or the Northwest before the 1600s is open for scholarly debate, but after permanent European settlements were established in North America, diseases afflicted those natives too. In short, in the century after European contact with the New World, vast regions were depopulated, losing 90 percent of their pre-1500 numbers, even if we do not know with certainty what the precontact population of the Americas was. Nonetheless, it does seem certain that tens of millions of people across the Americas had vanished.

Labor Supply Problems

Even without the Great Dying, the Spaniards would have had a labor problem in the New World because they themselves were not inclined to do manual labor, and getting the native Indians to work for them voluntarily proved problematic. Enslaving the Indians was also ruled out after a debate within the Catholic Church settled the debate over whether the Indians had a soul (ruling that they did). Although not slaves, Indians were compelled by Spaniards to work their fields or their mines in return for providing food, shelter, and Christianity in a system known as the *encomienda*. After the Conquest and the Great Dying, the *encomienda* system was supplemented by another, the *repartimento*. With Indians few and far between, the *repartimento* forced them into small towns laid out in the grid pattern familiar to Spaniards. The combination of these two provided food and clothing for the conquistadors and their followers.

Silver

The "discovery" of the Americas was of course an accident. Columbus sailed west to get to Asia, and on the way stumbled across a huge new continent.

But the reason he sought Asia was shared by those who followed him to America: to get rich. Not only did the Spaniards stumble onto America, they stumbled across huge amounts of gold and silver that the Aztecs and the Incas had fashioned into works of art, power, and utility that were theirs for the taking after the Aztecs and Incas had been defeated.

A shortage of Indian labor was not a problem when all the Spaniards had to do was loot the silver and gold already collected in Tenochtitlán and Cuzco (the former Inca capital in Peru), melt it down, and ship it off to Seville. The Great Dying thus was accompanied by a Great Plundering, and that is what characterized the Spanish approach to the New World economy for several decades after the conquest. But that soon changed with the discovery of huge deposits of silver ore in the former Incan empire (now in western Bolivia) and also in Mexico.

The biggest strike was at Potosí in 1545, which soon became a boomtown (at more than 13,000 feet elevation) with 150,000 people by 1570. Over the next century, thousands of tons of silver came out of Potosí, especially after the introduction of the mercury refining process. Indians worked in the mines and refined the ore, either because they were forced to do it or because they were drawn to the work and were paid wages. Where to the Spaniards Potosí was a source of fabled wealth ("to be worth a Potosí" became a stock phrase for being rich), to the Indian laborers it was "the mouth of hell." Mining was especially dangerous to begin with, but working with mercury was deadly (it is a poison); over the three centuries that Potosí was operating, it is estimated that eight million Indians—seven out of every ten working the mines—died.

Huge amounts of silver flowed out of the New World, half of it coming from Potosí alone: from 1503 to 1660, over 32 million pounds of silver and 360,000 pounds of gold were exported. But where did it all go? Who provided such an enormous demand for silver that Potosí would sprout in the middle of nowhere, and Spaniards were willing to work eight million Indians to death to get their hands on it? After all, the conquistadors had wanted gold, not silver. And yet here they were pumping out silver. Why? There are two parts to the answer to that question. China?!

The Spanish Empire and Its Collapse

With vast sources of newfound wealth apparently at their fingertips, Spain's rulers attempted to bring all of Europe under their dominion. The idea (and ideal) of empire was never far from the surface in sixteenth-century Europe. Indeed, ever since the fall of the Roman Empire, some Europeans had pined for the reestablishment of a universal political order based upon Christianity.

For a very long time, hopes rested with the Byzantine empire in the eastern Mediterranean, the defenders of Eastern Orthodox Christianity. But those hopes were dashed when the Ottoman Turks took Constantinople in 1453 and made it into a Muslim city.

Within western Europe, the idea of empire was enshrined in the Holy Roman Empire. More name and hope than reality, the title was revived in 962 when a semibarbarian Germanic invader took Italy and was crowned "Holy Roman emperor" by the pope. The title, mostly associated with Austria and Germany, persisted until 1806, even though Germany itself was politically fragmented even more than Italy.

But in the early 1500s, it looked like the Spanish might just succeed in creating a real empire in Europe. Ferdinand and Isabella's grandson, Charles V, inherited not just the Spanish crown, but claims to Habsburg lands spread throughout Europe (Austria, the Netherlands, Sicily, and Sardinia) as well as New Spain (Mexico) and New Castile (Peru) in the New World. The New World wealth that started flowing into Spain, at first from simply looting Aztec and Inca treasuries, but regularly after the mines at Potosí started operating, gave Charles V and then his successor, Philip II, the money to attempt to unify their lands. Between the Spanish monarchs and their attempts to unify their lands stood France and the Protestants in the Spanish-claimed territories in the Netherlands, with the English helping Spain's enemies as needed.

War followed war between Spain and France, and the Dutch war of independence (the Protestant Dutch versus the Catholic Spanish, especially heavy in the 1570s) too sapped Spanish strength. Despite the massive amounts of New World silver flowing into Spain, the wars proved so costly that the Spanish crown declared bankruptcy not just once but several times (first in 1557 and 1560, and numerous times thereafter). The English defeat of the Spanish Armada in 1588, followed by further Spanish defeats in Europe (the Thirty Years' War, 1618–1648) and in the New World too, sealed the fate of the Spanish attempt to create a European empire. Something new—a competitive system of sovereign nation–states—would take its place, and Spain would not be at its center. Many historians consider the end of the possibility of empire and the emergence instead of nation–states to be one of the critical turning points in West European history.[12] We will come to that later in this chapter. Now, we need to return to the second part of the answer to why there was such an interest in digging silver out of the New World.

China's Demand for Silver

Columbus risked the unknown of the Atlantic and Vasco da Gama charted new waters around the Cape of Good Hope to get direct access to the riches of Asia, bypassing the Ottomans and the rest of the Muslim world that controlled the overland routes from the eastern Mediterranean to Asia. Of course, Columbus never got to Asia (although he did think he got there, calling the Native Americans "Indians"), and when the Portuguese sailed into the Indian Ocean and the China Sea, they discovered they were poor and had little money with which to buy Asian spices and manufactured goods (so they extorted the goods with their "armed trading" protection racket). But when the Spaniards stumbled onto the silver of the New World, they found the key to accessing the wealth of Asia. Sort of.

The problem was the Spanish "owned the cow but did not drink the milk," as the saying went. True, the silver flowed from the New World to Seville. But the Spanish monarchs, especially Charles V and Philip II, were constantly warring in their efforts to unite Europe under their empire. The silver thus flowed out of Spain and into the hands of Dutch arms merchants and English and Italian financiers, who then used their newfound silver wealth to finance trade missions to China and the Indian Ocean. Moreover, the Spanish lacked direct access to Asia in any event, those routes being held by the Portuguese, the Dutch, the English, and the French, at least until 1571 when the Spanish seized Manila in the Philippines, established a colony there, and sent galleons loaded with silver directly from Acapulco to Manila.

All told, "approximately three-quarters of the New World silver production" over the three centuries from 1500 to 1800 eventually wound up in China.[13] The reason is that China had a huge demand for silver, both to serve as the basis of its monetary system and to facilitate economic growth. Because the Chinese valued silver, it was expensive there and very cheap in the Americas (after looting it, its cost was the cost of production, and that was very low as the deaths of the eight million Indian miners attest). Silver thus flowed from the New World, both through Europe and across the Pacific to the Philippines, all to China. As the largest and most productive economy in the world, China was the engine that powered much of the early modern economy, with New World silver providing the energy. It is not too much to say that without China, there would have been no Potosí (or at least a much smaller one). And without Potosí, the Spanish would not have attempted to create an empire in Europe. In short, silver "went around the world and made the world go round," in the words of a recent world historian.[14]

In the period from 1500 to 1800, the bulk of the world's population, economic activity, and trade remained Asian, despite the new beginnings made by Europeans in the New World and Asia.[15] In fact, Asia's proportion of world population rose from about 60 percent around 1500 to 66 percent in 1750 and 67 percent in 1800. Two-thirds of the world's population was Asian as late as 1800, with the bulk of that in China and India. As discussed in chapter 1, in the biological old regime, a growing population is evidence of success in developing additional resources to sustain the larger population.

But not only was Asia's population growing, so too was its economic production and productivity. In 1775, Asia produced about 80 percent of everything in the world, probably an increase from 1500. In other words, two-thirds of the world's population—Asians—produced four-fifths of the world's goods. Seen from another perspective, Europeans, at one-fifth of the world's population in 1775, shared production of one-fifth of the world's goods with Africans and Americans. Asia thus had the most productive economies in the three centuries after 1500.

Evidence for that can be seen in some surprising places, including the New World. In the 1500s, Chinese manufactured goods were so much better and cheaper than European ones that "they quickly ended the domination of markets there by commercial interests in Spain." The Spanish viceroy of Peru thus complained in 1594 to the authorities in Madrid:

> Chinese merchandise is so cheap and Spanish goods so dear that I believe it impossible to choke off the trade to such an extent that no Chinese wares will be consumed in this realm, since a man can clothe his wife in Chinese silks for 200 reales [25 pesos], whereas he could not provide her with clothing of Spanish silks with 200 pesos.

In Lima, the citizens also wore Chinese silks, and in Mexico City women wore dresses known as *China poblana*, which were, and remain, the "national dress" of Mexican women. Indeed, Chinese imports were so well made and cheap that they destroyed the Mexican silk industry, even as silk weaving increased because of cheap silk thread imported from China.[16]

The English too found cheap cotton textiles from India to be so superior to anything they could buy locally (either woolens or linens) that Indian imports climbed steadily during the seventeenth century. Indeed, the British were importing so much finished cotton from India by 1700 that it appeared to British textile manufacturers that their industry was doomed by the competition. So, instead of becoming more efficient producers to compete with India, in 1707 they successfully pressured the British government to embargo the importation of Indian cotton. French women found brightly painted Indian calicoes to be so fashionable that laws were passed in 1717 against wearing Indian cotton or Chinese silk clothing in order to protect the French home industry. One Paris merchant went so far as to offer to pay anyone 500 livres who would "strip . . . in the street, any woman wearing Indian fabrics."[17]

I will have more to say about the place of textiles in the story of industrialization in the next chapter. Suffice it to say here that in the global economy, and despite the wealth extracted from the New World, Europeans at the turn of the eighteenth century still were at a competitive disadvantage to Asians. In fact, one way to think about the global situation is that Europeans were so poor relative to Asia and still so peripheral to the real generators of industrial wealth and productivity that they competed mightily among themselves merely to gain the upper hand in dealing in Asian markets. Europe's peripheral position, in other words, heightened competition among European states, leading to attempts to find ways to accumulate wealth and power in a world still dominated by Asia. That is where the New World fits in again.

The New World Economy

Sugar and Slavery

Contributing to the making of the New World economy was the establishment and growth of a plantation system using imported African slave labor, initially for the production of sugar,[18] but eventually adapted to tobacco in the seventeenth century and cotton in the eighteenth century. The Portuguese played an essential role in this process by experimenting with the best way to exploit their colonial possession in Brazil. With so few Portuguese willing to migrate to Brazil, the Portuguese had no choice but to rely upon the native Tupi, who, to put it mildly, had little desire to work farms and instead fled into the forest. Even enslaving the Tupi did little to resolve the Portuguese labor shortage, which became acute after the introduction of European diseases further reduced the Tupi population. The solution was the use of African slaves.

Even before the discovery of the New World, the Portuguese had already worked out a slave-based plantation system for sugar production on the islands off the coast of Africa they had conquered in their quest for a sea route to Asia (borrowing from even earlier Spanish and Genoan success in the Mediterranean). The story of how that happened from the 1420s on is quite instructive for what happened later in the New World, for it involved the massive ecological change of tropical forests into sugar plantations, the enslavement and extermination of a native people (the Guanches), and then the importation of African slaves to work the sugar plantations.[19] All of this happened before Columbus stumbled on the Americas, but it did give the Portuguese experience in slave-based plantations, which they quickly adapted to the depopulated New World; by the 1580s, slavery and plantations were dominant features of the economy of Brazil.

The French and the English also soon created slave-based sugar plantations on Caribbean islands. Soon after the British took Barbados, in 1640, settlers started clearing the land for sugar plantations, with sugar exported to the home country in the 1650s. The sugar industry expanded rapidly, especially after Britain took the island of Jamaica—thirty times the size of Barbados—from the Spanish. The French also established sugar plantations in the Caribbean, starting on Martinique, exporting sugar back to France. By the late seventeenth century, so much English and French sugar was being exported back to the home countries that the competition drove Brazilian sugar from northern Europe. Ultimately, the British and French had so totally deforested several Caribbean islands for sugar that erosion wrecked the fertility of the soil (as in Haiti) and changed local climates as well.[20]

The number of African slaves taken to work the New World plantations is astounding, numbering over nine million people by the time the slave trade ended in the 1800s; by 1650, "Africans were the majority of new settlers in the new Atlantic world."[21] For nearly three hundred years, European slave traders, at first Portuguese and Dutch but eventually mostly the British, took thousands of African slaves every year to the Americas, leaving a lasting impact not only upon African but American (North and South) society as well. Although those effects are historically important,[22] here we are mostly interested in how the slave-based plantation system fit in with the world economy.

Two triangles of trade linked the Atlantic world, arising in the seventeenth century and maturing in the eighteenth century. The first, and by far the best known, linked England to Africa and the New World. Commodities from the Americas (not just sugar but timber and fish from North America too) went to England (and from there to its trading partners); finished goods (increasingly cotton textiles from India) were taken to Africa where they were exchanged for slaves; and slaves were taken to the Americas. The other triangle went in another direction. From England's North American colonies, rum went to Africa in exchange for slaves; slaves went to the Caribbean; and molasses (from sugar refining) went to New England to produce more rum.[23]

In all of these transactions, Europeans and North American colonists made money and accumulated wealth. The question of the extent to which slavery and the plantation economy benefited Europeans and allowed them to compete more effectively and in the world economy will be taken up in more detail in the next chapter. For now, we need note only that seventeenth- and eighteenth-century Europeans competed not only in a world economy dominated by Asian manufactures, but among themselves as well. The end of the Spanish attempt to create an empire in Europe soon led to the creation of a new system linking European states and pushing the development of the state and its power.

The European State System

Warfare defined the emerging European state system. Until the mid-seventeenth century, wars were mostly fought to stop the Spanish from establishing an empire or to support Protestants (in Holland and the German states) in their attempts to gain independence from the Catholic monarchs of Spain. From the 1648 Peace of Westphalia, which ended the Thirty Years' War, wars mostly involved France, whose fortunes had risen while Spain's declined, and then, from the late 1600s on, contests were mostly between France and England, culminating in the Seven Years' War (1754–1763), or what Americans call the French and Indian War, and leading to Britain's victory over France.

There are many things that are historically significant about wars among European states in the period we are considering in this chapter (i.e., from 1500 to 1775). First, the wars involved virtually all European states, tying them very clearly in a single system, especially after the Peace of Westphalia. That can be seen quite clearly in two schematic charts prepared by the historian Charles Tilly (see figure 3.1).[24] In these charts, which represent two different periods (Europe ca. 1500 and ca. 1650), the thin lines represent one war and the bold lines two or more wars between the states connected. Where there were two subsystems in 1500, with the western one focused on Italy, by 1650 all European states were embroiled in a common set of entanglements defined by war.

Second, wars in Europe led both to consolidation into increasingly fewer political units and to the development of a particular kind of national state as the most successful form of European state. Tilly's work again supplies the basic data. Beginning around 1000 C.E., the thirty million or so people who lived in the area we now call Europe lived in a bewildering array of political units headed by "emperors, kings, princes, dukes, caliphs, sultans, and other potentates." These titles, Tilly warns us, should not hide the fact of stupendous political fragmentation in Europe: in Italy alone there were two hundred to three hundred city–states. Five hundred years later, around 1500, "Europe's 80 million people divided into something like 500 states, would-be states, statelets, and statelike organizations." From then on, warfare reduced the number of European states until modern times when there were about thirty or so.[25]

Where the Spanish Habsburg empire proved to be too large and inefficient to mobilize its own resources against the English or the French, the wealthy

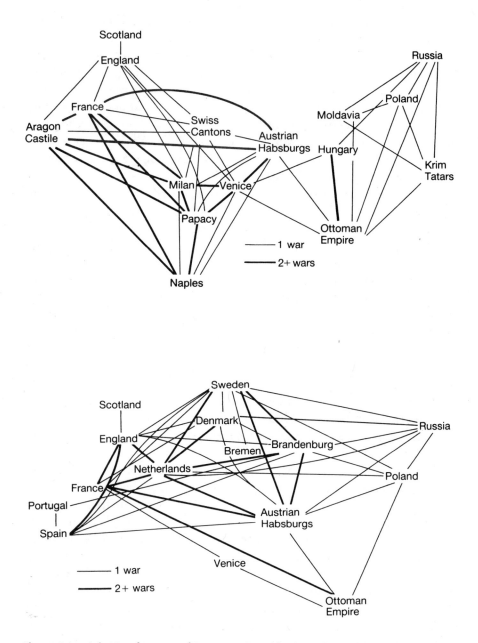

Figure 3.1.   Joint Involvement of European States in Great Power Wars, 1496–1514 and 1656–1674

Source: Charles Tilly, *Coercion, Capital, and European States, A.D. 990–1990* (Oxford: Basil Blackwell, 1990), 176–177.

city–states of Italy lacked the manpower to campaign outside of Italy against larger armies. Similarly, the various principalities of Germany, while strong enough to fend one another off, found it hard to keep larger states from interfering in their affairs. Small states like Sweden or Holland, which had some resources that allowed them to be international players in the seventeenth century, fell by the wayside in the eighteenth century as larger states came to dominate European politics. On the other hand, some large and populous states such as Poland, with a small nobility ruling over a large enserfed peasantry, could not field large enough armies to compete; Poland thus was partitioned at the end of the eighteenth century.

In this context, the third interesting consequence of war was the way it affected the internal evolution of European states, favoring some kinds but not others. The rulers of European states were not rich, and wars were expensive. Basically, European rulers could tap two sources of revenue. First, they could tax, but taxes usually met resistance from landowners. Hence, to gain the right to levy and use taxes, most European rulers had to negotiate with landowning elites, usually resulting in the establishment of some form of representative assembly that rulers were supposed to consult before imposing or raising taxes. Besides assemblies of landowners, the other institution growing up with taxation was the state bureaucracy necessary to assess and collect taxes from the known subject population, rather than "farming" the collection of taxes out to private parties. The tensions arising from both of these processes account for much of the internal political history of many European states in the centuries from 1500 to 1800.

A second source of revenue was loans from bankers or other wealthy people. The sixteenth-century Spanish monarchs, for instance, had to rely on loans to finance their wars, but much of the money came from bankers outside of Spain or Spanish control. All European rulers had to rely on both short- and long-term loans to prosecute their wars, and it thus became in their interest to encourage those with capital to reside in their cities. The English and the Dutch were most successful at this, in part because of their religious tolerance and willingness to take in wealthy Protestants and Jews unwelcome in Catholic lands. But even loans from one's own subjects had to be repaid, leading the British to institute "the national debt" in the late 1600s, an innovation of immense importance in enabling British power to expand.

England's national debt was in effect long-term loans secured by the Bank of England, or in other words "bonds." Other European rulers had often attempted to resolve their financial difficulties by consolidating short-term into long-term debt, but these were secured on the ability of the ruler to repay. The English innovation was to issue the bonds through the Bank of

England, established in 1694, and to guarantee them with the subscribed capital of the bank. The national debt not only provided British rulers with ready sources of cash for their wars, but also gave investors a relatively safe investment instrument, thereby attracting even more deposits to the Bank of England.

In summary, the wars of European states drove their expenses well above the amount of silver that was left in European hands after it was used to buy Asian products, leading to standing armies and navies, taxation and state bureaucracies to collect it, representative assemblies of various kinds demanded by the taxed subjects so they could influence the level of taxation (even though Europe's "absolute monarchs" tried mightily to ignore or shut down these institutions), public indebtedness, and the institution of the national debt. All of these activities were part of a "state-building" process in seventeenth- and eighteenth-century Europe.

State Building

European rulers would resort to force, if necessary, to gain access to the resources needed to conduct war, but rulers considered it preferable if their subjects would more voluntarily render those resources to the state. Rulers thus made various claims to legitimacy, that is, the idea that subjects should willingly obey their ruler. In the sixteenth and seventeenth centuries, these claims to legitimacy rested on religious grounds, expressed as "the divine right of kings," that is, that the Christian God gave them the right to rule. These religious claims also led European monarchs, in particular the Catholic ones, to expel non-Catholics from their territory. Spain's Ferdinand and Isabella's expulsion of the Jews and Muslims (who they called "Moors") was an early example, but so too was the late-seventeenth-century French prosecution of Protestants (the Huguenots). The Spanish Inquisition was also part of this process of ensuring that subjects throughout their realms in Europe and the Americas were Catholic and loyal.

The European Enlightenment of the late seventeenth and eighteenth centuries challenged the idea of the "divine right" of monarchs to rule, positing more democratic ones based upon the construction of the rights of the individual. Expounded most forcefully by the French "philosophes" in their struggle against the absolutisms of the French state and the Catholic Church, these ideas began to broaden the legitimate basis upon which a state could be established to include the consent of the governed, the "citizens." By the end of the eighteenth century and in the aftermath of the French Revolution of 1789, these were the ideas the French used to justify the execution of their monarchs and the establishment of a republic.[26]

In the competitive, war-driven environment in Europe, some states thus had advantages that led ultimately to a particular kind of state—one that had cities with large accumulations of capital and rural hinterlands with a population large enough to sustain armies—to become the most successful kind. For reasons that need not concern us, in the centuries after about 1000 C.E., cities in Europe tended to develop in a band extending north from Tuscany in Italy, across the Alps to Ghent, Bruges, and London; Paris also grew. To this day, this band is Europe's most urbanized zone. Cities provided the rulers of states encompassing them with opportunities to tax urban-to-rural trade, to gain access to funding from banks and thereby to avoid reliance on rural nobility for support, and generally to strengthen themselves: in general, to command more resources of all kinds, but especially money and men, than less-blessed competitors farther away from cities.[27] The rulers of two states in particular—England and France—proved to be most able to build that kind of state, combining the capital resources to be found in London or Paris with the manpower that could be tapped from the rural population. And, having built powerful states, England and France came to be intense competitors by the late seventeenth century.

The English proved willing and able to use state power for economic ends. In its struggles against Dutch competitors, the English had passed a series of Navigation Acts in the mid-seventeenth century designed to restrict the trade of their colonies in the New World to England only and to enforce those acts with force if necessary.[28] The Glorious Revolution of 1688–1689 brought Protestant monarchs to the English throne, who agreed to abide by the laws of a Parliament dominated by domestic manufacturing interests; in 1707 Parliament then passed laws restricting the importation of Indian cotton textiles into England in order to protect British manufacturers and to encourage the development of a British cotton textile industry. By 1700, then, England had a government that, in the words of one British historian, "was prepared to subordinate all foreign policy to economic ends. Her war aims were commercial" and her foreign policy "shaped" by pressure from manufacturers.[29]

Mercantilism

For its part, France too was building a strong state, and under the guidance of Jean-Baptiste Colbert, its minister of finance in the late seventeenth century, it implemented economic policies that came to be known as mercantilism. European rulers always seemed to be short of money to pay for their wars. Even the Spanish complained in the 1580s that "experience has shown that within a month or two of the arrival of a fleet from the Indies, not a farthing is to be seen." An English businessman likewise complained in the 1620s of the "scarcity of coin."[30] The reason is that although Europe's stock of money increased (especially from 1580 to 1620), by 1620 it probably declined as silver mining in Europe collapsed, American silver declined, and the outflow to Asia increased. Not only were European states competing on the battlefield, they were competing to attract and retain as much silver and gold bullion as possible.

In the intensely competitive European context, it appeared that one state could gain only if another lost: it was a war of each against all in which "looking out for number one" was the highest principle. And the best way for a state to gain advantage, according to mercantilist theory, was to attract and then to keep the largest possible quantity of the world's stock of precious metals, especially silver (and later, gold). The reason for the need for bullion reserves was simple: wars were very costly, arms had to be purchased, in many instances from weapons makers outside the monarch's own country,[31] and campaigning in a foreign country required vast amounts of silver or gold. To keep precious metals in one's own state therefore required economic policies that prevented them from flowing out in payment for, well, anything imported, especially for goods consumed and not used in war.

Thus European states imposed duties on virtually all imported goods, required that all goods be transported in their ships, and forced European New World colonists to trade only with the mother country, even if smuggling made such a policy somewhat porous. Mercantilist ideas also led to policies that states should use their own raw materials to manufacture within their own borders anything that was imported, an action we saw the English take in the early 1700s to keep Indian cotton textiles out. Although mercantilist policies did indeed lead to the establishment of industries in European states, industrialization itself was not the object: keeping gold and silver from flowing out of the state and enriching others was. European states were obsessed with their silver stocks: "the more silver, the stronger the state" was how a German once put it.[32]

In these inter-European wars, the fates and fortunes of various states rose and fell. As we have already seen, by the end of the sixteenth century, Spain's power had begun to wane, and Portugal proved to be too small to mount much of a challenge to the French (or Spanish) in Europe, or to the Dutch in Asian waters. The Dutch, being among the first Europeans to apply vast amounts of capital to their trading enterprises in both Asia and the Americas, saw their fortunes peak in the seventeenth century, just as the French and the British were gaining power. Ultimately, though, the Dutch did not have the manpower to build a standing army sufficiently large to counter the French, and they ultimately allied with the British to offset French power on the continent. By the eighteenth century, Britain and France were the two most powerful and competitive states. (See map 3.1.)

Map 3.1.   The World circa 1760

The Seven Years' War, 1756–1763

As the strongest and most successful European states, England and France competed not just in Europe but in the Americas and Asia as well. In the "long" eighteenth century from 1689 to 1815, Britain and France fought five wars, only one of which Britain did not initiate. Their engagement (with others) in the War of Spanish Succession was ended by the 1713 Treaty of Utrecht, which established the principle of the "balance of power" in Europe, that is, that no country should be allowed to dominate the others. However, periodic wars between the British and French continued.

But the most significant was the Seven Years' War of 1756–1763, or what Americans call the French and Indian War and interpret in terms of its impact on the American War of Independence of 1776–1783 against Britain. To be sure, the spark that led to war between Britain and France came in the American colonies, and it was in fact the twenty-two-year-old George Washington who lit it.[33] But it became a global engagement—perhaps the first real world war—with British and French troops fighting in the backwoods of the American colonies, in Canada, in Africa, in India, and in Europe. The outcome was disastrous for the French: they lost their colonial claims in both

North America (the British got Canada) and in India, leading to greater British power and position in both parts of the world.[34]

By 1775, therefore, the processes of state building in Europe had led to the creation of a system defined by war, which favored a particular kind of state exemplified by the ones built in Britain and France. Balance of power among sovereign states, not a unified empire, had become the established principle, and Britain had emerged as the strongest European state. But that does not mean that it was the strongest or richest state in the world—far from it. To be sure, Mughal power in India was declining in the early 1700s, and as we will see in the next chapter, the British were able to begin building a colonial empire there. But the British were still too weak to be able to contest China's definition of the rules of trade in Asia. When they tried, most famously in 1793 under Lord Macartney's mission, the Chinese emperor sent them home with a stinging rebuke, and the British could do nothing about it. However, the British Isles were fortunate enough to be the location for the start of the Industrial Revolution, which was gaining steam even as Lord Macartney was sailing back to London. And when the British learned to apply the tools of the Industrial Revolution to war, the global balance of power between Britain and China tipped. That is the story of the next chapter.

Notes

1. For a scholarly comparison of these two very different political economies see R. Bin Wong, *China Transformed: Historical Change and the Limits of European Experience* (Ithaca, N.Y.: Cornell University Press, 1997), part 2.

2. See Takeshi Hamashita, "The Intra-Regional System in East Asia in Modern Times," in Peter J. Katzenstein and Takashi Shiraishi, eds., *Network Power: Japan and Asia* (Ithaca, N.Y.: Cornell University Press, 1997), chap. 3.

3. See Geoffrey Parker and Lesley M. Smith, eds., *The General Crisis of the Seventeenth Century*, 2d ed. (London: Routledge, 1997).

4. For some exceptions, see C. A. Bayly, *Imperial Meridian: The British Empire and the World, 1780–1830* (London: Longman, 1993).

5. Recent archaeological finds at Caral in Peru may well push back the dates for the establishment of cities and long-distance trade to about 2600 B.C.E. For an initial report on this research, see the *Los Angeles Times*, April 27, 2000, p. 1.

6. Humans may have migrated to the Americas as early as 35,000 years ago, but the consensus among scholars is about 15,000 B.C.E. See Richard E. W. Adams and Murdo J. MacLeod, eds., *The Cambridge History of the Native Peoples of the Americas*, vol. 2, part 1 (New York: Cambridge University Press, 2000), 28.

7. Pronounced "Me-shee-ka." Nineteenth-century historians began calling these people Aztecs, after the name of the place from which they supposedly originated, Aztlan.

8. War prisoners played an important role in Mexican religious practice. The Mexica believed—or at least their priests told them—that their gods had set the universe into motion by their individual sacrifices, and that to keep the world going, in particular to ensure that the sun came up every morning, it was imperative to honor the gods through ritual sacrifice of human beings. Bloodletting on the central altar in the city thus was a daily ritual. Additionally, the Mexica developed an especial fondness for the god of war, Huitzilopochtli, who demanded extra sacrifices. When the temple to this god was completed in 1487, reportedly 80,000 people were sacrificed to the god.

9. For additional insights, see Jared Diamond, *Guns, Germs, and Steel* (New York: W. W. Norton, 1998), chap. 3.

10. Bruce G. Trigger and Wilcomb E. Washburn, eds., *The Cambridge History of the Native Peoples of the Americas*, vol. 1, *North America* (Cambridge: Cambridge University Press, 1996), part 1, 361–369.

11. Leslie Bethell, ed., *The Cambridge History of Latin America*, vol. 2 (Cambridge: Cambridge University Press, 1984), chap. 1.

12. For a brief summary, see Thomas A. Brady, Jr., "The Rise of Merchant Empires, 1400–1700: A European Counterpoint," in James D. Tracy, ed., *The Political Economy of Merchant Empires: State Power and World Trade 1350–1750* (Cambridge: Cambridge University Press, 1991), 117–160.

13. Dennis O. Flynn and Arturo Giráldez, "Spanish Profitability in the Pacific: The Philippines in the Sixteenth and Seventeenth Centuries," in Dennis O. Flynn, Lionel Frost, and A. J. H. Latham, eds., *Pacific Centuries: Pacific and Pacific Rim History since the Sixteenth History* (London: Routledge, 1999), 23.

14. Andre Gunder Frank, *ReOrient: Global Economy in the Asian Age* (Berkeley: University of California Press, 1998), 131.

15. See Frank, *ReOrient*, chap. 4 for the data cited in these paragraphs.

16. *Cambridge History of China*, vol. 8, part 2, 400–402.

17. Quoted in Fernand Braudel, *Civilization and Capitalism 15th–18th Century*, vol. 2 (New York: Harper and Row, 1981), 178.

18. The story of sugar and slavery can be found in Sidney W. Mintz, *Sweetness and Power: The Place of Sugar in Modern History* (New York: Viking Press, 1985), and in Bethell, *The Cambridge History of Latin America*, vols. 1–2.

19. See Alfred Crosby, *Ecological Imperialism: The Biological Expansion of Europe, 900–1900* (Cambridge: Cambridge University Press, 1986), chap. 4.

20. Richard Grove, *Green Imperialism: Colonial Expansion, Tropical Island Edens and the Origins of Environmentalism, 1600–1800* (Cambridge: Cambridge University Press, 1995), chap. 6.

21. John Thornton, *Africa and Africans in the Making of the Atlantic World, 1400–1800*, 2d ed. (Cambridge: Cambridge University Press, 1992), 14.

22. See Herbert S. Klein, *The Atlantic Slave Trade* (Cambridge: Cambridge University Press, 1999); Thornton, *Africa and Africans in the Making of the Atlantic World*.

23. As described in an exhibit at Britain's National Maritime Museum: "The slave trade was part of a global trading system. British products and Indian goods were shipped

to West Africa and exchanged for slaves. The slaves were taken to the Americas in return for sugar, tobacco, and other tropical produce. These were then sold in Britain for processing into consumer goods, and possible re-export."

24. Charles Tilly, *Coercion, Capital, and European States, A.D. 990–1990* (Oxford: Basil Blackwell, 1990), 176–177.

25. Tilly, *Coercion, Capital, and European States*, 38–43. Tilly says twenty-five to twenty-eight states in 1990, numbers preceding the 1991 breakup of the Soviet Union and its former client states.

26. For an instructive history of the development of the idea of popular sovereignty in England and its American colonies, see Edmund S. Morgan, *Inventing the People: The Rise of Popular Sovereignty in England and America* (New York: W. W. Norton, 1988).

27. Tilly, *Coercion, Capital, and European States*, 47–54. The proximity to these cities, according to Tilly, led to the formation of three different kinds of European states. Wealthy cities could afford to hire their own mercenary armies (the "capital-intensive" path to state formation); rulers far away from cities and their capitals had to rely on force mobilized from a rural nobility (the "coercion-intensive" path) to build states, while those with a combination of cities and their dependent countryside used a combination. Tilly argues that the latter, exemplified by England and France, proved to be the most successful kind in the competitive European state system.

28. On the Navigation Acts, see John J. McCusker and Russell R. Menard, *The Economy of British America, 1607–1789* (Chapel Hill: University of North Carolina Press, 1985), 46–50.

29. Eric Hobsbawm, *Industry and Empire* (New York: Penguin, 1968), 49.

30. Quoted in Geoffrey Parker, "The Emergence of Modern Finance in Europe 1500–1730," in Carlo M. Cipolla, ed., *The Fontana Economic History of Europe*, vol. 2 (Glasgow: William Collins Sons, 1974), 530.

31. "Much of what Philip [II of Spain] needed for his armies was not available within peninsular Spain. His repeated efforts to establish factories producing cannon and other needed commodities always failed to flourish. Perversely, from a Spanish point of view, it was exactly in places where the king's will was not sovereign that economic activity and arms production concentrated. . . . Thus, for example, the bishopric of Liege, adjacent to the Spanish Netherlands but not under Spanish rule, became the major seat of armaments production for the Dutch wars, supplying a large proportion of the material needed by both the Spanish and the Dutch armies." William McNeill, *The Pursuit of Power: Technology, Armed Force, and Society since A.D. 1000* (Chicago: University of Chicago Press, 1982), 113.

32. Werner Sombart, quoted in Braudel, *Civilization and Capitalism*, vol. 2, 545.

33. See Fred Anderson, *Crucible of War* (New York: Alfred A. Knopf, 2000), for an engaging narrative of these events and of George Washington's role.

34. According to E. J. Hobsbawm, "The result of this century [18th] of intermittent warfare was the greatest triumph ever achieved by any state [Britain]: the virtual monopoly among European powers of overseas colonies, and the virtual monopoly of world-wide naval power." Quoted in Andre Gunder Frank, *World Accumulation 1492–1789* (New York: Monthly Review Press, 1978), 237.

CHAPTER FOUR

The Industrial Revolution and Its Consequences, 1750–1850

In 1750, every one of the world's 750 million people, regardless of where they were or what political or economic system they had, lived and died within the biological old regime. The necessities of life—food, clothing, shelter, and fuel for heating and cooking—all came from the land, from what could be captured from annual energy flows from the sun to the earth. Industries too, such as textiles, leather, and construction, depended on products from agriculture or the forest. Even iron and steel making in the biological old regime, for instance, relied upon charcoal made from wood. The biological old regime thus set limits not just on the size of the human population, but on the productivity of the economy as well.

All of this would change in the century from 1750 to 1850 when people increasingly used coal to produce heat and then captured that heat to fuel repetitive motion with steam-powered machines.[1] The use of coal was a major breakthrough, launching human society out of the biological old regime and into a new one no longer limited by annual solar energy flows. Coal is stored solar energy, laid down hundreds of millions of years ago. Its use in steam engines freed human society from the limits imposed by the biological old regime, enabling the productive powers and the numbers of humans to grow exponentially. The replacement—with steam generated by burning coal—of wind, water, and animals for powering industrial machines constitutes the beginning of Industrial Revolution[2] and ranks with the much earlier agricultural revolution in importance for the course of history. How and why it happened and what consequences it had thus are vitally important matters in world history and will be the focus of this chapter.

To understand the Industrial Revolution, we will use once again the tool of "conjuncture," that is, the coming together at a particular point in time of otherwise separate historical developments and processes. In the case of the Industrial Revolution, the conjuncture involves the playing out around the world of growth potential in the biological old regime, the extension of European state conflicts around the globe, the peculiar nature of New World colonies, and the chance location of, and challenges for, operating coal mines in England. In particular, I will consider the ways in which cotton textiles and the British need for coal contributed to the Industrial Revolution.

Cotton Textiles

The Industrial Revolution is commonly thought to have begun in eighteenth-century England with the mechanization of the process for spinning and weaving cotton thread and cloth. The spinning jenny, the water frame, and the "mule" all have been taken as evidence of English inventiveness and hence contribute to a Eurocentric storyline of the rise of the West. The problem is, while it is true that England was the first place to revolutionize cotton manufacture by using steam-powered machinery, how and why it happened can only be understood in a global context.

In the late seventeenth century, the English developed a strong desire for the Indian cotton textiles commonly known as calicos. As one man observed: "On a sudden we saw all our women, rich and poor, cloath'd in Callico, printed and painted; the gayer the better." Another complained: "It crept into our houses, our closets and bedchambers; curtains, cushions, chairs, and at last beds themselves were nothing but Callicoes or Indian stuffs. In short, almost everything that used to be made of wool or silk, relating either to dress of the women or the furniture of our houses, was supplied by the Indian trade."[3] These observations by contemporaries around 1700 raise some interesting questions: Why were the English importing so much Indian cotton? How did it get there? How did they then create and industrialize a cotton textile industry?

The reason the English imported so much Indian cotton around 1700 is because it was of high quality and lower price than domestically produced textiles (in particular linen and wool). It felt good next to the skin, it was lightweight for summer wear, it could accept bright dyes for color, and most of all, it was less expensive than anything the English could manufacture themselves. Indeed, India around 1700 was the largest exporter of cotton textiles in the world and supplied textiles not just to meet English demand, but throughout the world as well. Southeast Asia, East and West Africa, the Mid-

dle East, and Europe were major export markets, in addition to the large domestic Indian market. No wonder that the demand for Indian cotton in the
eighteenth century was "greater than all the weavers in the country can manufacture," and that India accounted for fully one-quarter of the world manufacturing output in 1750.[4]

Like so many things desired by Europeans and supplied by Asians—at first
luxury items for the elite such as silk or porcelain, but increasingly products
like tea from China for a mass market[5]—cotton textiles were produced well
and cheaply in India. The British textile manufacturers focused on the
"cheap" part and complained that with relatively higher wages, British manufacturers could not compete. India had a competitive advantage-in the
eighteenth century, being able to undersell in the world market virtually any
other producer of textiles. Some thought the reason for cheap Indian textiles
was because of a low living standard, or a large population earning depressed
wages, but all of those have been shown to not be true: Indian textile workers in the eighteenth century had just as high a standard of living as British
workers.[6] So, if it was not a low standard of living that gave India its competitive advantage, what did?

In a word: agriculture. Indian agriculture was so productive that the
amount of food produced, and hence its cost, was significantly lower than in
Europe. In the preindustrial age, when working families spent 60–80 percent
of their earnings on food, the cost of food was the primary determinant of
their real wages (i.e., how much a pound, a dollar, a real, or a pagoda could
buy). In India (and China and Japan as well), the amount of grain harvested
from a given amount of seed was in the ratio of 20:1 (e.g., twenty bushels of
rice harvested for every one planted), whereas in England it was at best 8:1.
Asian agriculture thus was more than twice as efficient as British (and by extension European) agriculture, and food—the major component in the cost
of living—cost less in Asia. Thus although nominal wages may have been
lower in India, the purchasing power—the real wage—was higher in India.

In the biological old regime, productive agriculture was Asia's competitive
advantage, even in industry. The causal chain went like this: high per-acre
yields → low-priced food → relatively low wages → comparative advantage.
In England, the causal chain was like this: low per-acre yields → high-priced
food → relatively high wages → comparative disadvantage. The question
then becomes, how did the British begin to reverse this comparative disadvantage?

In part, as we saw in the previous chapter, they did it by raising tariffs on
the imports to Britain of Indian textiles, that is, protectionism. Had the
British not done that in the early eighteenth century, there is little reason to

believe they would have made much progress in competing against Indian producers and establishing much of a cotton textile industry in the first place. But also, the British had colonies in the Americas and acquired their "jewel" in India. Both became intimately connected with the story of the rise of a cotton textile industry in Britain.

India

Indeed, where England had very little by way of overseas empire in 1650, it soon began putting one together, preying on Portuguese and Spanish possessions in the East and West Indies (i.e., India and the Caribbean), competing with the Dutch in both regions of the world, and battling France in the eighteenth century. Curiously, though, the agents for this extension of European interstate conflict around the world were not at first the governments of European states but private trading companies, the first being the Dutch Vereenigde Oost-Indische Compagnie (VOC, East India Company), the English East India Company (EIC), and the French Compagnie des Indies.

Although each was formed at different times and had slightly different organization, all were private companies chartered by their governments and given monopoly rights to trade with Asia, all in keeping with mercantilist ideas. They also differed from mere trading expeditions in that they were formed with a permanent capital and stock that could be traded—to that extent, the East India companies are the forerunners of the modern corporation, and their success at organizing trade and raising profits meant that the corporation would play an increasingly important role in European industrialization. But in the seventeenth and eighteenth centuries, their purpose was to reap profits from trade with Asia.

The Dutch VOC, though, seeing itself as an extension of Protestant Dutch interests and hence deeply hostile to the Catholic powers of Spain and Portugal, saw trade and war as intimately connected. In a terse 1614 letter to his directors, the Dutch VOC governor-general observed: "You gentlemen ought to know from experience that trade in Asia should be conducted and maintained under the protection and with the aid of your own weapons, and . . . [s]o trade cannot be maintained without war, nor war without trade."[7] The Dutch then effectively pursued this strategy throughout the seventeenth century, taking Malacca from the Portuguese, seizing Java and making it into a sugar-producing colony, and trying to establish a colony on the Chinese island of Taiwan.

The English EIC, by contrast, was more interested in trade and the profits of trade than in war, at least at first. In the century after its founding in 1600, the directors insisted that "our business is trade, not war."[8] To avoid conflicts, the English EIC concentrated trade in India where Indian states were weak and European competitors few, especially in Bengal and Madras. But by the late seventeenth century, that began to change as the French established forts nearby. And when the British and French warred in Europe, their forces (however small) clashed in India, with the French usually getting the upper hand because they began enhancing their war-making capability by enlisting Indians as regulars, known as Sepoys, into their army. In the 1750s the British EIC followed suit, and by the eve of the Seven Years' War, each had nearly ten thousand men in arms—mostly Indians—on the Indian coast.

In the meantime, the political and military power of the great Mughal empire had seriously declined. At its height it was capable of mobilizing perhaps a million troops; after the death of its last great leader, Aurangzeb, in 1707, the empire declined with regional political and military leaders asserting their independence from the Mughals. One of those leaders, the nawab of Bengal, took control of the British trading port at Calcutta and demanded increased payments from the EIC for the privilege of trading there.

The British resisted, sent a force of some two thousand men under the leadership of Robert Clive, and together with other Indian forces opposed to Bengal, defeated the nawab's French-assisted forces at the Battle of Plassey in 1757. They captured and executed the nawab, got a more pliable replacement, and by 1765 received the right to collect tax revenue—a huge sum—from Bengal. In the meantime, of course, the Seven Years' War had begun, and British and French forces had at it up and down the Indian coast, with the British winning a decisive victory over the French at Pondicherry in 1760. This was the start of the British empire in India, and over the next fifty years the extent of British control widened with the entire subcontinent becoming a formal colony in 1857. (See map 3.1.)

The Seven Years' War—or more precisely, the British victory in the Americas and in India—is important to the story of how Britain became a cotton textile producing, rather than importing, country. Recall that the British government had banned the importation of Indian textiles in 1707 for the purpose of allowing its domestic cotton industry to get going, which it did, in the area around the town of Manchester. But because of technical difficulties in copying Indian dyeing techniques and because of its higher wages/higher prices, Manchester produced mostly for the British home market, still being bested in the world market by Indian textiles traded by the EIC. For the British cotton textile industry to grow, it therefore needed export markets. And there was a growing market in the New World because of its peculiar institutions of slavery, plantations, and mercantilist trade restrictions.

The New World as a Peculiar Periphery

European New World agriculture from the beginning was export oriented. Throughout the Caribbean and South America, mostly all sugar, tobacco, and cotton was produced on plantations that used African slaves because of labor shortages caused by the Great Dying and the unwillingness of Europeans to migrate to the New World. Unlike peasants in India and China or serfs in eastern Europe, African slaves in America did not grow much of their own food. Food, especially fish and grain, had to be imported, mostly from the North American colonies. Slaves also had to be clothed, creating a demand for cheap cotton textiles. Additional quantities of Indian textiles were traded in West Africa for slaves who were then sold in the Caribbean. New World products—sugar, tobacco, raw cotton—were taken back to England.

At each point in the triangular Atlantic trade, the English made profits and by colonial legislation tried to ensure that the New World would remain producers of raw materials only and consumers of the industrial products of Britain.[9] Smuggling or trading with the enemy, whether Dutch or French, was pervasive, but by the early eighteenth century, "colonial trade conformed in almost every particular to the navigation system . . . [and] smuggled goods accounted for a tiny fraction of all quantities handled." Of course, the colonists in both the Caribbean and North America were Englishmen, and they too looked for ways to profit from a system that denied other nationals, especially the Dutch or the French, from getting a piece of Britain's colonial trade.[10]

This triangular trade and in particular the linkage between the slave trade and textiles fueled the growth of British shipping and established Manchester as a center of cotton textile manufacture. Raw cotton was imported mostly from the Levant in the Ottoman empire and the British colonies in the Caribbean, and by the 1780s it was spun into thread in newfangled "factories" using water power and employing hundreds of workers in one place. As the Manchester manufacturers became more proficient and the prices of their textiles declined, they even exported them to Africa, especially whenever Indian textiles were expensive. The real boom to British cotton textile production came after American independence in 1793 when Eli Whitney's invention of the cotton gin made it possible to use short-staple and much cheaper American cotton. When another series of innovations derived from the application of steam power, as we will see shortly, mechanizing both spinning and weaving over the years from 1815 to 1840, the productivity of the Manchester textile factories surged again, resulting in ever lower prices and the ability to out-compete Indian textiles in the world market.

When that happened, the British became advocates of "free trade" and abandoned both mercantilist theory and practice and tariffs on imports. Indeed, "free trade" became the ideological mantra of imperial Britain at the height of its global power in the nineteenth century. Mercantilism, at least as it applied in the Atlantic world, had been dead since the victory of the Americans in their War of Independence from Britain. To the British, their former American subjects and colonists became "foreigners, subject to all the provisions of the Navigation Laws,"[11] which restricted the importation of raw cotton, potentially strangling the British textile industry and giving rise to calls for "free trade." Free trade with the new United States after 1783 showed the fallacy of the argument that British manufactures could grow only with a monopoly on colonial markets, and the American South with its cotton plantations worked by African slaves and their descendants became the major supplier of raw cotton to the mills of Manchester.

Although this story of the rise to global competitiveness of the British cotton textile industry sounds Eurocentric, it really is not, for British success was contingent upon a number of worldwide developments that were not of their own making. In the first place, the British were at a competitive disadvantage to Indian producers and would have remained so except for several coincidences. The Glorious Revolution of 1688–1689 brought to power a government willing to use state power to protect its domestic manufacturers; and the New World developed as a peculiar periphery that, by the accident of the Great Dying and colonial legislation, provided a market for British manufactured goods. In the second place, the British were fortunate to develop a usable coal-fueled steam engine, which further revolutionized cotton textile production, making it even more productive and its products so cheap that the British could undersell Indian textiles not just in Africa but, interestingly, in India as well. For that part of the story, we now look at the innovations in coal and steam engines.

New Sources of Energy and Power

Until about 1800, the story of cotton textiles for the most part remains one that unfolds within the biological old regime; that is, everything about it depended on the annual flows of solar energy and their capture by humans. To be sure, the early British "factories" had begun to use water power, but there was a limit to how much that could increase cotton textile production. Indeed, there is every reason to think that cotton textile production would have reached serious limits within the biological old regime, leading not to an industrial revolution but to an economic dead end, had it not been for coal, the steam engine, and iron and steel production that truly launched the Industrial Revolution and allowed Britain to break out of the constraints imposed by the biological old regime. To see how and why, we need to take a closer look at what was happening to the most advanced biological old regime economies, starting with China and then looking at England. What we will see is that all old regime economies were beginning to push up against serious ecological constraints that would have stopped all of them from developing an industrial revolution. Except for a few chance occurrences and a vast global conjuncture, we all now might still be living in the biological old regime.

China

Two favored explanations of the Industrial Revolution in Europe have focused on population dynamics and the growth of free markets. By various techniques and practices, mostly late marriage, European families were able to keep their sizes smaller than "naturally" possible. Smaller family size meant a smaller population overall, leaving greater surpluses in the hands of families to invest in improving agricultural and industrial productivity. Fewer people working harder to make their investable surpluses grow—an "industrious revolution," it is said—grew inexorably into the Industrial Revolution.[12]

The market-driven storyline of industrialization suggests that the establishment and growth of markets for commodities, land, labor, and capital in Europe enabled European producers to be much more efficient and hence to accumulate sufficient capital to invest in improving agricultural and industrial productivity. Also necessary for the success of markets was a state that protected (or at least respected) private property rights. This combination likewise, according to the Eurocentric version of the origins of the modern world, grew more or less naturally into the Industrial Revolution.

Of course, the population- and market-driven storylines of industrialization are not incompatible, and many historians have melded them together in explaining why Europeans were uniquely capable of launching an industrial revolution. As proof, they often point to China as a counterexample. China, it is alleged, had "a preindustrial demographic regime," in which nothing was done to keep birthrates down. Hence, population surged, eating up any surplus above subsistence and rendering the investments necessary for an industrial revolution impossible.[13] Similarly, it is alleged, China was "despotic": it had a state that meddled in private affairs, property rights were not respected, and markets could not operate efficiently. Hence, it is concluded, there was no possibility for an industrial revolution.

There is only one thing wrong with these assumptions about what "went wrong" in China: they are wrong. As I will show below, Chinese families in fact had numerous ways—albeit different from Europeans—of limiting their size and hence keeping the overall Chinese population above subsistence levels. Also, Chinese markets of all kinds not merely existed, but arguably functioned better and more efficiently than those in Europe. If both of those are true for China, then their value as "explanations" for why the Industrial Revolution occurred in Europe is questionable. To see why, we must take a closer look at China.

As mentioned earlier in this chapter, agriculture in China (as well as in Japan and numerous other parts of Asia) was highly productive, harvesting twenty bushels of rice for every one sown. Rice has the unique capability of gaining nutrients not directly from the soil, but from the water (and so it is grown in "paddies"), eliminating the need for the land to lie fallow, as was the custom in Europe, to regain its fertility. Additionally, Chinese farmers had learned how to prepare the soil, to irrigate, to fertilize, and to control insect pests in order to maximize the harvest yield. Moreover, farmers in the southern half of China could get two or sometimes three harvests per year from the same plot of land, drawing the amazement of early-eighteenth-century European travelers to China. "By what art can the earth produce subsistence for such numbers [of people]," asked the Frenchman Pierre Poivre in the 1720s.

> Do the Chinese possess any secret arts of multiplying grain and provisions necessary for the nourishment of mankind? To solve my doubts I traversed the fields, I introduced myself among the laborers, who are in general easy, polite, and knowledgeable of the world. I examine, and pursue them through all their operations, and observe that their secret consists simply in manuring the fields judiciously, ploughing them to a considerable depth, sowing them in the proper season, turning to advantage every inch of ground which can produce the most considerable crop, and preferring to every other species of culture that of grain, as by far the most important.[14]

Such an impressively productive agriculture certainly allowed the Chinese population to grow, from 140 million in 1650, to 225 million in 1750, and then to 380–400 million by 1850. Numbers like these also convinced European observers, in particular Adam Smith and Thomas Malthus, whose ideas about markets and population have so shaped Eurocentric views of the modern world, that the Chinese just could not control their population growth. Malthus believed that populations like the Chinese who could not control their growth would overshoot the capability of the land to support their numbers until "negative" population checks, such as famines or wars, reduced the population size. Malthus also believed that Europeans avoided those fates by having "preventative" checks on population growth.

Where Malthus certainly was right about Europeans, he was wrong about the Chinese. The fact is, they could—and did—control their family size, although in ways quite different from the Europeans. Although almost all Chinese women married and married early, Chinese families developed many methods for controlling the number of children. Abstention from having sexual relations, especially early in the marriage, was a preferred mechanism and was enforced by married couples living with their parents. Infanticide, especially of daughters, was another means to limit family size, leading as well to a gender-unbalanced population of more men than women, and hence of forced celibacy for many poorer men. As James Lee and Wang Feng summarize the Chinese demographic system:

> In contrast to the European system, in which marriage was the only volitional check on population growth, the Chinese demographic system had multiple conscious checks, and was therefore far more complex and calculating than Malthus or his successors thought. As a result . . . population never pushed the economy to subsistence levels.[15]

Nevertheless, because of the productivity of agriculture and the ability of the Chinese economy to produce more than enough food for its population, the population did in fact grow, and as mentioned above, it grew rapidly from 1750 to 1850.[16] In the densely populated core areas of the Pearl River delta in south China, along the southeast coast, and in the Yangzi River delta, populations did reach the size where people started migrating out into less-populated areas. Sometimes these regions had exceptionally fertile soil that could be brought into production by clearing the land, as in Hunan up the Yangzi River from Shanghai, or in the West River valley in Guangxi province, or sometimes the land that was brought into production was more marginal and less fertile, as in the Jiangxi highlands on the southern bank of the Yangzi River.[17]

Wherever new land was being brought into agricultural production, especially by 1800 when it was land that was not as fertile or productive as land in the densely populated core regions, that was an indication that the limits of growth within the biological old regime were being reached. That does not mean that a Malthusian disaster was imminent—the Chinese were in fact very much in control of their reproductive capabilities—but that good agricultural land was becoming in short supply. The reason for that is that the four necessities of life—food, clothing, shelter, and fuel—all came from the land and hence were in competition. Clearing land for food decreased the amount of wood available for fuel, either to cook and heat homes or to make charcoal for industrial purposes. Switching land from cotton to rice production also put pressure on the supply of the raw material for clothing, while doing the opposite would decrease the amount of food available. There just was not much room for maneuvering when the limits of the biological old regime were being reached, as they were in China in the late eighteenth century, and, as we will see, in Britain too.

It was not just that meeting the needs for sustained population growth meant increasing pressure on the land and decreases in other things at the expense of food, but that to keep food production increasing while at the same time keeping supplies available for clothing, shelter, and fuel meant that greater and greater amounts of labor and capital had to be expended in agriculture just to keep pace. For instance, clearing land was expensive and so too was building irrigation works or terracing fields from hills, all of which improved the output of Chinese agriculture in the eighteenth and nineteenth centuries. Allocating more labor also could increase output, and Chinese farming families did that too: planting rice in nurseries and then transplanting it to the fields or picking insects off rice plants by hand, for instance, also increased agricultural yields and sustained a growing population.

Markets

Another way the Chinese economy improved both overall production levels and productivity was by the use of markets, especially for agricultural commodities. It used to be thought that markets were first and most highly developed in Europe (reading backward from the the Industrial Revolution to find reasons why it happened there first). But in the past twenty years, historians of China have shown how fully developed and efficient the markets were in eighteenth- and nineteenth-century China. Peasant farmers in the Pearl River and Yangzi River deltas, for instance, came to specialize in sericulture (that is, the whole process of producing silk), raising silkworms and growing the mulberry trees with which to feed the silkworms, boiling the cocoons to obtain the silk threads, then spinning, weaving, and dyeing the silk. Other areas might specialize in cotton, sugarcane, or other nonfood agricultural crops.

Such specialization meant that those peasant producers had to obtain their food from other sources, usually places upriver that came to specialize in rice that could easily export it on boats to the more densely populated core regions. Massive investments in canals by both private parties and the state vastly extended and improved the Chinese inland water transportation system, linking China from Tianjin in the north to Guangzhou in the south by water. Efficient water transportation facilitated the movement of grain throughout the Chinese empire, the growth of markets, and provided the material foundations for maintaining some of the world's largest cities.

Initially, the Chinese state intervened in the food markets quite regularly to ensure that peasant producers and urban consumers alike would be ensured adequate food supplies,[18] but by the mid-eighteenth century the Chinese state was increasingly willing to allow markets and merchants to handle the movement of grain across huge distances—up to a thousand miles—from where it was produced to where it was consumed. Measures of the efficiency of these markets show that they were more efficient than contemporary markets in France, England, or the United States.[19] Additionally, Chinese markets for land, labor, and capital all functioned well, and in some ways more efficiently than comparable markets in European countries.[20]

In short, eighteenth-century China looked as "developed" as any other developed part of the world, whether measured by levels of agricultural productivity, sophistication of manufactures and markets, or levels of consumption. Chinese families regulated their size and were responsive to changing economic opportunities, limiting their size when those opportunities diminished in order to maintain consumption above subsistence levels; specialization of function gave rise to markets and a highly commercialized economy; and an extensive water-based transportation system allowed the efficient movement of goods and people throughout the empire.

Yet China's highly developed market economy did not lead to an industrial breakthrough. Instead, by the nineteenth century, there were plenty of indicators that China was pushing up against ecological constraints imposed by the biological old regime. In several areas, fuel became short in supply in the early 1800s, with peasant families turning to rice straw and chaff for heating and cooking rather than wood. Moreover, some market exchanges between densely populated core regions and developing peripheral areas also served to slow Chinese economic growth.

One of the advantages of markets and a good transportation network is that they allow some areas to specialize in what their natural resources make most profitable and to exchange that produce with others, enabling both to be more productive and allowing everyone's income to rise. At least that is the theory, and to a point that is the way they functioned in China. However, the exchanges began to break down regarding the exchange of raw cotton from cotton-producing regions in return for manufactured goods, cotton textiles in particular, from the highly developed core regions in the lower Yangzi and Pearl River deltas.

Throughout China, rural families were free to decide what and how much to grow and how to allocate family labor on the farm. To this extent they differed markedly from African slaves in the New World, or serfs in eastern Europe, both of whom had their freedom curtailed and production decisions made by their owners or overseers. Thus those Chinese peasants who migrated to more peripheral areas, like their counterparts in the more developed cores, were free to make their own decisions. Increasingly, what they decided was that it was in their interest to spin and weave their own cotton textiles for their own use and for local exchange, rather than concentrating on rice or raw cotton and importing the finished goods. In effect, large parts of rural China underwent a process of "import substitution," producing their own textiles. Not only did they reduce the amount of raw cotton sold to the textile-producing centers, but they also increased the area given over to cotton and hence decreased the amount of rice they were willing to export as well.[21]

The freedom of Chinese peasant families thus may have spurred what might be called "self-sufficient proto-industrialization" in peripheral areas, but that acted as a constraint on the growth of an industrial cotton textile industry in China's core regions. Contributing to the willingness of Chinese peasant families in peripheral areas to spin and weave their own textiles may have been the long-standing norm that "men plow, women weave." It was not just that "women weave," but that they weave in the household. Chinese families thus placed a high value on mothers and daughters staying at home to do the weaving, rather than leaving home to work in a factory, as English and Japanese girls did.[22] Paradoxically, the freedom of producers throughout China's core and peripheral regions, when compared with the limited freedoms of slaves and serfs in the European system, constrained China's ability to continue developing a textile industry in its most highly developed core regions.

In summary, China had a highly developed market economy within the constraints of the biological old regime. Nonetheless, that regime placed ecological limits upon growth, and the freedom of Chinese peasants coupled with practices governing the sexual division of labor, all combined, meant that China was bumping up against the limits of growth by the mid-1800s. Food, clothing, shelter, and fuel competed for land, and to get more from the land, the Chinese lavished increasing amounts of labor on agriculture. The dynamics of specialization, increased market exchanges, and improved transportation in the context of the biological old regime and the particularities of China's situation was pushing it toward an increasingly labor-intensive agriculture, rather than toward an industrial revolution.

England, Redux

Surprisingly, a Chinese-like labor-intensive fate may well have awaited England and the other developed parts of Europe as well. Instead, England underwent an industrial revolution that changed everything, not just for England, but for the world. Part of the reason is that Britain had a "peculiar" periphery in the New World: slavery, mercantilist colonial legislation, and then the expansion of cotton plantations in the American South after independence created a very large market for British cotton textiles, thereby stimulating and sustaining the growth of the cotton textile industry in Manchester. Paradoxically, greater freedom for China's peasant families in China's periphery meant that they could choose not to buy cotton textiles imported from their textile centers, but instead produce them themselves. New World slavery not only kept demand for British cotton textiles high, it also supplied the raw cotton cheaply. Additionally, Britain's wars with France from 1689 to 1815 "virtually eliminated all rivals from the non-European world, except to some extent the young United States."[23]

British colonies and textiles went together. By 1840, Britain was exporting 200 million yards of cotton textiles to other European countries, but 529 million yards to Asia, Africa, and the Americas (excluding the United States). Between 1820 and 1840, the tables turned in terms of Britain's relationship with Indian cotton textiles. Whereas England had imported so much Indian cotton cloth in the early 1700s that its government had to ban imports, in the 1800s Britain began exporting cotton textiles to its new colonial possession: only 11 million yards in 1820, but 145 million by 1840. In the process, India's great cotton textile industry declined, leading to what some historians call "the de-industrialization of India."[24]

Coal, Iron, and Steam

Despite the impressive growth of Britain's cotton textile industry, a leading British historian doubts that textiles alone would have led to an industrial revolution. True, Britain's cotton textile industry accounted for nearly all economic growth there until the 1830s. Cotton textiles also called into existence a new class of urban industrial workers and created the "factories" and horrendous injustices captured by Charles Dickens in his various novels. But all of these could not transform the British economy from one that was mired in the biological old regime to one that was freed from those constraints. For that to happen a whole new source of power was needed: coal-fired steam power.[25]

Unlike the story of cotton textiles, the story of how a coal and steam industry developed in England is mostly unique to England, and it shows how close England was to following in China's footsteps toward labor-intensive agriculture. For like China, population growth and agricultural development put pressure on the land resources of England. Indeed, by 1600 much of southern England had already been deforested, largely to meet the needs of the growing city of London for fuel for heating and cooking.

Fortunately for the British, veins of coal were close enough to the surface of the ground and close enough to London to create both a demand for coal and the beginnings of a coal industry. By 1800, Britain was producing ten million tons of coal, or 90 percent of the world's output, virtually all destined for the homes and hearths of London. As the surface deposits were depleted, mine shafts were sunk, and the deeper they went in search of coal, the more the mines encountered groundwater seeping into and flooding the mine shafts. Mine operators had a problem, and they began devising ways to get the water out of the mines.

Ultimately what they found useful was a device that used steam to push a piston. Early versions of this machine, developed first by Thomas Newcomen in 1712 and then vastly improved by James Watt in the 1760s, were so inefficient that the cost of fuel would have rendered them useless, except for one thing: at the mine head, coal was in effect free. Newcomen's (and later Watt's) inefficient steam engines thus could be used there. Between 1712 and 1800 there were 2,500 of the contraptions built, almost all of which were used at coal mines. But even that does not yet explain the Industrial Revolution, because the demand for coal (and hence steam engines) was fairly limited until new applications were devised. The one that proved most important was the idea of using the steam engine not just to draw water out of coal mines, but to move vehicles above ground.

The real breakthrough thus came with the building of the first steam engine railway. Along with digging deeper, coal miners had to go farther from London to find coal deposits and thus had high expenses for transporting the coal overland from the pithead to water. Fixed steam engines were being used to haul coal out of the mines and to pull trams short distances. But at a mine in Durham in the north of England, the idea of putting the steam engine on the tram carriage and running it on iron rails became a reality in 1825 with a seven-mile line connecting the mine directly to the coast. The first railroad was born.

Where in 1830 there were a few dozen miles of track in England, by 1840 there were over 4,500 miles, and by 1850 over 23,000 miles. The prodigy of the coal mine, the railroad fueled a demand for more coal, more steam engines, and more iron and steel: each mile of railroad used 300 tons of iron just for the track. Between 1830 and 1850, the output of iron in Britain rose from 680,000 to 2,250,000 tons, and coal output trebled from 15 million to 49 million tons.[26]

Steam engines also transformed the cotton textile industry, vastly increasing output. The spinning of yarn was first to be "industrialized" using water power; in 1790 Samuel Crompton's "mule" was adapted for steam power, resulting in a hundredfold increase in thread output over a worker on a manual spinning wheel, such as was still in use in India and China. So much thread was produced that weavers could not keep up, leading to innovations in that part of the industry, including the use of steam to power the looms, so much so that by the 1820s there were few hand weavers left. So large was Britain's textile industry that of the twelve million men, women, and children in England in 1830, a half million—mostly women and children—were employed in the textile mills.

Recap: Without Colonies or Coal

The Industrial Revolution is usually portrayed as the story of the invention and use of laborsaving devices that so dramatically increased the ability of people to produce that human society was placed upon a path of ever-increasing productivity, overall societal wealth, and higher standards of living. To a certain extent, that is true enough, in particular when thinking about the cotton textile industry. There, British producers—faced with competition from low-priced Indian products and their own high-wage labor force—had to find ways of lowering their costs of production, and hence they turned to mechanization.[27] However, without steam power, that process might well have played itself out as England used up all available locations for water-powered mills. For without coal and steam, cotton textiles alone could not transform the British economy from one limited by the constraints of the biological old regime to one liberated from it by the new sources of stored energy. Indeed, if there is any image that portrays "industrial revolution," it is that of smokestacks rising above a factory.

As Kenneth Pomeranz argued in The Great Divergence, a better way to think about the Industrial Revolution is that it proceeded by finding land-saving mechanisms. For throughout the Old World, from China in the east to England in the west, shortages of land to produce the necessities of life were putting limits on any further growth at all, let alone allowing a leap into a different kind of economic future. This understanding of the ecological limits of the biological old regime opens a new window onto the explanation of how and why the Industrial Revolution occurred first in England.

Steam could have been produced using wood or charcoal, but that would have required vast forests, and by the end of the eighteenth century, forest covered but 5–10 percent of Britain. Under the best of circumstances, using charcoal to produce iron in 1815 would have yielded but 100,000 tons or so, a far cry from the 400,000 tons actually produced and the millions soon needed for railroads. Tens of millions of additional acres of woodland would have been needed to continue to produce iron and steel.[28] That might have been feasible, but converting land from agricultural purposes back to forest would have had other rather dire consequences. Thus without coal, and the historical accident that it was easily found and transported in England, steam and iron and steel production would have been severely curtailed.

Similarly, Britain's New World colonies provided additional "ghost acres" beyond its borders that allowed the first part of the story of industrialization, that of cotton textiles, to unfold. To feed its textile mills, in the early 1800s Britain was importing hundreds of thousands of pounds of raw cotton from the New World, mostly from its former colonies in the new United States, but also from its Caribbean holdings. If the British had been forced to continue to clothe themselves with wool, linen, or hemp cloth produced from within their own borders, it would have required over twenty million acres. Similarly, Britain's sugar imports from its colonies provided substantial calories to its working population, all of which would have required more millions of acres.[29] The point is this: without coal or colonies, the dynamics of the biological old regime would have forced Britons to devote more and more of their land and labor to food production, further constraining resources for industrial production and snuffing out any hope for an industrial revolution, much as what happened to China in the nineteenth century.

Science and Technology

Eurocentric explanations of the Industrial Revolution typically invoke the "scientific revolution," the immensely interesting and ultimately very important development beginning in the sixteenth century, whereby some Europeans began to think of nature as a separate entity that could be understood and modeled mathematically. Although it is quite true that science has come to be an integral part of the world, and while it has come to play a leading role, especially from the late 1800s on, in developing new industries,[30] there is little evidence to tie European science to the beginnings of the Industrial Revolution or to the technologies that fueled it. The reasons are several.[31]

Let us start by defining science as the intellectual enterprise of understanding the natural universe, and technology as the means by which humans gain mastery over natural processes for their own productive or reproductive ends. As long as the Industrial Revolution was believed to have been spurred by the search for laborsaving devices, it might have made sense to see the development of technology as critically important. But as discussed above, the critical shortage was land, not labor, and hence it was coal and colonies that eased that shortage and allowed Britain to industrialize first. In fact, the principles of technologies used in the Industrial Revolution were well known in China; what explains their development in England and not China, as suggested above, were the particular circumstances in England that made the fuel for the first, extremely inefficient steam engines effectively free. China did not have that good fortune.

Even if we grant new technologies—in particular steam engines and iron and then steel—an important role in the Industrial Revolution, there is little evidence that the mechanics and tinkerers who developed those machines were "scientists" or even had any scientific training at all. Indeed, seventeenth- and eighteenth-century science had been most useful as a political tool wielded against the twin pillars of the old regime in Europe, monarchs and the Catholic Church. Finally, there is little reason to think of "science" as specifically or uniquely European; rather, scientific ideas flowed across the Eurasian continent, especially between China and Persia, and the European Renaissance itself progressed in large part by rediscovering Greek texts preserved in Muslim libraries.[32]

Industrialization in Britain thus was contingent upon a host of factors, although the scientific revolution was not one of them. In the New World, the Great Dying created a demand for labor that was ultimately satisfied by African slaves, creating both a peculiar institution and a peculiar periphery that produced agricultural products for export (especially sugar and cotton) but needed to import food and clothing. In Europe, the sixteenth-century failure of the Spanish to create a continental empire led to a state system marked by interstate conflict, competition, and warfare that produced winners and losers, with Britain and France emerging in the eighteenth century as the primary players. In Britain, deforestation to heat the growing city of London produced a demand for coal, which the accidents of geography placed within easy reach. In Asia, the decline of the Mughal empire in the early 1700s allowed British, Dutch, and French East India Companies to compete for access to Asian products, and the victory of the British in the Seven Years' War led to the exclusion of France from both the New World and India. And finally, China's demand for silver and the fortuitous New World supply of it provided Europeans with a means by which to buy spices and industrial goods produced in Asia. To conclude this chapter, we return to the China story.

Tea, Silver, Opium, Iron, and Steam

The 1760 British victory over the French in India, the subsequent growth of a British colony there, and the defeat of the British by their American colonists in the War of Independence focused British attention once again on Asia and trade there. Despite the mechanization of Britain's textile industry and the sale of vast amounts of cotton textiles to India, Britain still could not find any way to sell much of anything to the Chinese. To make matters worse, the British had developed a taste for tea, and they began buying large amounts of it from China. Fortunately, the British had access to lots of New World silver: one of the terms of the 1713 Peace of Utrecht gave Britain the right of *asiento*, that is, to provide slaves to Spain's New World colonies, receiving in return New World silver. And that silver was used to buy Chinese tea—lots of it.[33]

Tea

The Chinese had been producing tea from the leaves of a particular evergreen bush for over a thousand years and had perfected the process of selecting, drying, and brewing the leaves into a mildly stimulating hot beverage. The British East India Company discovered that there was a market for tea in England, and soon it began importing chests of it back home. At first tea was drunk mostly by the upper classes (which remains with us in the practice of "high tea") because it was relatively pricey, but as the EIC increased the amounts it bought for the English market, its price declined to the point that common people could also afford it. Workers especially came to appreciate its mildly stimulating effect, and when textile factories and coal mines increased both the numbers of workers and the length of the workday, workers increased their consumption of tea. Fortified with sugar from the colonies and milk from local dairies, tea also became a major source of calories to sustain the growing British industrial workforce. Where Britain imported five million pounds of tea in 1760, by 1800—when the textile mills were growing rapidly—they imported more than twenty million pounds, maybe twice that if smuggled tea is included.[34] By 1800, textile workers and coal miners were spending 5 percent of their income just on tea (10 percent if sugar is added).[35]

With British merchants sailing up and down the Chinese coast trying to find cheaper sources of tea than that available through official channels, and periodically insulting Chinese sensibilities and practices, in 1760—the same year that the British were defeating the French and consolidating their empire around the world through the Seven Years' War—China's rulers restricted all foreign trade, especially that conducted by the British, to the single south China port of Guangzhou. For the next eighty years, the "Guangzhou system," established by China and conducted by the rules it alone set, governed trade between England and China.

The British periodically tried to negotiate their way out of what to them was a restrictive arrangement, but to no avail. The largest and most famous of these missions came in 1793 when Britain sent Sir George Macartney to

China to try to open regular diplomatic relations and to gain more open access to Chinese markets. After being shown the imperial splendors of Beijing and the summer palaces of the Chinese emperor, Macartney was sent packing. China's emperor Qianlong then sent a letter to King George III. Dismissing British pleas for more trade, the emperor told King George that "Our Celestial Empire possesses all things in prolific abundance and lacks no product within its borders," and ordered the British to obey the laws and customs of the Chinese empire.[36] Although this view of China's economy and its place in the world is belied by its need for imports of silver and exports of tea, silk, and porcelain, it did reflect the emperor's assessment of the relative strength of China vis-à-vis Britain. For despite their growing industrial power, the British still were no match for the Chinese in Asia. But that would change over the next forty years.

Silver

As tea consumption in England increased, and as the ability of the British to command New World silver shrunk, in part because of the American Revolution, mercantilist fears of what the continued outflow of silver to China would mean for British power prompted the British to find substitutes for silver that the Chinese would accept for the tea. Pianos and clocks held limited interest in China, and there was not a demand for woolens in south China. Unlike the rest of the world, the Chinese also had no need for Indian cotton textiles, since they had their own advanced cotton textile industry. By the late eighteenth century, about the only commodity the British East India Company could take to China in lieu of silver was raw cotton from its colony in India. But still that was not enough, and silver continued flowing into China, leaving the EIC and the British government with problems arising from the outflow of silver.[37] As it turned out, the British colonialists in India were able to produce another commodity for which there was a suitable demand in China to finance British purchases of tea: the addictive drug opium.

Opium

Many societies, China included, had long used opium for medicinal purposes, and so there was a small market there. In 1773, the British governor-general of India established an opium monopoly in Bengal, charged with increasing production of the drug there and pushing its sale in China. Finding some success even though the Chinese had prohibited opium smoking, the British expanded their market in China by distributing free pipes and selling the drug to new users at very low prices. Sales leapt in 1815 after a general lowering of opium prices, again in 1830 when Indian opium from another area was allowed into the EIC pipeline, and yet again in 1834 after the British government, now favoring "free trade," abolished the EIC monopoly on trade with Asia and private traders leapt into the trade. Americans too had been bringing opium from Turkey to China, adding yet another source of supply.

Huge numbers of Chinese became addicted to the drug: up to 100,000 in the city of Suzhou, and hundreds of thousands more in the port city of Guangzhou. As tens of thousands of chests containing about 154 pounds of opium flowed into China, silver began flowing out, reaching 34 million ounces per year during the 1830s. The Chinese recognized they had a serious drug problem, and the court debated how to handle it. One side argued that the drug should be legalized, its trade and distribution regulated by the state, and treatment centers established to wean the addicts from the drug. The other side argued that the drug trade was both immoral and illegal, and that it should be stopped by halting its import and punishing the foreign merchants who trafficked in it. In the late 1830s, the latter argument won out, with the emperor appointing Lin Zexu a special commissioner with the power to do whatever it took to end the opium traffic.

Commissioner Lin proceeded to Guangzhou, investigated the situation, and, appalled at what he believed to be the immorality of the British and American drug dealers, composed a letter to Britain's Queen Victoria asking that she control her countrymen. The letter was never delivered. He also decided to blockade the foreigners in their warehouses on an island in the river next to Guangzhou, insisting that they would be allowed to leave only if they turned over their stocks of opium and pledged never to traffic in the drugs again. After gaining their acquiescence on the first count, in June 1839 Commissioner Lin dissolved 21,000 chests of opium in irrigation ditches, and, before opening them to be washed into the sea, said a prayer asking the creatures of the sea to forgive him and to move away from the coast for a while.

That was, unfortunately, not the end of the matter. Further clashes between Chinese and British forces near the island of Hong Kong, continued Chinese blockade of the foreign trading warehouses in Guangzhou, and agitation within Britain by moneyed interests representing both the China traders and the cotton textile manufacturers of Manchester to open China's markets to British goods ("400 million customers will keep the mills of Manchester running forever!"), led to the British decision to send a naval expeditionary force to China.

Iron and Steam

Thus was launched the Opium War of 1839–1842 between Great Britain and China. Although the details of this war are interesting, for our purposes two are worth discussing in a bit more detail. The first has to do with the British use against China of a new kind of warship, the first of which was called the *Nemesis*.

The *Nemesis* was the first all-iron gunboat designed specifically for fighting in the rivers of Asia, although it turned out that it was the private British East India Company, not the British navy, that commissioned it. The British Admiralty preferred wooden sailing (and some steam-powered) ships as the mainstay of the navy, which had already come to "rule the waves," as the British described their dominance of the Atlantic and Indian Oceans. The admirals were not convinced that smaller, steam-propelled iron ships would be of much use to them in their defense of the high seas from other Europeans, so it was the East India Company that contracted secretly with the Birkenhead Iron Works of Liverpool to build the new ships. Compared with other warships these were relatively small: 184 feet long by 29 feet wide, only 11 feet deep and drawing but 5 feet of water. Powered by a 120 horsepower steam engine, the novelty of the ship is that it was completely made of iron—no wood whatsoever.

The East India Company was very interested in developing river gunboats by which to extend its colonial holdings in India and elsewhere in Asia. According to an account of the *Nemesis* published in 1844, the outbreak of war with China "was considered an extremely favourable opportunity for testing the advantages or otherwise of iron steam-vessels; and the numerous rivers along the coast of China, hitherto very imperfectly known, and almost totally unsurveyed, presented an admirable field for these requirements."[38] The EIC was also interested in demonstrating the speed by which it could convey goods, people, and mail from India around the Cape of Good Hope to England. And finally, the owner of the ironworks was interested in demonstrating the viability of his iron warships to the admiralty in order to secure future contracts.

The *Nemesis* was built in three months and arrived off the coast of China in late 1840. It soon saw action in operations in the Pearl River, destroying several Chinese war junks because of its ability to maneuver against the current and wind and its shallow draft, and it played a major role in 1842 in blockading the intersection of the Yangzi River and Grand Canal, which carried much of the waterborne commerce of the empire in central and north China and then in threatening to bombard China's southern capital at Nanjing. Effectively defeated and knowing that they were, China's rulers sued for peace. The Treaty of Nanjing, signed in 1842 between China and Great Britain, ended the Opium War, but signified the beginning of a century of Western aggression against China.

By its terms, this treaty was the first of what came to be known as the "unequal treaties" by which Western powers (including the United States) over the next sixty years extracted concessions from China, curtailing both the sovereignty of China's government and its ability to raise tariffs to protect its own industries. Instead, China ceded territory to the British (Hong Kong), paid a $21 million indemnity in Mexican silver to cover the losses of the British drug traffickers, and opened more ports to Western commerce. The opium traffic was not legalized as a result of the first Opium War, but it was after the next war in 1858–1860.

Although the use of the *Nemesis* was not the only reason the British were able to defeat China in the first Opium War, the *Nemesis* did symbolize the immense changes that had occurred in Britain in the forty years since Lord Macartney had been sent packing in 1793. Quite forcefully, of course, the *Nemesis* represented the application of the tools of the Industrial Revolution—iron and steam—to the tools of war in general, but specifically to the European's colonial ventures in Asia and later Africa. Indeed, much of the history of European advances against Asian and African governments and peoples for the remainder of the nineteenth century was a variation on that theme.[39]

But the interests of Britain's iron and steam producers were not the only ones served by going to war with China, for the British colonial government in India and the EIC depended on opium for revenue. Also, European governments (and mostly their militaries) were quite interested in developing and testing new technologies in war, and certainly that was the case with the Opium War. But Britain's cotton textile manufacturers also clamored for war, hoping to open the Chinese market to their exports. With the entire industry now mechanized and powered by steam engines, the Manchester cotton manufacturers were confident they could undersell anybody on the planet, and so they agitated for "free trade" to prove it. Finally, Britain's colonial government in India was interested in the outcome of the war. Two-thirds of the "British" troops used in the Opium War were Indians from the British colonies in Madras and Bengal, proving that native troops could be used to fight under British command. Indeed, as a French historian remarked: "It was as if the British had subjugated the Indian peninsula simply in order to use its resources against China."[40]

Conclusion

In the course of human history, the Industrial Revolution equals or surpasses that of the agricultural revolution in importance. Where agriculture allowed people to capture the annual energy flows of the sun, allowing human populations to rise and civilizations to flourish, albeit within the limits of the biological old regime, the Industrial Revolution has enabled human society to escape from the constraints of the old regime and to build whole new economies and ways of organizing human life on the basis of stored sources of mineral energy, in particular coal and oil. The lifestyle in the world we inhabit is made possible by the immense increase in material production spawned by the Industrial Revolution. Those who think that computers have ushered in a new, postindustrial stage in human history have been rudely awakened, especially in 2001 during the energy blackouts in California's Silicon Valley, to the fact that computers need—and consume—huge amounts of electricity produced by fossil fuels.

Where we have thousands of years of perspective on the results and consequences of the rise of agriculture, the industrial world is barely two hundred years old. Since we are still in the midst of it, we cannot yet say where it ultimately is leading us. For the same reason, explanations of the Industrial Revolution must remain somewhat tentative. Nevertheless, it seems to me that it can only be understood in a broad global and ecological context.

Globally, European textile manufacturers in the seventeenth and eighteenth centuries were at a disadvantage to Indian and Chinese competitors whose calicoes and silks were of higher quality and much cheaper than anything they could produce. Support from a government willing to use force and arms to protect its domestic manufacturers, coupled with colonial legislation in the New World, enabled British cotton manufacturers to exclude Indian cotton textiles and to gain a market for their own goods and a source of cheap raw materials.

Ecologically, Old World (and biological old regime) economies from China to England alike were beginning to experience shortages of land. Increased market size and division of labor allowed China and England alike, for instance, to wring greater efficiencies out of the biological old regime economy, but supplying the necessities of life all required land. Without coal or colonies, the Chinese were forced to expend greater amounts of labor and capital on improving output from land, where the British were released from that constraint by New World resources and the ready availability of coal.

To be sure, British manufacturers and inventors rose to the challenges they faced, especially with regard to coal mining and the development of the steam engine. But there is no reason to think that the Chinese or Indians (or other people with advanced old regime economies, like the Japanese, for instance) would not also have been able to solve those problems in similar ways. They simply didn't have colonies or easily accessible supplies of coal.[41]

Notes

1. Actually, as early as the tenth century, the Chinese had developed both an iron and steel industry, and a coal industry to support it, but both died out by the fourteenth century. See Robert Hartwell, "A Revolution in the Iron and Coal Industries during the Northern Sung," *Journal of Asian Studies* 21, no. 2 (February 1962): 153–162.

2. Like the term "agricultural revolution," some have objected to the use of the term "revolution" to describe this process. Because I think the effects were indeed revolutionary, and because of long-standing usage, I will continue to use the term here. For a discussion of the issues surrounding the use of the term, see E. A. Wrigley, *Continuity, Chance, and Change: The Character of the Industrial Revolution in England* (Cambridge: Cambridge University Press, 1988), chap. 1.

3. Quoted in Prasannan Parthasaranthi, "Rethinking Wages and Competitiveness in the Eighteenth Century: Britain and South India," *Past and Present* 158 (Feb. 1998): 79.

4. Parthasaranthi, "Rethinking Wages and Competitiveness in the Eighteenth Century."

5. For the particulars of how consumer tastes created demand for imports, see Carole Shammas, *The Pre-Industrial Consumer in England and America* (Oxford: Oxford University Press, 1990).

6. Parthasaranthi, "Rethinking Wages and Competitiveness in the Eighteenth Century," 79.

7. Geoffrey Parker, "Europe and the Wider World, 1500–1750: The Military Balance," in James D. Tracy, ed., *The Political Economy of Merchant Empires: State Power and World Trade 1350–1750* (Cambridge: Cambridge University Press, 1991), 179–180.

8. Parker, "Europe and the Wider World," 180.

9. Eric Williams, *Capitalism and Slavery* (Chapel Hill: University of North Carolina Press, 1994 [1944]), 56.

10. John J. McCusker and Russell R. Menard, *The Economy of British America, 1607–1789* (Chapel Hill: University of North Carolina Press, 1985), 46–49, 77, 161.

11. McCusker and Menard, *The Economy of British America*, 121.

12. Jan deVries, "The Industrial Revolution and the Industrious Revolution," *Journal of Economic History* 54 (1994): 249–270.

13. See Kenneth Pomeranz, *The Great Divergence: China, Europe, and the Making of the Modern World Economy* (Princeton, N.J.: Princeton University Press, 2000), 40–41 for a discussion and critique.

14. Quoted in Robert B. Marks, *Tigers, Rice, Silk and Silt: Environment and Economy in Late Imperial South China* (Cambridge: Cambridge University Press, 1998), 284–285.

15. James Z. Lee and Wang Feng, *One Quarter of Humanity: Malthusian Mythology and Chinese Realities* (Cambridge, Mass.: Harvard University Press, 1999), 105.

16. The idea that China experienced an eighteenth-century "population explosion" has been questioned in F. W. Mote, *Imperial China 900–1800* (Cambridge, Mass.: Harvard University Press, 1999), 743–749, 903–907.

17. See Marks, *Tigers, Rice, Silk and Silt*; Peter Perdue, *Exhausting the Earth: State and Peasant in Hunan, 1500–1850* (Cambridge, Mass.: Harvard University Press, 1987); Anne

Osborne, "The Local Politics of Land Reclamation in the Lower Yangzi Highlands," *Late Imperial China* 15, no. 1 (June 1994), 1–46.

18. Pierre-Etienne Will and R. Bin Wong, *Nourish the People: The State Civilian Granary System in China, 1650–1850* (Ann Arbor: University of Michigan Press, 1992).

19. See Marks, *Tigers, Rice, Silk and Silt*, chap. 8.

20. Pomeranz, *The Great Divergence*, chap. 2.

21. Pomeranz, *The Great Divergence*, 242–243.

22. Francesca Bray, *Technology and Gender: Fabrics of Power in Late Imperial China* (Berkeley: University of California Press, 1997); Jack Goldstone, "Gender, Work, and Culture: Why the Industrial Revolution Came Early to England but Late to China," *Sociological Perspectives* 39, no. 1 (1996): 1–21; Pomeranz, *The Great Divergence*, 249–250.

23. E. J. Hobsbawm, *The Age of Revolution, 1789–1848* (New York: New American Library, 1964), 51.

24. The causes are a subject of intense debate: Did the British cause it, or were there other reasons? For a brief summary of the debate, see Pomeranz, *The Great Divergence*, 294.

25. E. J. Hobsbawm, *Industry and Empire* (New York: Penguin Books, 1968), chap. 2.

26. Hobsbawm, *The Age of Revolution*, 63–65.

27. See Andre Gunder Frank, *ReOrient: Global Economy in the Asian Age* (Berkeley: University of California Press, 1998), 297–317.

28. E. A. Wrigley, *Continuity, Chance, and Change: The Character of the Industrial Revolution in England* (Cambridge: Cambridge University Press, 1988), 54–55; Pomeranz, *The Great Divergence*, 59–60.

29. Pomeranz, *The Great Divergence*, 274–276.

30. For a succinct discussion, see Harry Braverman, *Labor and Monopoly Capitalism: The Degradation of Work in the Twentieth Century* (New York: Monthly Review Press, 1975), Part 2, "Science and Mechanization," 155–250.

31. David Landes developed this point in *The Unbound Prometheus: Technological Change and Industrial Development in Western Europe from 1750 to the Present* (Cambridge: Cambridge University Press, 1969), esp. 61, 104.

32. For good discussions of these issues, see Frank, *ReOrient*, 185–195, and Pomeranz, *The Great Divergence*, 43–68.

33. A different way of looking at the flows of silver to China has been proposed by Dennis O. Flynn and Arturo Giraldez in "Cycles of Silver: Global Economic Unity through the Mid-18th Century," *Journal of World History* 13, no. 2 (Fall 2002): 391–427. Rather than seeing demand for tea as causing Britons to pay for it with silver, Flynn and Giraldez argue that China's demand for silver created a higher value for it there, compared with gold, than in Europe. China's problem was how to "buy" silver from the British, finding tea the best commodity available. From this perspective, the Chinese in effect "hooked" the British on tea, stimulated a demand for the mild stimulant there, and then reaped the benefit of silver flowing into its economy.

34. Sidney W. Mintz, *Sweetness and Power: The Place of Sugar in Modern History* (New York: Viking Press, 1985), 112–113.

35. Frederick Wakeman, Jr., *The Fall of Imperial China* (New York: Free Press, 1975), 123.

36. The entire letter can be found in Harley Farnsworth MacNair, *Modern Chinese History: Selected Readings* (Shanghai: Commercial Press, 1923), 2–9.

37. There was actually a very complicated triangular trading system involving not just EIC merchants, but private Indian and Scottish merchants as well, by which raw cotton was taken to China, tea purchased in China and then sold in London. See Wakeman, *The Fall of Imperial China*, 123–125. Moreover, the innovations of the EIC in creating convertible paper notes to enable the stockholders to realize profits back in London probably had begun to lessen the importance of actually moving silver around the world to settle accounts. Nonetheless, the British government apparently continued to act as though that was happening and that it was a problem.

38. W. D. Bernhard, *Narrative of the Voyages and Services of the Nemesis, from 1840 to 1843; and of the Combined Naval and Military Operations in China*, Vol. 1 (London: Henry Colburn, 1844), 4.

39. See Daniel Headrick, *The Tools of Empire: Technology and European Imperialism in the Nineteenth Century* (New York: Oxford University Press, 1981).

40. Louis Dermigny, quoted in Parker, "Europe and the Wider World," 184.

41. For the argument and supporting evidence leading to this conclusion, see Pomeranz, *The Great Divergence*. For an abbreviated version, see Kenneth Pomeranz, "Two Worlds of Trade, Two Worlds of Empire: European State-Making and Industrialization in a Chinese Mirror," in David A. Smith, Dorothy J. Solinger, and Steven C. Topik, eds., *States and Sovereignty in the Global Economy* (London: Routledge, 1999), 74–98. For a critique of this thesis see P. H. H. Vries, "Are Coal and Colonies Really Crucial? Kenneth Pomeranz and the Great Divergence," *Journal of World History* 12 (Fall 2001): 407–446.

CHAPTER FIVE

The Gap

In the eighteenth century, China, India, and Europe (and probably Japan as well, though it has not been discussed) were broadly comparable in terms of the level of economic development, standard of living, and people's life expectancies. As can be seen in figure 5.1, India, China, and Europe each claimed the same share—about 23 percent—of the total gross domestic production (GDP)[1] of the world. Together, those three parts of the world thus accounted for 70 percent of the economic activity in the world in 1700. A similar story can be seen in figure 5.2. In 1750, China produced about 33 percent of all the manufactured goods in the world, with India and Europe each contributing about 23 percent, totaling almost 80 percent of world industrial output. By 1800, the story is much the same, although India's share begins to decline while that of Europe begins to climb.

By the early 1800s, though, figures 5.1 and 5.2 chart a different story, as the share of global GDP and manufacturing output claimed by Europe begins to rise rapidly, while that of China stalls and then falls rapidly by 1900, as does that of India. By 1900, India accounts for barely 2 percent of world manufacturing output, China about 7 percent, while Europe alone claims 60 percent and the United States 20 percent. In 1900, Europe and the United States together account for 80 percent of all manufacturing activity.

Figures 5.1 and 5.2 thus chart the course of a great reversal in world history. Where India and China accounted for a little over half of the wealth in the world in the eighteenth century, by 1900 they had become among the least industrialized and the poorest. Their shares of world GDP did not fall as far as their shares of world manufacturing output, though, largely because their populations continued to grow. Indeed, as figure 5.3 shows, from 1750 to 1850, China's population shot ahead of both India and Europe, where they

Figure 5.1.   Share of World GDP, 1700–1890

Source: Mike Davis, *Late Victorian Holocausts* (London: Verso, 2001), 293.

had been broadly comparable since 1400. With growing populations and less wealth being created, Chinese and Indians became relatively poorer over the course of the nineteenth century, as Europeans and Americans became wealthier. Moreover, since neither China nor India were industrializing, as we will see, cities there could not accommodate those larger populations, thereby intensifying rural poverty.

The charts thus show the emergence during the nineteenth century of a large and growing gap between the West and the rest of the world, here epito·mized by India and China. "To explain this gap, which was to grow wider over the years," the eminent historian Fernand Braudel once said, "is to tackle the essential problem of the history of the modern world."[2] Braudel himself was quite modest about his own ability to explain "the gap," recognizing that when he wrote (in the late 1970s) more was known about the history of Europe than about India, China, or the rest of what has become known as the "under-developed" or "third" world. One thing, though, did seem clear to him: "[T]he gap between the West and the other continents appeared *late in time,* and to attribute it simply to the rationalization of the market economy, as too many of our contemporaries are still inclined to do, is obviously oversimplifying."[3]

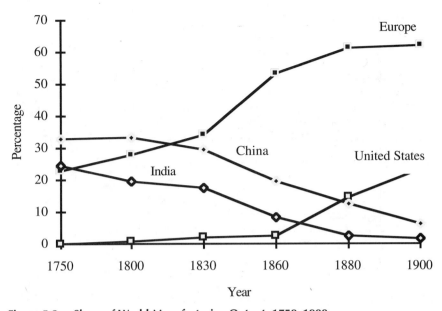

Figure 5.2. **Share of World Manufacturing Output, 1750–1900**

Source: Derived from data in Paul Kennedy, *The Rise and Fall of Great Powers* (New York: Vintage Press, 1989), 149.

By that, Braudel was indicating his dissatisfaction with the various Eurocentric explanations of "the gap" examined in the previous chapter. Most particularly, he thought that explanations that looked just at the emergence and "rationalization" of a market economy in Europe were too simplistic. Indeed, as pointed out in the previous chapter, China had a very well-developed market economy by the eighteenth century, and yet it came out on the losing end of the growing gap. This chapter examines the reasons why not only China and India, but much of the rest of Asia, Africa, and Latin America, became increasingly poor relative to Europe and the United States during the course of the nineteenth century.

In this chapter we will see how opium, guns, el Niño famines, and new industrial technologies corresponded to Europeans' colonial ventures, especially railroads, the telegraph, and quinine. What I will not resort to are the various Eurocentric explanations for Europe's increasing wealth and power vis-à-vis the rest of the world. There just is no evidence that Europeans were smarter, had a superior culture (that is, one that sustained if not created an industrial economy), or were better managers of natural and human resources than Chinese, Indians, or New Guineans for that matter. Instead, Europeans

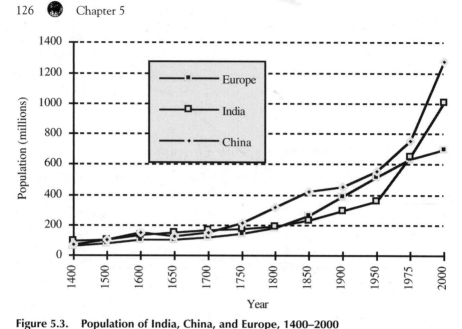

Figure 5.3.   Population of India, China, and Europe, 1400–2000

Source: Colin McEvedy and Richard Jones, *Atlas of World Population History* (New York: Viking Penguin, 1978); United Nations, *2000 Revision of the World Population Estimates and Projections* (http:www.un.org/esa/population/wpp2000at.xls).

had colonies that supplied them with huge amounts of "free" energy (sugar, cotton, timber, codfish), and in the case of the British in particular, the good fortune to have coal deposits lying close to the surface and to the centers of population and manufacturing that needed new sources of energy when their forests were used up.

The story of the nineteenth century largely concerns the process by which the world became divided into the developed and the underdeveloped, the rich and the poor, the industrialized and what became known as the "third" world.[4] Of course, from the ecological perspective used in this book, the gap also reflects the division of the world into those parts that remained within the biological old regime (which became increasingly poor) and those parts that began to escape the limits the biological old regime placed on material production (both industrial and agricultural). Moreover, the gap that emerged in the nineteenth century was not just between different parts of the world, but also within the societies we have been discussing. Industry produced not just wealth and power for some nations, but especially for some people within those countries—those who owned the new means of production. On the other hand, for those who worked in the mines and the factories, industry produced new jobs, but also new forms of work, urban experiences, and understandings of poverty. Indeed, women and children formed a significant portion of the new industrial workforce, especially in textiles and even coal mines, bringing them out of the home and onto the historical stage where their voices could be more clearly heard.

Opium and Global Capitalism

This narrative of the origins of the modern world started in the early 1400s with China's demand for silver to use in its economy, which, together with that of India, constituted the major source of wealth and industrial production in the early modern world. China's demand for silver set into motion a series of developments that led, willy-nilly, to most of the major events discussed so far in this book. Without China's demand for silver, it seems fair to say, the European role in the world economy would have been greatly diminished. As it was, China's demand for, and New World supplies of, silver enabled Europeans to enrich themselves by gaining access to Asian commodities and trade networks.

Similarly, Chinese demand in the nineteenth century for another commodity—this time the addictive drug opium—also played a major role in structuring the world economy. To be sure, the importation and consumption of opium did not have the positive effects on China's economy that silver imports had had four hundred years earlier. Furthermore, the demand for opium was driven by the needs of forty million addicted consumers, rather than state needs for its economy. Nonetheless, Chinese demand for opium in the 1800s did stimulate worldwide economic activity.

Despite Britain's defeat of China in the first Opium War (1839–1842), Britain had not forced China to legalize the sale and distribution of opium. Nonetheless, the new British colonial possession of Hong Kong provided a convenient base of operations free from Chinese harassment. For the next twenty years, Hong Kong was the hub of the British drug trade. British trading companies imported about 50,000 chests of opium annually (6.5 million pounds) for sale to Chinese customers.

As opium flowed into China, silver flowed out, and great fortunes were built, not just in England but in the United States as well. With American independence, U.S. merchant ships immediately started competing with British merchants in Asian waters; the first U.S. ship arrived in China in 1784, one year after independence. By the early 1800s, Americans were intimately involved with the opium trade, particularly the Russell Company, with American sources of opium located in Turkey, while the British maintained their monopoly on Indian opium. Profits from the American opium trade added to the endowments of prominent East Coast universities, padded the fortunes of the Peabody family in Boston (and hence the Peabody Museum) and the Roosevelt family in New York, and provided capital for Alexander Graham Bell's development of the telephone. (See map 5.1.)

After a second war with China (the so-called Arrow War of 1858–1860, named after a British vessel), the British forced China to legalize the sale of opium. Although this opened up more markets in China for the drug, the centrality of Hong Kong in the trade declined as British and American ships called directly at more Chinese ports opened to trade. As new sources of opium in India were developed and the markets there opened up, Persian, Indian, and Chinese merchants entered the trade. By the 1870s, the Chinese too began poppy cultivation and opium manufacturing, especially in the interior provinces previously little connected with the booming coastal trade. Perversely, this "import substitution" occurred in many of the same places that Chinese peasant farmers earlier had exercised their freedom in choosing to plant cotton. In many of these places, cash cropping of poppies thus expanded at the expense of crop farmland, giving peasant farmers greater cash income but heightening their risks if food supplies failed.

By the late 1800s, so much opium was entering China or being produced there that 10 percent of China's population, or forty million people, were users, with as many as half of those "heavy smokers." At the turn of the twentieth century, China was consuming 95 percent of the world's opium supply, with predictable social, economic, and political effects. Nearly every city had its opium dens, and the sale and use of opium had entered the fabric of Chinese life. Where opium smoking had started as an elite habit, it became an item of mass consumption. Indeed, even into the twentieth century, poppy cultivation and opium manufacturing in China provided China's governments with revenue and peasant farmers with cash income.[6]

After we take a look at what happened in India and then examine the process of industrialization in Europe, I will return to a consideration of how very important China's consumption of opium was to the world economy in the late nineteenth century. For now, suffice it to note that while the Chinese themselves bore some responsibility for bringing the drug plague on themselves, British guns had forced open the door in the first place, and then China and India took particular (peculiar) roles in the global economy as producers and consumers of opium.

India

Most of the opium consumed in China came from India, where British colonial policies combined with Chinese demand for the drug created an agricultural export industry. Opium production in India became one of its major exports in the nineteenth century, and this is part of a larger story of the transformation of India from one of the world's greatest industrial centers in the seventeenth and eighteenth centuries to a primarily agricultural economy by the mid-1800s. Indeed, India's cotton textile industry was so thoroughly destroyed by the 1820s that historians have talked about the "deindustrialization" of India, even as they have continued to debate its causes.

As we have had occasion to note in previous chapters, Indian cotton goods enjoyed a worldwide market, with Africans, Europeans, and American slaves all purchasing and wearing Indian textiles. In the early 1700s, as we have seen, the British erected trade barriers to keep Indian textiles out. Still, Indian textiles found other markets, and the textile districts in Bengal, Madras, and elsewhere were kept quite busy producing for the world market. Two things changed all that.

First, in 1757 the British East India Company (EIC) acquired its first colonial beachhead in Bengal, and in 1765 it gained the right to collect land taxes from much of Bengal. This windfall gave the private EIC the revenues both to increase its purchases of Indian textiles and, more ominously, to raise and pay for its own army of "Sepoys," or Indians enlisted in an army commanded by British officers. The EIC then used that army to extend its control over other parts of India. The disarray of Indian political power, the jockeying for power among Indian princes, the uncertain but certainly declining power of the Mughal emperor, and the ambitions of Hindu warrior princes all created a climate in which the scheming of the EIC, backed by its army, resulted in the gradual extension of its control throughout most of India by the 1830s. Additional large-scale and costly wars brought EIC control over the Punjab and Sindh (areas that became Pakistan after 1947). By the mid-1800s, the British had colonized India.

Second, the Industrial Revolution resulted in greatly reduced costs for Britain's manufactured goods, cotton textiles in particular. Not only did British cotton textiles begin to win global market share from Indian textiles because of lower price, India itself became an important market for British cotton textiles. Where in the eighteenth century British tariffs had kept Indian textiles out of England, British colonial policy in India removed tariff barriers to British manufactured textiles. With lower prices, British manufactured textiles flooded the Indian market. Between 1800 and 1810, production and export of Indian cotton textiles continued to fall while the import of British manufactures into India continued to grow. By 1820, millions of Indian weavers had been thrown out of work, their looms stood still, and their houses empty: "By the year 1833, the process of 'deindustrialization' of Bengal . . . went quite far. India lost a great art and the artisans lost their employ-ment. The housewife's spindle seldom now twirled on the cotton-floor."[7]

Instead of exporting finished goods, India then began to export raw cot-ton, first to China and then to England. Former Indian cotton weavers either emigrated or took up new occupations, many turning to farming. When they did, they had to farm something that could be sold, because the British East India Company collected taxes in money, not rice or cotton. Thus old and new Indian farmers turned to cash crops such as indigo, sugarcane, cotton, and poppies from which opium was made. The "ruralization of India" was complete.

If this story of India's decline to what we would now call a third world country—one producing raw materials for export so it can import manufac-tured goods from the "developed" world, thereby becoming locked into "un-derdevelopment"—appears to be one merely of "economics," it was not. Rather, it was planned to work that way for the benefit of Britain, especially after the EIC monopoly on trade in Asia was abolished in favor of the free trade principles first championed by Adam Smith in 1776 in his famous book *The Wealth of Nations*.

Combined with David Ricardo's concept of "comparative advantage," free trade and minimal government intervention in the economy were intended to transform India into a producer of food and raw materials for export. Tar-iffs were to be abolished, the colonial government obviously would not move to protect either the cotton textile weavers or to promote a policy of indus-trialization (for that would be "redundant" and compete with the British do-mestic industry), and "free" markets would ensure that food and raw materials moved out of India to Britain and that Indians purchased British industrial products. Indeed, from the mid-1800s on, India reliably consumed 25–35 per-cent of Britain's exports.[8] The principles of "free trade" enforced by the colo-nial government set India on the path to becoming a third world country. We will see later in this chapter how that, coupled with the effects of el Niño droughts, completed India's transition to a third world nation.

Suffice it to say here that the deindustrialization of India, coupled with China's demand for opium, provided the British and their global capitalist system with immense profits. So great were these opium profits that the en-tire structure of the world trade patterns was reversed. From 1500 to 1800, Europeans had gained access to Asian trade with New World silver, and sil-ver flowed in great quantities to India and China. Opium tipped that flow in the opposite direction, with silver flowing into British hands. Without opium, historian Carl Trocki argues, "there probably would have been no British Empire."[9]

Industrialization Elsewhere

As the first to industrialize and to apply the fruits of industrialization to its military, Britain established itself as the most powerful nation in the world, and as long as Britain maintained its industrial lead over all the others, its military power remained unchallenged as well. By 1830, Britain had a virtual monopoly on industrial production of iron, steam engines, and textiles, and it used that power to sell its products throughout the world and build the world's largest empire, encompassing not just India but other parts of Asia as well. Its paramount position led to calls to lift tariff barriers on the import of food and other raw materials so it could expand its industrial system even faster. As we saw with India, global "free trade" became Britain's program for action. However, if Britain's imposition of the principles of "free trade" on India had contributed to its third-world-ization, Britain could not do so to several other European countries or to its former colony, the United States.

The European state system, defined as it was by the frequency of war among European states (and with independence, the United States too), created strong competitive pressures for others to follow Britain's lead, especially in the quest for new colonial possessions. As Britain's overseas empire grew, other European states tried desperately to improve their militaries to compete in Asia, Africa, and Latin America. Try as the British might to prevent the transfer or export of its industrial technologies, France, the United States, and Germany soon began to industrialize. And in the second half of the nineteenth century, two additional countries—Russia and Japan—began rapid industrialization, largely in order to maintain their independence from West European countries. If industrialization in Britain had arisen from a conjuncture of forces that no one could have predicted, after it happened its results could be replicated as the result of plans implemented by strong governments forced to compete with Britain and one another. With few exceptions, then, industrialization elsewhere proceeded with a heavy role for the state.

France

Even in the early stages of British industrialization, the French government (and others) attempted to gain access to Britain's industrial know-how by stealing information, bribing manufacturers, or hiring British industrialists. France got its start in textiles and iron and steel this way, but it was seriously hobbled by the lack of large (and easily worked) coal deposits, periodic revolutionary upheavals and war (1789–1815, 1848–1851, and 1870–1871), and a relatively backward agriculture. Nevertheless, the decision of the French government in 1842 to build a national railroad system, completed in the

1860s,) spurred France's industrialization. Unlike the private ownership of railroads in England, in France the government provided the capital to build them, then privatized them on ninety-nine-year leases. Stimulated by the national market made possible by the railroad, other parts of the French economy also industrialized, or at least standardized. Nonetheless, France remained much less able to produce industrial products, leaving it at a disadvantage both to Britain and to other countries as they industrialized.

The United States

Industrialization in the United States centered on the Northeast and the Ohio River valley, and, like Britain, relied mostly on private capital, not government initiative. Textiles were among the first industries to industrialize, and New England—with supplies of raw cotton from slave-worked plantations in the South—soon competed with British textiles both in the U.S. and world markets. The state used tariffs to protect the young American industry, and the Bank of the United States provided some capital for canals and railroads. Beginning in the 1830s, local rail lines were built, and by the 1870s the transcontinental railroad spanned the continent, providing a huge demand for iron, steel, and steam-powered locomotives. The Civil War (1860–1865) spurred Northern industrialization, and, as we will see later in this chapter, contributed to the industrial production of guns and a more industrial way of warfare.

Americans also pioneered the application of industry to agriculture. Where the British allowed their agricultural sector to decline, preferring to import cheap food from eastern Europe, Ireland, and the United States, and where French peasants acquired a tenacious hold on their minuscule landholdings as a result of the Revolution of 1789, which hindered their ability to buy or use modern farm implements until well after the end of World War II in 1945, the United States had vast plains and little labor to work them. Horse-drawn and then later steam- and gasoline-powered harvesters and combines (built by the Chicago magnate Cyrus McCormick) produced such huge agricultural surpluses that the United States became (and remains to this day) a major exporter of food in global markets.

Germany

Unlike Britain, the United States, or France, until 1870 Germany was not actually unified under a single state but rather was divided among numerous principalities, each with its own ruler but speaking a common language that ultimately provided a basis for national unity. This political disunity hampered German efforts to industrialize. Indeed, the lack of a single state meant that the German textile industry did not have tariff protection against British imports, leading to the destruction of German textile production by the 1830s. A customs union in the 1830s, followed by the abolition of serfdom in the 1840s and the building of railroads in the 1850s, provided sufficient unity for industrialization in some areas to begin, in particular the coal- and iron-rich Ruhr River valley.

Industrializing later than Britain, France, and the United States, Germany was at a competitive disadvantage and could not industrialize following the same route (i.e., textiles to iron and steel). Instead, after unification in 1870, Germany emphasized heavy industry (iron and steel) to sustain its national railroad program and to support the growth of its military. The development of the Bessemer process for making steel combined with innovations in large-scale business organization pioneered by the Krupp metallurgy and armament works spurred rapid German industrialization in the 1870s and 1880s. Germans also linked their universities to industrial research, leading to whole new chemical and electrical industries, and for the first time explicitly applying science to industrial development.

Russia

Of the European countries with the biggest obstacles to overcome in order to industrialize, Russia stands at the head of the list. Profoundly rural, peasants had been enserfed to noble estate owners until their emancipation in the early 1860s, leading to yet another form of rural society with nobles still owning the land and former serfs renting it. For centuries, Russia had exported grain to western Europe and had imported fineries consumed by the nobility. Russia also had vast natural resources—forests, coal, iron ore—that attracted West European investors who extracted them and sold them to the industrializing countries. Despite having a large army and being considered one of the "powers" of Europe (mostly because of its size and population), Russia in the nineteenth century was beginning to take on third world characteristics: exporting food and raw materials, having little or no industry of its own, and relying on others for whatever manufactured goods it could afford to import.

All of this began to change in the 1880s when the Ministry of Finance, headed energetically after 1892 by Count Sergei Witte, launched a massive railroad-building program followed by heavy industry (coal, iron and steel, and oil). Where Russia had less than 700 miles of railroads in 1860, it had 21,000 by 1894 and 36,000 by 1900, the longest stretches reaching eastward into Siberia, thereby tying that vast region and its resources closer to the needs of the industrializing parts of Russia. Like Germany and France, the Russian government, rather than private capital, played a major role in these first stages of Russia's industrialization, creating banks, hiring foreign engineers, and erecting high tariff barriers to protect its new industries from foreign competition.

Count Witte was quite clear on the reasons for Russia's crash industrialization program: to escape colonial-like relations with western Europe.

> Russia remains even at the present essentially an agricultural country. It pays for all its obligations to foreigners by exporting raw materials, chiefly of an agricultural nature, principally grain. It meets its demand for finished goods by imports from abroad. The economic relations of Russia with western Europe are fully comparable to the relations of colonial countries with their metropolises. The latter consider their colonies as advantageous markets in which they can freely sell the products of their labor and of their industry and from which they can draw with a powerful hand the raw materials necessary for them.

But Russia would not become a semicolony, Witte argued, because "Russia is an independent and strong power. . . . She wants to be a metropolis [i.e., colonial power] herself."[10]

Japan

Unlike Russia, Japan had few natural resources that an industrial economy needed, in particular coal and iron ore. Moreover, in the mid-1800s it was still following a policy of "closed country" implemented two hundred years earlier. When U.S. Commodore Matthew Perry steamed into Tokyo Bay in 1853 demanding that Japan open itself up to "normal" international commerce ("or else . . ."), it came as a huge shock to Japan's leaders. Knowing what had happened to China at the hands of the British in the Opium War, Japan's leaders decided to negotiate an opening to the West, leading both to increased trade and contact between Japanese and Westerners, but also to the collapse of the old regime in 1868.

The new regime that replaced it, called the Meiji era after the reign title of the new (and very young) emperor Meiji (r. 1868–1912), after some fits and starts, set about dismantling the old feudal system and establishing a strong, centralized state that took on the task of industrializing Japan when private capital failed to take up the challenge. However, with few natural resources and with tariffs limited by the treaties imposed on it by the United States, Japan's industrialization took a peculiar path. Having to first export in order to import industrial raw materials, Japan turned to its silk industry, standardizing and mechanizing as much as possible to sell in the world market, taking their market share from the Chinese and the French. In the 1880s and especially the 1890s, Japan developed a cotton textile industry, again designed for export in order to acquire the foreign exchange with which to purchase industrial raw materials—coking coal and iron ore—for a heavy industry strongly tied to the needs of its military. To compete in world textile markets, Japan kept its workers' wages very low, employing large numbers of girls and women and prohibiting the formation of labor unions.

This strategy paid off handsomely. Its military was strong enough to defeat China in an 1894–1895 war and then a decade later to defeat Russia. Recognizing Japan's military might, in 1902, the British concluded a military pact with Japan, and in 1911 the Western powers renounced the unequal treaties that had limited Japan's ability to control its own tariffs. By 1910, Japan had the industrial capacity and technological know-how to produce the world's largest warship, the *Satsuma*. Even as China and India continued to decline relative to the West, Japan's industrialization by 1900 was an early indication that the West would not continue to dominate the world through a monopoly of industrial production, but that prior patterns of Asian vitality would begin to show through.

As this brief survey suggests, among the requirements for industrialization was a strong state determined to create the material prerequisites for powerful armies. For differing reasons and at various times, France, Germany, Russia, and Japan were able to build strong states. Those parts of the world that had weak states (e.g., most of Latin America or the Ottoman empire), states that were becoming enfeebled (e.g., China), states that had been colonized (e.g., India, much of Southeast Asia, and, as we will see, Africa), or even stateless people within empires who wanted independence (as we will see below) were doomed to remain in the biological old regime, at best exporting raw materials or food to the industrialized world.

New Dynamics in the Industrial World

By 1900, 80 percent of world industrial output came from Europe and the United States, with Japan contributing another 10 percent: China contributed 7 percent and India 2 percent, totaling 99 percent of all industrial production. Thus the one hundred years from 1800 to 1900 saw a great reversal, with Europe and the United States taking the pride of place previously held by India and China. Part of the immense gap between the wealthiest and poorest parts of our world thus can be explained by industrialization and the escape of some parts of the world—in Europe, the United States, and Japan—from the constraints of the biological old regime. Actually, of course, it is more correct to say that industrial output came from selected regions, not entire countries: parts of New England in the United States, Manchester or other parts of northern England, the Rhineland in Germany, Milan in northern Italy, and so on. For even within those industrializing and increasingly rich countries, there remained impoverished regions.

In the biological old regime, the size and quality of agricultural harvests determined the economic health, wealth, and well-being of a society: the larger the harvest, the more food, the lower wages, the more competitive industry, and so on. Of course, the opposite was also true. Although climate and the vagaries of the weather certainly had a major impact on agriculture, people's ingenuity, social organization, and hard work could minimize adverse climatic effects. But still, the biological old regime set the tune by which agrarian economies danced.

That was (and is) not so with the new industrial economies. Having escaped from the limits of the biological old regime and its dynamics, the new industrial economies were entering into uncharted waters that became ever more uncertain as more of Europe industrialized. So, in the nineteenth century, the industrial world began to experience a new kind of regulator on economic activity: boom and then bust. As more and more factories were built to produce the same commodity, especially in different countries, global supply at times vastly outstripped demand, leading to falling prices to clear the inventory buildup. Competitors slashed prices by slashing wages, further depressing demand, at least for consumer goods, leading to a "recession," or depending on how long it lasted, a "depression." The first recession occurred in 1857, and it was fairly short lived, followed by a resumption of the economic boom, which lasted until the early 1870s. But then in 1873 another recession began, which lasted, in some historians' views, until 1896; during those twenty years, prices in Britain fell by 40 percent.

Until the 1870s, most industrializing countries had followed Britain's lead in favoring international free trade, for all in one way or another had benefited. But the slump of 1873 changed that, with Germany and Italy raising tariffs to protect their textile industries, followed in the 1890s by France, the United States, and, as we have already seen, Russia. Japan was forbidden by treaty from raising tariffs. Expectedly, as a result of the new tariffs, British exports to the United States and the industrializing parts of Europe dropped, creating a sizable balance-of-payments problem for Britain and fueling calls within Britain for protectionist tariffs. Had that happened, the industrializing world might have entered a period of sharp contraction into something like the exclusive trading blocs that arose in the 1930s in the wake of the Great Depression, followed by the horrors of World War II. Global capitalism may well have been strangled shortly after its birth.

Except that Britain's huge trade surpluses with Asia, India, and China in particular, made possible by the opium trade, kept the system from crashing. With these huge trade surpluses, Britain was able to settle its debts to the United States and Germany, in particular, keeping capitalist development alive there (and elsewhere in Europe).[11] In a very real sense, China's consumption of opium, and British traffic in the drug, is one of the factors that kept the capitalist world economy going through the recession of 1873–1896.

Although the industrializing world did not collapse into exclusive (and possibly warring) economic trading blocs, the slump did sharpen competition and tension between industrializing countries in the late nineteenth century. As we will see later in this chapter, this contributed to the "New Imperialism" of the period, where European countries and the United States competed to grab large parts of the world to create, or add to, their colonial empires.

The Social Consequences of Industrialization

The Industrial Revolution transformed—and still is transforming—the patterns of life. Just as the Neolithic agricultural revolution 13,000 years earlier transformed the relationships of people to one another and the environment, so too did the Industrial Revolution. Work, families, cities, time, culture, values, and more changed with the industrial mode of production. Although the precise ways these changes worked themselves out varied from place to place, there were broad similarities. In the place of fields and farms, there were factories; in the place of seasons and annual festivals as the markers of time, there came the hour and the time clock; in the place of large families, there came small ones; in the place of stability, there came change.

Factories and Work

Industrialization in the first instance called into being a large new working class largely concentrated in growing cities. Indeed, a common measure of industrialization is the percentage of a country's population living in cities. For England, 50 percent lived in cities by 1850; in Germany that mark was reached by 1900, in the United States by 1920, and in Japan by 1930. For new workers, especially those fresh from the farms, factories imposed a new concept of work on them. Machines dictated the pace of work, supervisors set rules for eating and bodily functions, and owners set wage rates as low as possible to ensure high profits.

Factories were not pleasant places, and it is hard to imagine anyone actually choosing to work there rather than outdoors in the fields. But, in England at least, prior changes in agriculture had pushed large numbers of peasants off the land *before* the Industrial Revolution occurred. There were, therefore, lots of poor and barely employed people in London glad to take a job even if the wages met bare subsistence needs.

Because of the misery of working conditions, "disciplining" the labor force to the new rhythms of the workplace and ensuring that they returned day after day became the task of "management," which grew as a new occupation and formed the backbone of the new "middle class." Much of the early British workforce—especially in textiles but also in the mines—was composed of women and children who could be more easily managed than men. Although that changed over time and more men than women composed the English working class by 1900, in Japan girls and young women too formed the backbone of the textile workforce. There, hard-pressed rural families "contracted" their daughters out to textile mills: the family patriarch got the pay (in annual installments) and the girls got work and the promise of life in safe dormitories until they were ready to marry.[12]

Women and Families

Industrialization remade the family. In agrarian societies, farming families were units of both production and consumption. Urban industrial life increasingly removed production from families, changing roles and relationships among men, women, and children. Where women and children initially worked in factories (giving us the horror-filled novels of Charles Dickens such as *David Copperfield* and *Oliver Twist*), legislation restricting children's and women's labor turned factories into workplaces for men. A woman's place was redefined as being in the home and taking care of domestic affairs, even while taking in laundry or other odd chores to help make ends meet. Prohibited from working until age twelve or thirteen, the task of children became (minimally) to master an elementary school education. As children came to be seen as causing family expenses and not contributing to family income, the number of children married couples were willing to have began to decline, especially in the period after 1870, and families got smaller.

Resistance and Revolution

Factories were battlefields for daily confrontations, sometimes small and sometimes large, between workers and the factory owners or their representatives. Simply not returning to work was one form of resistance, but then one would forfeit what pay was owed. Working as slowly as possible was another response, as was sabotage of the machinery to stop it, if even for a little while. With time, workers discovered that collective action could win them higher wages, better conditions, or shorter hours, but usually only after long, bitter, and often bloody strikes.[13]

It is little wonder that the new urban hellholes and factories produced not just commodities flooding world markets but organized resistance to factories and to the capitalist system. Early opponents were simply repelled by the smoke-belching factories, the "unnatural" modes of work, and the impact they were having on family life, calling instead for more "natural" ways of organizing work. The most rigorous and long-lasting challenge to the capitalist mode of production, though, came from ideas propounded by Karl Marx and his lifelong collaborator Friedrich Engels.

Publishing *The Communist Manifesto* in 1848, Marx and Engels (whose father owned a textile mill) tossed down the gauntlet:

> A specter is haunting Europe—the specter of communism. . . . The history of all hitherto existing society is the history of class struggles. . . . Our epoch . . . shows . . . this distinctive feature: it has simplified the class antagonisms. Society as a whole is more and more splitting into two great hostile camps, into two great classes directly facing each other: *bourgeoisie* [capitalist class] and *proletariat* [working class]. . . . What the bourgeoisie . . . produces, above all, is its own grave diggers. Its fall and the victory of the proletariat are equally inevitable.[14]

And for a few months in 1848, it looked like Marx's predictions might have been coming true. Throughout western Europe, revolts of the laboring poor toppled governments in France, the Italian states, the Habsburg empire, and Switzerland, threatened the established order in Spain and Denmark, and shook Ireland, Greece, and Britain. Although the political demands of the rebels mostly envisioned greatly extended democratic rights for working people, nonetheless, the more comfortable middle class and especially the factory-owning capitalist class felt threatened and so supported the suppression of the revolts. But the growing division of society into warring classes—even the threat that that would happen—presented a serious problem to the rulers of European states.

Nations and Nationalism

States, or what we now more commonly refer to as "governments," have been around for a long time and have taken a number of forms. In this book, we have talked mostly about agrarian and conquest empires, especially in Asia and Mesoamerica, and about the various monarchies and principalities in Europe and their transformations into centralized states under the pressures of war. The process of European "state building," which was discussed in chapter 4, it might be remembered, resulted in fairly large territorial states that had both the population and the wealth to sustain competitive interstate pressures, with seventeenth- and eighteenth-century Britain and France building the most successful states.

In the nineteenth century, states underwent additional changes, becoming much closer in form and function to twentieth-century states, and became linked with another force, that of nation-building, or nationalism, giving us the modern nation–state. Where the modern state can be defined, the concept of nation is a little bit harder, since exceptions always seem to be found. But let us start by defining the modern state as a territory (usually contiguous) over whose inhabitants the government ruled directly through salaried bureaucrats, not through intermediaries or agents such as aristocrats with their own power bases, enforcing uniform administrative and institutional arrangements and taking notice of its subjects or citizens, generally through representatives (elected or otherwise).[15] The French Revolution of 1789 and the extension of some of its ideas, especially that of people's right to be politically active "citizens" rather than merely the "subjects" of their sovereign, and that of universal administrative codes and direct contact between state and citizen to other parts of Europe by the French general/emperor Napoleon in the early 1800s (the Napoleonic Code) were especially important in the genesis of the modern state.

The idea of "nations" and "nationalism," on the other hand, arose only after modern states and industrial society had emerged.[16] States were confronted with a dilemma, especially acute after the French Revolution called into question all the traditional sources of state legitimacy (divine ordination, dynastic succession, or historic right), of how to ensure loyalty to the state and the ruling system. This question became critical as industrialization created new social classes, especially the urban working class and the capitalist class, and the revolts of the early 1800s culminating in the mass uprisings of 1848. To the rulers of nineteenth-century European states, huge schisms were appearing among their peoples and between the people and the state, threatening to bring the states down.

Also, industrialization created new forms of communication, especially the railroad and the telegraph, which in turn spawned economic and emotional needs among people who seemed to share common bonds of language and culture but did not have a unified state—in particular the various German and Italian states. This gave rise to the idea that a "nation"—that is, a "people" sharing a common language and culture—ought to have a single, unified state. This kind of European nationalism fueled many movements in Europe from 1830 to 1880 of state-building on the basis of a "nation" and "national boundaries." This was most strikingly illustrated by the Italian nationalist Mazzini and his call for "every nation a state; only one state for the entire nation."

This idea then informed the rulers of states, who were feeling pressured by the revolutionary uprisings from below, and offered them a way to begin ensuring the loyalty of "their people." The problem these rulers faced, though, was twofold. The first aspect was how to get their people to identify themselves as a "nation" and then how to link that identity with the state. For this, public education (at first elementary but in the twentieth century increasingly secondary too) was especially useful and so too were historians in constructing celebratory "national histories."[17]

Some territorial states, though, had been constructed with more than one "nation" in them. Great Britain was formed with the union of Scotland and England, but also included the Welsh and Irish. The Russian empire as it expanded in the eighteenth and nineteenth centuries came to be known as "the prison house of nationalities." The Balkans were an especially nettlesome place for the Ottoman empire, with Slavs, Serbs, Croats, Bosnians, Albanians, and Macedonians under the rule of Turks. One possible solution to this problem of multiple ethnicities, or nations, within one state was the French and American one of defining "the people," not in ethnic, religious, or even linguistic terms, but in political terms: "Americans are those who wish to be [Americans] . . . French nationality was French citizenship; ethnicity, history, the language or patois spoken at home, were irrelevant to the definition of 'the nation.'"[18]

This kind of multiethnic, multilinguistic, multireligious, "deliberate political option" nationalism waned in the nineteenth century, especially after the 1870s and 1880s. On the one hand, European states (and the United States) found it more convenient to invent nationalist traditions and to inculcate those into their populations, creating an imagined but nonetheless real nationalism. On the other hand, people who considered themselves "nations" but without states—Zionists, Irish, Serbs—began agitating for their own states. In short, nationalism of an exclusive, ethnic, and cultural kind—one that says "my people are great"—began to shape Europe in the second half of the nineteenth century, contributing to the way Europeans related to the rest of the world, to the pressures leading to World War I in the early twentieth century, and to the modern nation–state, with all its contradictions, ambiguities, and power over people.

Nationalism, economic competition among European states, internal social tensions arising from industrialization, and strategic considerations led to several wars among European states in the nineteenth century and to wars of imperialist expansion against Asians and Africans in the last thirty years of the century. The largest inter-European war was the Crimean War of 1854–1856, pitting Russia on one side against an alliance of Britain, France, and Turkey and resulting in the deaths of over 600,000 soldiers on all sides. Russia's loss contributed to its decision to eliminate serfdom and to industrialize. The American Civil War (1860–1865) killed additional hundreds of thousands of men. Finally, the nationalist unifications of Italy and Germany contributed to four more major European wars, culminating in the Franco-Prussian War of 1870–1871. Nationalism thus was injected into the ongoing tensions among European states, helping recruit young men into their armies, but also contributing to racist ideas about the superiority of Europeans and inferiority of others, especially Africans and Asians.

The Scrambles for Africa and China

After the Franco-Prussian War, Europeans for the most part stopped warring against one another (at least until 1914 and the outbreak of World War I) and instead directed their military power against China, Southeast Asia, the Middle East, and Africa.[19] Competition among European powers thus was displaced into those parts of the world we now call the third world, contributing to their decline into that status.

Africa

For centuries, Europeans found penetration of Africa to be almost impossible: various diseases endemic to the tropical parts of the continent, especially malaria, restricted slave-trading Europeans to coastal enclaves free from the disease. By the nineteenth century, steamships may have permitted access to the interior on Africa's various rivers, but malaria still killed most of the explorers. Although the cause of malaria was not discovered until 1880 and the means of transmission by mosquito not uncovered until 1897, a process of trial and error led to the realization by the mid-nineteenth century that the bark of the cinchona tree native to South America contained quinine, a substance that prevented malaria. British military personnel then successfully planted cinchona seeds in India and by the 1870s had greatly increased the supply of quinine to their troops. The subsequent European "scramble for Africa" may have been initiated in the 1870s by French insecurities arising from their defeat by the Germans in 1871, by the bizarre and secretive scheming by Belgium's King Leopold II,[20] and by British determination to protect their colonial interests in India, but all of those motivations would have been irrelevant had it not been discovered that quinine prevented malaria, or for the development of steamboats that could open the rivers, or for new technology in guns that killed more efficiently. The new technologies mattered.

In earlier chapters we traced some of the developments in the technology of guns, which remained fairly stable from the early 1500s to the early 1800s and featured the muzzle-loading musket. Muskets took several minutes to load, made huge puffs of smoke when fired, and were barely accurate even within a few hundred yards. Military tactics took account of these shortcomings, but clearly more accurate guns with greater range and less evidence of having been shot (thereby concealing the soldier's position) would be vast improvements.

Those improvements came rapidly after 1850 with the "rifling" of the barrel to improve accuracy, the creation of paper and then copper cartridges ignited by smokeless powder and inserted by breech loading, and the invention of mechanisms for repeating fire. The American Civil War and a European arms race in the 1860s and 1870s revolutionized guns and vastly increased the ability of European soldiers to kill rapidly, from a distance of a couple of thousand yards, and in any weather. The pinnacle of perfection came in the 1880s with the invention of a reliable machine gun, named after its inventor Hiram Maxim.

By the 1870s, Europeans thus had the "tools of empire" with which to engage and defeat Africans on African soil. Africans put up valiant and stiff resistance, but their technology was no match for the Maxim gun. The most famous and perhaps deadly instance was at the 1898 Battle of Obdurman where British troops confronted the 40,000-man Sudanese Dervish army. As described by Winston Churchill, the future British prime minister, the Dervish attack was quickly repulsed by Maxim guns mounted on river gunboats: "The charging Dervishes sank down in tangled heaps. The masses in the rear paused, irresolute. It was too hot even for them." On shore, the British "infantry fired steadily and stolidly, without hurry or excitement, for the enemy were far away and the officers careful." To the Sudanese "on the other side bullets were shearing through flesh, smashing and splintering bone; blood spouted from terrible wounds; valiant men struggling on through a hell of whistling metal, exploding shells, and spurting dust—suffering, despairing, dying." After five hours, the British lost 20 soldiers; 10,000 Sudanese were killed.[21] As a saying had it:

> Whatever happens, we have got
> the Maxim gun, and they have not.[22]

With such a technological advantage, by 1900 most of Africa had been divided up among a handful of European powers, in particular Britain, France, Germany, and Belgium, with Portugal hanging on to its seventeenth-century colonial possession in Angola. Only Ethiopia, under the extraordinary leadership of King Menelik, defeated the weakest European power, Italy, and thereby maintained its independence.[23] (See map 5.1.)

China

If dreams of vast stores of raw materials fueled imperialist dreams of Africa, for China it was access to its market. As Britain's cotton textile industrialists dreamed, "if we could add but one inch to the shirt of every Chinese, we could keep the mills of Manchester running forever." Although the market for "400 hundred million customers" continually evaded Europeans, their quest to "open" China was pressed throughout the nineteenth century, culminating in the "scramble for concessions" at the end of the century.

Following the Opium War (1839–1842), China was torn by a massive civil war, the Taiping Rebellion (1850–1865). Fueled by impoverished peasants and displaced workers and led by a man who believed himself to be the younger brother of Jesus Christ with a mission to establish the Heavenly Kingdom on Earth, the Taipings nearly swept the Manchu rulers of the Chinese empire from the historical stage. Combining appeals for a new, just social order resting on land reform, equality among all peoples (both social classes and genders within China, and nations globally), and ousting China's Manchu rulers, the Taipings swept up from south China to capture the southern capital of Nanjing on the Yangzi River. But for squabbling, bizarre behavior, and some poor strategic decisions among the Taiping leadership, China's modern history might have been very different from how it turned out. As it was, conservative landowners created their own armed forces, defeated the Taipings, and saved the Manchu regime.

Enfeebled by the civil war (during which some twenty million may have died), hobbled by the treaties imposed by the British after the two Opium Wars, and now committed to reviving the old agrarian regime to satisfy the demands of the landowners who saved the dynasty, the Manchus began a program of limited military modernization called "Self Strengthening" to protect themselves against foreign aggression. Although having some success at building what appeared to be a modern military, China nonetheless was subject to constant foreign pressure from not just the British, but from the Russians, French, Germans, and, as they industrialized, the Japanese. The latter two were to be responsible for sparking the "scramble for concessions," which led to the partition of China among "the Powers" in 1900.

Industrializing late, Japan too harbored imperialist expansion plans, directing its attention to Korea and the island of Taiwan. Although China considered Korea to be part of its tributary system and thus subordinate to it, Korea nonetheless had its own internal politics. When those sharpened and resulted in various insurrections in the 1880s and 1890s, the Japanese took the opportunity to support the side opposed to the Chinese. When China intervened (as it thought it had the right to) in 1894, war between China and Japan broke out. Surprising most observers, Japan rather handily defeated the Chinese in a major naval battle, bringing the war to an end.

Determined to press its advantage over a weakened and demoralized opponent, Japan extracted numerous concessions from the Chinese, including a huge $300 million indemnity, the island of Taiwan and the Liaodong Peninsula in Manchuria, the "independence" of Korea (thereby allowing Japan to exercise its influence over it), and the right of Japanese nationals to open factories and own mines in China. Russia, which opposed Japan's interests in Manchuria (its expansion into Siberia created its own interest in Manchuria), then convinced the Germans and French to join with it to force Japan to return Manchuria to Chinese sovereignty.

Succeeding in doing so and humbling Japan, the Russians earned the gratitude of China's rulers, who in turn granted the Russians concessions to develop a railroad in Manchuria. The Germans, who wanted a naval port in China to equal the British, French, and Russians, asked China for a base as a reward for their role in turning back the Japanese, but were rejected. But then, in 1898, using the murder of two German missionaries in China as a pretext, Germany seized a harbor on the Shandong peninsula and forced China to lease the harbor to it for ninety-nine years. This act unleashed "the scramble for concessions" in which all the other powers also extracted ninety-nine-year concessions from the Chinese government, "slicing China like a melon," as the phrase at the time had it. By 1900 it looked as if China too would be divided up into colonial possessions, as Africa had been.

But Britain needed "open trade" in China to keep its global empire working. Fortunately for the British, the United States had just acquired a colonial presence in the Philippines as a result of the 1898 war with Spain and was easily convinced to carry the torch for "open trade" for all powers in China. Expressed as the Open Door Notes of 1900, the United States articulated a policy, for various reasons and rather surprisingly accepted by the other powers, which kept China from being colonized and kept it open so it could be equally exploited by all the powers, Japan and the United States included.

Map 5.1   The World circa 1900

El Niño Famines and the Making
of the Third World

Although industrialization, improvements in military technology, strategic jockeying among "the powers," and the economic slump, which began in the 1870s, go a long way toward accounting for the dominance of Europeans, Americans, and Japanese over Africans, Asians, and Latin Americans, there was as well an ecological dimension to the making of the third world and the gap between the industrialized and unindustrialized parts of the world.

Where the very success of China's economy in the biological old regime had begun putting stress on its forest reserves by 1800, leading to serious deforestation by the middle of the nineteenth century, other parts of Asia and Latin America were deforested by other processes. In India, forests in the peninsula were cleared long before the population began to grow around the middle of the nineteenth century. Warring Indian princes cleared forests to deny their enemies cover, a policy of "ecological warfare" that the colonizing British also carried out with gusto. Additionally, dislocated peasant farmers cleared land, and there was some commercial logging in the north as well. All of these contributed to the extensive deforestation of India by the late nineteenth century.[24]

In Latin America, different processes led to massive deforestation. There, colonial powers, intent upon extracting raw materials and transforming their Latin American holdings into sugar or coffee plantations, cleared forests. In Brazil, the great forests of the Atlantic seaboard were first cleared for sugar plantations. In the early 1800s, Brazilian landowners switched to coffee crops. As a tree (not native, but imported from Ethiopia), coffee presumably could have been planted and replanted on the same land, given adequate care to the fertility of the soil. But as it turned out, landowners preferred to deplete the soil and after thirty years or so to clear another patch of virgin forest. "Thus coffee marched across the highlands, generation by generation, leaving nothing in its wake but denuded hills."[25] And on Caribbean islands, French and British colonists in the eighteenth century removed so much forest for sugar plantations that even then observers worried that it was causing the climate for the islands to change, getting drier and drier with every stand of forest cut down.[26]

By the last quarter of the nineteenth century, then, large parts of Asia and Latin America experienced significant environmental damage caused by deforestation and the depletion of soil fertility.[27] Of course, being agricultural societies, these changes put additional stresses on the biological old regime, making them even more susceptible to climatic shock and increasing the possibility of widespread famine.

Mostly, harvest failures were localized affairs. But in the late nineteenth century, a climatic phenomenon we now know as el Niño (or by its more scientific name, ENSO, for el Niño–Southern Oscillation) intensified to the greatest extent in perhaps five hundred years, affecting vast portions of the planet. Where el Niño brings excessive rainfall to the wheat belt of North America and does not affect Europe at all, it means drought for vast portions of Asia, parts of northern and western Africa, and northeast Brazil, and flooding for Argentina. Three times—in 1876–1879, 1889–1891, and 1896–1902—el Niño droughts afflicted the future third world. The particularities of how el Niño affects Asia, Africa, Latin America, and North America, coupled with the workings of a world economy designed to benefit the industrializing parts of Europe and North America, and the aggression of the "New Imperialism" against Asians and Africans combined in a historical conjuncture of global proportions to spell famine and death for millions of people.

In all, an estimated thirty to fifty million people died horribly in famines spread across Asia and parts of Africa and Latin America. But these deaths were not just caused by the natural effects of el Niño, no matter how powerful they were in the late nineteenth century. Rather, as historian Mike Davis describes in a recent book, these massive, global famines came about as a result of el Niños working in conjunction with the new European-dominated world economy to impoverish vast swaths of the world, turning much of Asia, Africa, and Latin America into the "third world." In Asia, governments were either unwilling or unable to act to relieve the disasters. The British colonial rulers of India were more intent on ensuring the smooth workings of the "free market" and their colonial revenues than in preventing famine and death by starvation or disease. There, people died in sight of wheat being loaded onto railroads destined for consumption in Britain, and the colonial authorities spurned famine relief in the belief that it weakened "character" and promoted sloth and laziness. In China, the Manchu government, switching resources and attention from the interior to the coasts where foreign pressure was greatest, had neither the ability nor the resources to move grain to the isolated inland province of Shanxi where the drought and famine was the most severe. Likewise in Angola, Egypt, Algeria, Korea, Vietnam, Ethiopia, the Sudan, and Brazil, el Niño–induced drought contributed to famines that weakened those societies and their governments, inviting new waves of imperialist expansion and consolidation.[28] The gap between the industrialized and future third world had crystallized.

Although it may appear to have been a historical accident that those late-nineteenth-century el Niños hit Asians, Africans, and Latin Americans hard while improving harvest yields in the American Midwest and bypassing Europe altogether, the socioeconomic impact they had was the result of the historical processes discussed in this and the previous chapter. All of these adversely affected regions either had weak states (and largely weakened because of imperialist aggression) that could not act either to industrialize or to provide famine relief to their people, or they had colonial governments (especially the British in India) whose policies had the same results. Thus at the beginning of the twentieth century, large parts of the world and its people were condemned as best they could to fend off the worst effects of the biological old regime. It is hardly surprising that the life expectancies and life chances of people there were much less than those in the industrialized parts of the world. "The gap" was—and remains—a life-and-death matter.

Social Darwinism and Self-Congratulatory Eurocentrism

By 1900, Europeans and their North American descendants controlled, directly or indirectly, most of the world. That fact did not escape their notice, and the British in particular celebrated it throughout their empire on the occasion of the fiftieth and sixtieth anniversaries of Queen Victoria's reign in 1887 and 1897 respectively—and in the midst of the late-nineteenth-century famines discussed above. With the advances of science since the middle of the nineteenth century, the ease with which the Maxim gun cut down Sudanese, and the famine deaths of millions of Asians, some Europeans now thought that they had a scientific explanation for the rise of the West and the "backwardness" of Asians, Africans, and Latin Americans: social Darwinism and eugenics, or scientific racism.

Charles Darwin had argued in his famous 1859 book *The Origins of Species* that evolution and the development of new species occurred by the processes of natural selection and the survival of the fittest species. Darwin soon extended the argument to humans, tracing human origins to apelike creatures. Then, in the late nineteenth century, Darwin's ideas about evolution were applied to societies. "Social" Darwinism purported to explain why some people were wealthy and others poor (virtue versus sloth), and why some societies were "advanced" and others "backward."[29] With Africans appearing to fall down dead at the sight of Europeans, with Indians (both kinds, in India and in North America) and Chinese dying by the millions from disease or during the el Niño famines, the idea that evolution could be applied to human society and the relationship between different races was believed to be true by large numbers of Europeans and North Americans. Both millionaires and Europeans, especially the white northern ones, according to Herbert Spencer, the foremost champion of social Darwinism, can be explained by natural selection:

> The poverty of the incapable, the distresses that come upon the imprudent, the starvation of the idle, and those shoulderings aside of the weak by the strong which leave so many in shallows and miseries are the decrees of a large, far-seeing benevolence.[30]

To social Darwinists, the poor, the Asians, the Africans, and the Native Americans thus all deserved their dismal fates—it was "natural." In a world in which the gap between the rich and the poor within European and American societies and between the wealthiest and poorest parts of the world had become glaring, social Darwinism was a comforting ideology for those on top of the world.

In Latin America, especially in Mexico and Brazil, ruled by light-skinned descendants of Europeans, a further extension of the idea of social Darwinism proved attractive. Eugenics, originally the selective breeding of plants and animals to produce the best stock, came to be applied to the belief that the condition of humans could be improved *only* through genetic manipulation, by increasing valuable human traits associated with North Europeans and eliminating those associated with the poor and the nonwhite. So, to "improve" the stock of their human populations, Mexican and Brazilian governments embarked on programs to encourage the migration of light-skinned Europeans to their countries so that their populations could be "lightened," they thought, just like adding a bit of milk to coffee. In Europe and the United States, eugenics contributed to racist ideas about the natural superiority of whites and the inferiority of southern and eastern Europeans, in addition to Asians, Africans, and Native Americans. And of course, this kind of pseudoscience turned into twentieth-century genocide in the hands of the Nazi leader Adolf Hitler.

Conclusion

And so we have come full circle, with the concoction at the beginning of the twentieth century of explanations for the rise of the West that now seem silly (and dangerous), but which were accepted as "true" by many people in the wealthiest and most powerful parts of the world. Of course, we can now see that these ideas (discussed in more detail in the introduction) are more ideology than historical truth. For the rise of the West is more the story of how some states and peoples benefited from historically contingent events and geography to be able, at a certain point in time (a historical conjuncture), to dominate others and to accumulate wealth and power. There is no more mystery in it than that, and by coming to grips with the contingent nature of the wealth, power, and privilege of the West, those who have benefited should be humbled by the actual sources of their good fortune, and those who have not should take heart that in the future new contingencies may well favor them. Europe was not always dominant or even bound for that destiny, even though Eurocentric ideologies of the past century may have propounded that myth.[31]

Notes

1. GDP is the total value of all goods and services produced in an economy, usually delimited by national boundaries.

2. Fernand Braudel, *Civilization and Capitalism 15th–18th Century*, vol. 2, Sian Reynolds, trans. (New York: Harper and Row, 1982), 134.

3. Braudel, *Civilization and Capitalism*.

4. The term "third world" came about after World War II in the context of the Cold War between the United States (and its European allies) and the Soviet Union, the first and second worlds respectively. To chart a path with some independence from

both the Americans and the Russians, "developing" but poor nations like India, Egypt, and Indonesia came to be known as the third world. By the 1970s, even poorer parts of the world, Africa in particular, became to be seen as the fourth world. All of these terms reflect the divisions of wealth and power that have come to define the modern world.

5. Carl A. Trocki, *Opium, Empire, and the Global Political Economy: A Study of the Asian Opium Trade, 1750–1950* (London: Routledge, 1999), 126.

6. See Edward R. Slack, Jr., *Opium, State, and Society: China's Narco-Economy and the Guomindang, 1924–1937* (Honolulu: University of Hawaii Press, 2001).

7. For the story of the rise and decline of India's cotton textile industry, at least in Bengal, see Debendra Bijoy Mitra, *The Cotton Weavers of Bengal 1757–1833* (Calcutta: Temple Press, 1978), 98.

8. S. Ambirajan, *Classical Political Economy and British Policy in India* (Cambridge: Cambridge University Press, 1987), 54–55.

9. Trocki, *Opium, Empire, and the Global Political Economy*, xiii, 8–9.

10. Sergei Witte, "An Economic Policy for the Empire," in Thomas Riha, ed., *Readings in Russian Civilization*, 2d ed. (Chicago: University of Chicago Press, 1969), vol. 2, 419. Had it not been for Russia's defeat by Germany in World War I and the successful Bolshevik (Communist) Revolution of 1917, Witte's plans may well have transformed Russia in ways he had envisioned. As it was, the capitalist countries of western Europe and the United States cut the new Soviet Union off from loans and other forms of direct foreign investment that Witte's plan had depended on for industrializing Russia. Instead, the Soviet Union had to pioneer a new path, epitomized from the late 1920s on as a succession of "Five-Year Plans," where the funds for investment in industry were squeezed from a newly collectivized agriculture. Despite the expropriation of private property in both cities and the countryside, the abolition of free markets, and hence the creation of a "planned economy" run by communist bureaucrats, the Soviet Union did achieve remarkable levels of industrial growth, especially of heavy industry, all the way to the beginning of their involvement in World War II.

11. A. J. H. Latham, *The International Economy and the Underdeveloped World 1865–1914* (London: Rowman & Littlefield, 1978), 175: "China's large trade deficit [caused by opium] in these years was an important feature of the international economy."

12. For Japan, see Mikiso Hane, *Peasants, Rebels, and Outcasts: The Underside of Modern Japan* (New York: Pantheon, 1982).

13. For the United States, see Jeremy Brecher, *Strike* (San Francisco: Straight Arrow Books, 1972).

14. Karl Marx and Friedrich Engels, *The Communist Manifesto* (New York: Washington Square Press, 1964), 57–59, 78–79.

15. This definition is based on E. J. Hobsbawm, *Nations and Nationalism since 1780*, 2d ed. (Cambridge: Cambridge University Press, 1992), 80.

16. Ernest Gellner, *Nations and Nationalism* (Ithaca, N.Y.: Cornell University Press, 1983), esp. chaps. 1 and 7.

17. See Joyce Appleby, Lynn Hunt, and Margaret Jacob, *Telling the Truth about History* (New York: W. W. Norton, 1994), chaps. 2 and 3.

18. Hobsbawm, *Nations and Nationalism*, 88.

19. See, for example, Brian Bond, ed., *Victorian Military Campaigns* (New York: Frederich Praeger, 1967).

20. The fascinating story is told in Adam Hochschild, *King Leopold's Ghost: A Story of Greed, Terror, and Heroism in Colonial Africa* (Boston: Houghton Mifflin, 1998).

21. Quoted in Daniel Headrick, *The Tools of Empire: Technology and European Imperialism in the Nineteenth Century* (New York: Oxford University Press, 1981), 118.

22. That ditty may have captured the balance of power at that moment between Africans and Europeans, but overall the balance between Europeans and others, especially those who used guerrilla tactics against European armies, was rapidly narrowing and would disappear altogether in the twentieth century. Where British armies at the end of the eighteenth century could defeat Indian armies six or seven times as large, by the early nineteenth century they could defeat Indian armies only twice as large. Finally, by the 1840s, the British had to use armies equally as large and with superior firepower to defeat Indian armies. Clearly, future third-worlders could quickly acquire use of the most advanced European arms to eliminate the European technological advantage. By the 1950s and 1960s, as both the French and then the United States were to learn in Vietnam, an occupied people determined to gain independence could effectively employ guerrilla tactics to stymie even the most advanced armies. To defeat that kind of mobilized population would have required five to six times as many troops as the guerrilla army, and by the late 1960s it was clear that the American public would not allow an escalation of troop strength from 500,000 to several millions. Given those military and political realities, the American defeat in Vietnam was a foregone conclusion. On the declining arms advantage of European armies in Africa and Asia, see Philip D. Curtin, *The World and the West: The European Challenge and the Overseas Response in the Age of Empire* (Cambridge: Cambridge University Press, 2000), chap. 2.

23. The West African state founded by returned American slaves, Liberia, too was independent, as was a small part of Morocco.

24. C. A. Bayly, *Indian Society and the Making of the British Empire* (Cambridge: Cambridge University Press, 1988), 138–139.

25. Warren Dean, *With Broadax and Firebrand: The Destruction of the Brazilian Atlantic Forest* (Berkeley: University of California Press, 1995), 181.

26. Richard H. Grove, *Green Imperialism: Colonial Expansion, Tropical Island Edens and the Origins of Environmentalism, 1600–1860* (Cambridge: Cambridge University Press, 1995), chaps. 5 and 6.

27. For the story of global deforestation, see Michael Williams, *Deforesting the Earth: From Prehistory to Global Crisis* (Chicago: The University of Chicago Press, 2003).

28. Mike Davis, *Late Victorian Holocausts: El Niño Famines and the Making of the Third World* (London: Verso Press, 2001).

29. See especially Michael Adas, *Machines as the Measure of Men: Science, Technology, and Ideologies of Western Dominance* (Ithaca, N.Y.: Cornell University Press, 1989).

30. Quoted in Eugen Weber, *A Modern History of Europe: Men, Cultures, and Societies from the Renaissance to the Present* (New York: W. W. Norton, 1971), 1001.

31. For a discussion of the role of racism in motivating Europeans to conquer foreign land, see John M. Hobson, *The Eastern Origins of Western Civilization* (Cambridge: Cambridge University Press, 2004), chap. 10.

CHAPTER SIX

The Great Departure

Introduction to the Twentieth Century

By 1900, the major elements of the modern world had been created. Nation–states had become the most successful organization for controlling territory and had been adopted throughout much of Europe and the Americas. Some of those nation–states had industrialized (notably western Europe, the United States, and Japan) and had harnessed that newfound industrial power for imperialist military and economic purposes to colonize most of Africa and much of Asia. Europeans, Americans, and Japanese had developed racist ideas of their superiority—the whites' arising from a Christian "civilizing" mission coupled with social Darwinism, and the Japanese from their purported uniqueness in Asia, which contributed to their colonizing programs, and a belief that the world order was as it should be—with them on top.[1]

Yet the twentieth century brought remarkable change. To be sure, we still live in a world of nation–states, of industry, and of a growing gap between the richest and poorest parts of the globe. But the early twenty-first century differs fundamentally from that of the early 1900s. During the last century, whole new industries developed, dramatically restructuring the industrial world—oil and the automobile; electricity and the telephone, radio, television, and computers; motors and the airplane, jet engines, and space travel as well as washing machines and vacuum cleaners; and the germ theory of disease and inoculation against it, to mention just a few scientific discoveries that would transform lives throughout the world. These clusters of innovations created consumption patterns that required energy from burning vast quantities of cheap fossil fuels.[2]

In addition to technological change, by the middle of the twentieth century, western European states would be dislodged from dominance. World War I (1914–1918) shook the imperialist order of the late nineteenth century to its foundations, and had major consequences for the shape of the twentieth century as a century of war and violence. But it was World War II (1939–1945) that destroyed not only the old European colonial order but also the new Japanese empire and gave rise to a bifurcated world dominated by two superpowers: the United States and the Soviet Union (the USSR, or Union of Soviet Socialist Republics). During the twentieth century, nearly two hundred million people were killed in war, revolution, genocide, and other human-caused mass deaths.[3] Two world wars, punctuated by a global economic breakdown, constituted thirty years of crisis from 1914 to 1945. That "thirty-year crisis" of the modern world destroyed Europe's global dominance and Japan's Asian empire, made way for the rise of two new superpowers (the United States and the Soviet Union) and their "Cold War," and created a host of newly independent former colonies seeking to unlock the secrets of industrial development.

In two great waves, one following the end of the Second World War in 1945 and the other the end of the Cold War in 1991, the world became increasingly interconnected: ideas, capital, and labor moved with increasing rapidity and ease around the globe. This globalization, largely under U.S. auspices and with the specific goal of spreading capitalism and the institutions that protect it around the world, has benefited some, but not most, contributing to a continued and deepening gap between the wealthiest and poorest parts of the world.

Among the great changes to the modern world in the twentieth century—perhaps the most significant in the long run—will be the impact humans have had on the environment. In the pursuit of rapid economic development in the capitalist world, the socialist world, and the third world alike, the relationship of human beings to the natural environment has changed to the point where human activity now affects global ecological processes. Just as the use of fossil fuels in the nineteenth century freed industrial production and economic growth from natural constraints, so too in the twentieth century did synthetic fertilizer increase food supplies, sending the world's human population soaring. The combination of both rapid industrial and population growth in the twentieth century marks a "great departure" of humans and our history from the rhythms and constraints of the biological old regime. That story starts with the invention of synthetic fertilizer.

Nitrogen, Gunpowder, and Fertilizer

At the dawn of the twentieth century, social Darwinism and racism blinded Europeans to two dangers. First, they could not believe that the "advanced, progressive, civilized" races of the world (i.e., the whites) could go to war amongst themselves; that myth would come crashing down in World War I, and with it the vision of the omnipotence of Europe. Second, they could not conceive that the poor, backward, black, brown, and yellow peoples would ever be able to militarily challenge their European masters. That myth began to crumble in 1905 when Japan defeated Russia, but it would take successful revolutions and wars against Europeans to finally dispel it and bring down the old colonial order. One of the main reasons twentieth-century wars were so destructive is that the machinery of death was industrialized.

The peculiar thing about the technologies of war that imperialist states wielded against Asians, Africans, and indigenous peoples of the Americas through the nineteenth century is that the manufacture of a crucial element— gunpowder—was dependent upon extremely slow processes of nature. For all the steel, steam, and guns that their factories could produce, Europeans could not manufacture nitrates, the stuff that made gunpowder explode—they had to find it in the natural world. The critical element in nitrates is nitrogen, and although European scientists had figured that out, they had difficulty discovering how to take nitrogen from the air and "fix" it into a solid, usable substance.[4] Paradoxically, coal, steam, iron, and steel had enabled the industrializing countries to escape from some of the limitations of the biological old regime, but the gunpowder they used to dominate the rest of the world was still based on it.

Nitrogen is crucial to the growth of plants and is essential to the creation of the amino acids that sustain animal, including human, life. Life on earth is part of a global nitrogen cycle by which the vast sources of nitrogen in the atmosphere become available to plants, and through them, to animals. Certain plants—legumes like beans, peanuts, and clover—fix nitrogen to the soil, and that helps fertilize fields and improve crop yields, making more food available to humans. Lightning strikes too can produce small amounts of nitrates. But the largest sources of naturally occurring nitrates are produced as animal waste. Farmers around the world, knowing that, have long applied animal (and human) manure to their fields. These naturally occurring sources of nitrogen sustained life, but they also limited the size of the human population by limiting the amount of food that could be produced. As long as humans depended upon nature to supply nitrogen, they remained constrained within the rhythms and processes of the biological old regime.

Ironically, that same substance—nitrates—was essential to improving agricultural yields *and* to making explosives.[5] Paradoxically then, both the size of the global human population and its ability to conduct modern warfare depended on, and were limited by, nature. That fact led to a global search for naturally occurring deposits of nitrates, mostly in the form of bat and bird guano. Guano was excrement that under certain conditions—in particular the absence of rain that would otherwise dissolve the droppings and their precious nitrogen—could accumulate over time. Caves were one place that bat guano could build up, and then be extracted by guano miners to make fertilizer and, increasingly in the nineteenth century, gunpowder. But it turned out that the largest supplies of bird guano had accumulated over thousands, if not millions, of years on the arid Chincha Islands off the coast of Peru.

The first clump of Peruvian guano was brought to Europe in 1804 by the German naturalist and world explorer Alexander von Humboldt, and then extracted in ever greater amounts and exported by British merchants. By 1890, the supplies of Peruvian guano were mostly exhausted, but another natural source (sodium nitrate, or "saltpeter") that could be mined was found in southern Peru; in 1879 Chile had gone to war with Peru to gain control of the sodium nitrate, and exported it to the industrializing world, which used it to make both fertilizer and gunpowder. In 1900, for instance, the United States used about half of its imports of Chilean sodium nitrate to make explosives. Food or explosives? For the imperialist powers of the world, that was a tough enough position, but it was exacerbated further by the fact that Chile had a monopoly on the largest naturally occurring source of sodium nitrate. Moreover, for the saltpeter to get from Chile to Europe or the United States, it had to be shipped. Sea power was thus crucial to maintaining supplies of sodium nitrate, and any imperialist power vulnerable to a maritime blockade would be severely weakened, its food production and munitions industries held hostage to Chilean sodium nitrate. That was particularly true with Germany. And it was there that the most intense search for a way to produce nitrates industrially was underway by the turn of the twentieth century.

It was not that other nations' scientists were unaware of the importance of the problem, for they certainly were. But Germany's vulnerabilities made the problem pressing. In 1909 a chemist named Fritz Haber synthesized ammonia (which contains nitrogen that could be processed into nitrates) in his laboratory, and a year later the issues of industrial production were resolved by Carl Bosch of the German firm BASF. The process of synthesizing ammonia, known as the Haber-Bosch process, shaped the subsequent course of world history.

The synthesis of ammonia made possible the growth of the world's human population. Coupled with the expansion of farmland, the fertilizers from guano and saltpeter had enabled the world population to increase from about one billion in 1800 to 1.6 billion by 1900. But by 1900, most of the good arable land in the world was already being farmed, so that increased food production could come most readily from the application of additional fertilizer; but, as we have seen, most of the naturally occurring guano had already been used up, and global military competition ensured that substantial amounts of saltpeter went to various states' munitions industries. One expert has concluded that using the materials and techniques available in the biological old regime to improve agricultural output, the world's population might have increased at most to 2.8 billion people. The Haber-Bosch process for synthesizing ammonia made it possible to increase the food supply and support the world's current population of about 6.2 billion people. In other words, in the twentieth century, the population of the world increased from about 1.6 to 6.2 billion (or 4.6 billion more people, most of them since 1950) largely because of the Haber-Bosch process. That increase in the human population alone makes the twentieth century unique in all of human history.[6] The synthesis of ammonia and the consequent industrial production of fertilizer freed human population growth from the natural limits of the biological old regime. More than that, it also made possible the industrial production of explosives, and, because Germany was the first to use this new technology, increased the confidence of its military leaders. And that was to be a crucially important factor contributing to the outbreak of world war in 1914.

The Thirty-Year Crisis (1914–1945)

By 1900, there was precious little of the world left to be dominated by the imperialist powers; the largest chunks that were not yet spoken for were the Chinese and Ottoman empires. As for China, the Open Door Notes of 1900 led the imperialist powers to conclude that a weak Chinese state would enable them to enjoy the benefits of their "spheres of influence" without any one of them actually having to conquer and govern China, a task made all the more difficult by the competing powers, including the United States and Japan, aspiring to dominate the region. Indeed, it was hoped that the acceptance of the Open Door Notes had cooled competition among the imperialist powers in Asia and removed an irritant and possible cause of war.

World War I

A general war among the European powers would indeed break out, but the spark was ignited not in Asia, but in the Balkans, in southeastern Europe. In July 1914, a Serbian nationalist assassinated the heir to the Austrian throne,

Archduke Ferdinand, and his wife, while they were visiting the city of Sarajevo, an administrative center in Bosnia that had recently been absorbed by the Austria-Hungarian Empire. Supported by Germany and intending to cause a war and increase the size of its empire, Austria sent an ultimatum to Serbia, which in turn was supported by Russia.

What made this little confrontation in the Balkans so explosive was that in the previous years, imperialist rivalries and European power politics had led to a system of alliances, largely fueled by French and Russian fears of the rising economic and military power of Germany. In the early 1900s, Britain joined France and Russia to form the "Triple Entente," while Germany and Austria-Hungary formed the Central Powers. Thus Austria counted on German support in attacking Serbia, while Russian support for Serbia soon brought France and Britain into the equation.

When Russian and German armies mobilized to support their allies, all of Europe soon was at war. Then Britain's new ally in Asia, Japan, declared war on the Central Powers, the Ottoman empire sided with Germany for fear of being partitioned by the Entente powers, Britain's dominions (Canada, Australia, New Zealand) mobilized, Britain and France mobilized armies and resources from their colonies, and soon the whole world outside of the Americas was warring or mobilized to support Europeans at war with each other. And by 1917, the United States too, previously insulated from self-destructive European wars by the Atlantic, entered the war in support of Britain and its allies. By the time an armistice was called on November 11, 1918, over ten million soldiers had been killed, and upwards of twenty million had been maimed, blinded, or otherwise wounded.

It had been the bloodiest conflict the world had ever seen, in large part because industrialization had made war more destructive than ever. Not only did Fritz Haber's invention free the production of explosives from natural constraints,[7] Haber also discovered how to manufacture various poisonous gasses that then were used in the trench warfare of World War I, and later by Hitler's Nazi regime in the extermination camps. Tanks, submarines, and great battleships increased the carnage.

Viewed in long-term historical perspective, the "Great War," as World War I was then known, was the beginning of the end of the European-dominated world order, an end that ultimately would take the Great Depression and another world war to complete. However, as the First World War ended, that outcome was not clearly in sight.

The 1917 entry of the United States on the side of Britain and France assured the defeat of Germany and Austria. America had troops, war material, and an awesomely productive industrial economy to throw into the war effort. It also cost the United States over one hundred thousand dead and two hundred thousand wounded, a small fraction of the casualties suffered by the main European contenders, but enough to guarantee a seat at the Versailles Peace Conference called to draw up the terms ending the war. Germany had not surrendered, but had agreed to an armistice and thus hoped to have a voice in what would happen to it after the war; that was not to be, as the losers were treated as losers. The British and French colonial subjects who had fought for their colonial rulers in the war thought they would get enhanced treatment, especially when they heard about U.S. President Wilson's "Fourteen Points" that included a call for respecting nations' sovereign rights; but that was not to be either. The various Arab peoples who were encouraged to revolt against the Ottomans in return for British and French promises of independence were likewise disappointed. And China, which had joined on the side of Britain and France (sending young men to France to work at factory jobs) in the hopes of regaining control of German concessions in Shandong province, would get a different lesson.

Instead of a more equitable settlement implicit in all of these hopes and aspirations, Britain, France, and Japan acted as victorious imperialists whose main task was divvying up the spoils of war. France took back Alsace-Lorraine from Germany, Germany was forced to pay huge war reparations, the Austria-Hungarian empire was taken apart, with the new states of Czechoslovakia, Hungary, and Yugoslavia being formed, and Poland was reconstituted, also with parts of Germany. Instead of China recovering its own Shandong peninsula from a defeated Germany, control passed to Japan, which had entered the war on the winning side.

After the League of Nations was formed, Britain and France used it to gain "mandates" to control the Middle Eastern remnants of the Ottoman empire: France got Syria, Britain carved out Iraq, and neither Arab Palestinians nor Jewish Zionists got Palestine, which became a British mandate. Vietnamese who had helped the French, and Indians who had supported the British, also were slapped down by their colonial masters. However, actions by the victorious imperialist powers at the end of World War I provoked reactions that could not be contained, as German resentment built and provided support for Adolf Hitler and his Nazi program, and as national independence movements spurred opposition to imperialism and colonialism.

Revolutions

Added to that, the 1917 communist-led Bolshevik Revolution in Russia challenged the capitalist world order itself. Under the leadership of V. I. Lenin, the Bolsheviks seized power in October 1917 after the czarist regime had collapsed amidst disastrous defeats in World War I, and promptly signed a separate peace with Germany, taking Russia out of the war. Despite armed intervention and a civil war that followed, the Bolsheviks established the world's first communist-led state with the avowed intent of building socialism and seeing an end to the capitalist world. After Lenin died in 1923, Joseph Stalin consolidated power and led the Soviet Union on a crash industrialization project that he termed "socialism in one country," relying solely on Russian resources and having as little contact as possible with the capitalist world.

Revolution was shaking not just Russia, but other parts of the world as well in the years before and after World War I. In Mexico, moderate reform in 1910 was followed by peasant rebellions led by Emiliano Zapata in the south and Pancho Villa in the north that fueled the Mexican Revolution (1910–1920), ushering in land reform and limiting foreign ownership of Mexican natural resources. In China, revolutionaries toppled the Manchu dynasty in 1911, and after a decade of confusing warlord politics, two new political parties formed with explicitly nationalist goals. Cooperating in the 1920s to eliminate warlords, the revolutionaries threatened to break imperialist control of the modern sectors of China's economy. In Italy, a new movement—fascism—emerged that was both anti-communist and promised to avoid the miseries of capitalism by fostering national unity and the power of the state under a strong leader, Benito Mussolini.

Colonial Independence Movements

Post–World War I challenges to the imperialist world order came not just from revolutionary movements in Russia, China, Mexico, and Italy, but also from independence movements in Europe's colonies, most notably India. There, Mohandas Gandhi created a nonviolent independence movement stressing boycotts of British goods (especially cotton textiles) and salt. In the process, civil disobedience was born. Gandhi broke colonial laws and invited imprisonment for doing so, all in the name of Indian independence. A Hindu himself, Gandhi stressed the multiethnic scope of the anti-colonial movement by insisting that his Congress Party include Muslims and Sikhs in leadership positions as well.

In the face of setbacks and divisions among the imperialist powers in World War I, nationalism fueled anti-imperialist and anti-colonial independence movements not just in India and China, but in Egypt, Vietnam, and Palestine as well. Nationalism, which had developed in nineteenth-century Europe and Japan, in the twentieth century became a global force. Where in Europe nationalism was mostly a conservative force that emphasized cultural, linguistic, and religious commonalities to blunt the class conflicts that grew along with industrialization, in Asia and Africa nationalism would have an explicit anti-imperialist content, often fueling socially revolutionary movements. The modern world was being challenged.

Normalcy?

World War I had brought the capitalist world system to a point of crisis that was only postponed by the apparent "return to normalcy" of the 1920s in the industrialized world. Although Europe had been deeply shaken by the war and much of its productive capacity destroyed, loans from U.S. banks (in particular to Germany) kept sufficient liquidity for Europeans to buy American products, restoring prosperity to Europe and stimulating U.S. industry. U.S. capital was keeping the global system afloat, though few realized it at the time. After the conclusion of the Versailles Peace Conference ending World War I, President Woodrow Wilson's fond hope that the economic and political conditions causing war could be ameliorated through U.S. leadership of new international bodies such as the League of Nations was shattered when an isolationist Congress refused to approve U.S. participation.

There were other signs of serious problems in the industrialized world, especially in agriculture. Wartime demand and rising prices throughout Europe and the United States prompted farmers to increase production, while postwar inflation encouraged them to take loans to expand food production even more. By the early 1920s, there was serious overproduction of food (together with malnutrition and starvation in poor regions), a sharp decline in agricultural prices, and a spike in foreclosures as farmers had difficulty repaying loans. The increased supply of food on the world market came also from Australia and New Zealand, as well as the newly formed states of eastern Europe. To make matters worse, prices for coffee, sugar, and other agricultural and primary product exports that Latin American countries had relied upon also collapsed. By the late 1920s, few rural producers anywhere in the world could afford to buy manufactured goods.

The Great Depression of the 1930s

To protect their nation's manufactures, industrialized states began raising tariffs on imported goods, which further cut international trade in industrial goods. Loans that U.S. bankers had made to European countries were called in, and when that happened, investors panicked, leading to "Black Monday" in October 1929 when the U.S. stock market crashed. Wealth vanished overnight, banks failed, and the savings of millions evaporated. The world economy entered a vicious downward spiral in which factories laid off workers whose income and purchases shrunk. Lower demand led to further cuts in production—the only thing that was rising in the 1930s was the unemployment rate. In the industrialized world, between 22 percent of the workers (in Sweden) and 44 percent (in Germany) lost their jobs. The U.S. unemployment rate reached 27 percent.

By 1913, the United States had become the largest economy on earth, producing one-third of the world's output. World War I provided further stimulation, and by 1929 the U.S. economy had grown to an astounding 42 percent of world output. So, when the Great Depression hit America, it affected the entire world. U.S. imports crashed by 70 percent between 1929 and 1933, and its exports fell by half.[8]

The Great Depression thus was a global phenomenon. States in western Europe, Latin America, Asia, and Africa all suffered. Only the Soviet Union, which had cut itself off from the capitalist world and was trying, under Joseph Stalin, to build "socialism in one country," emerged unscathed. As the rest of the world was plunged into the Great Depression, the communist-led Soviet Union was experiencing rapid economic growth.

The Great Depression was a global crisis of capitalism, leading several states to abandon the pre–World War I model of unfettered capitalism. Some states experimented with reforms to provide a social safety net under the workers and farmers who suffered mightily (e.g., U.S. President Franklin D. Roosevelt's "New Deal"). In Germany, the reparations issue and the loss of territory after World War I, coupled with the crisis of the Great Depression, laid the groundwork for the 1933 rise to power of Adolf Hitler and his "Nazi," or National Socialist Party, which promised that a powerful state headed by a strong leader would get Germany out of the crisis it was in: by the mid-1930s, Germany's economy was indeed growing once again, and many Germans credited Hitler's national socialism with improving their lot. In Japan, where exports of silk to the United States shrunk as women cut back on stocking purchases, military leaders saw dependence on the world market as a strategic mistake and began to more aggressively move to a position of primacy among the powers in Asia, building on its formal colonies in Taiwan and Korea and extending its reach from 1932 with the creation of Manchukuo. By the early 1930s, nationalistic and militarily aggressive regimes had come to power in Germany and Japan.

By its actions toward China during World War I, Japan had signaled that it intended to be a major player among the imperialist powers in Asia. Although it was not strong enough in the 1920s to resist the combined power of Britain and the United States, when the world entered into the crisis decades of the 1930s, Japan extended its empire at China's expense and ultimately confronted the United States for control of the Pacific. While Japan and the United States jockeyed for dominance in Asia, they overlooked the growing power and world-changing significance of the Chinese communist movement that would establish China's independence in the wake of World War II, setting the stage for its rise to global power in the late twentieth century.

During the Great Depression, the global trading and monetary systems came apart; instead of seeking to increase international trade as a way out of the depression, those states that could severed ties to the global system and instead sought to gain as much independence from it as possible—the goal was "autarky." In the early 1930s, Britain attempted to protect its economy by binding its colonies ever tighter to the home market and discouraging other nations from trading there. The United States took similar actions with regard to its Caribbean and Philippine colonies as well as in Latin American countries. The Soviet Union already had successfully broken away from the international system. After Japan added Manchuria to its colonial empire, it continued to build its own "Greater East Asian Co-Prosperity Sphere." Italy expanded into North Africa, and Hitler's Nazi Germany looked to reconstitute an empire in central and eastern Europe, annexing Austria in 1938, dismembering Czechoslovakia in early 1938, and then taking the rest of it in early 1939. The global system disintegrated into competing and then warring blocs.

World War II

Britain and France had given guarantees of protection to Poland, so when Nazi armies invaded in September 1939, Britain declared war. The still-isolationist United States stayed out of the conflict, but when Japan attacked Pearl Harbor on December 7, 1941, it entered the war in both the Pacific and Europe. By then the Soviet Union too had become involved after Hitler broke a nonaggression treaty and attacked Russia in 1940. The communist-led Soviet Union then made common cause with capitalist Britain and the United States against the immediate threat, the Axis powers of Nazi Germany, Fascist Italy, and Imperial Japan.

The Second World War was even more destructive than the first. Not only were the numbers of dead and injured soldiers vastly greater, but civilians mobilized for the war effort (nearly all industrial production in the contending states was geared toward war) and then became targets as well. By 1943, the Allies (Britain, France, the United States, and the Soviet Union) had determined that only total, unconditional defeat of the Axis powers was acceptable, and by 1944 U.S. resistance to using military force against civilians was overcome. U.S. warplanes joined the British in the firebombing of Dresden in

Germany; then in Japan they firebombed Tokyo and sixty-three other cities, before dropping the first atomic bombs on Hiroshima and Nagasaki in August 1945.

If war was hell, "total war" was total hell. The Nazis, of course, had industrialized the death of six million Jews and other "undesirables," while the Japanese had conducted the "three all" (kill all, burn all, destroy all) campaigns against Chinese villagers, among other atrocities. More civilians and more troops died in the Second World War than in the First. The number is staggering. More than fifty million people around the world perished, with twenty million in the Soviet Union and ten million in China accounting for most of the war dead.

The Post–World War II World

The end of World War II in 1945 would be much different from the end of World War I. There was no "armistice," or standing down of armies; total war yielded total defeat—the unconditional surrender of Germany (in June 1945) and Japan (in September) to the victors. Perhaps most importantly, European states (victors as well as vanquished) would not have the ability to reconstitute their colonial empires—over the course of the coming decades, Asian and African colonies would become independent states. In Asia, Japan's colonial empire was also dismantled during the U.S. occupation of Japan in the years from 1945 to 1952. A civil war in China would bring the Chinese Communist Party to power in 1949. In short order, the former colonial world and a communist-led China began aggressive pursuit of economic "development" with an emphasis on industrialization.

Hitler's national socialism, Italy's fascism, and Japan's statist development models, while successful in getting those states out of the Great Depression faster than European and American states, also led them to war and defeat. Europe's colonial model also was discredited and destroyed. Left standing and considerably strengthened by the end of World War II and the thirty-year crisis were the United States and the Soviet Union, the two rising powers of the postwar world. Indeed, the defeat of Nazi Germany would not have been possible without the Soviet Red Army, just as the United States was primarily responsible for the defeat of Japan.

For different reasons, both the United States and the Soviet Union had strongly anti-colonial ideologies and were opposed to European states maintaining their colonies, and that fact contributed to the surge of postwar anti-colonial movements in the colonies. But they also had vastly different social and economic systems—one primarily free market capitalism (the United

States) and the other state-planned socialism (the Soviet Union)—which each sought to project as a global model. The United States wanted to end colonialism not simply because it believed in the inherent right of national independence, but because it could then get access to those markets and raw materials denied it by colonial preference systems. The Soviets believed that ending colonialism would further the likelihood of socialist transformations in the colonies, a necessary step on the way to a communist world.

Although both were anti-colonial, their very different visions of the place of newly independent colonies in the world led to tensions between the United States and the Soviet Union that would produce the "Cold War," an arms race with horrifying new nuclear weapons that each side realized could never be used, but which could deter the other from attacking. "MAD," it was called: "mutually assured destruction." So the military standoff between the United States and the USSR would not result in actual "hot" war, but a "cold" war, one that would provide the context for most of the post–World War II world until the collapse of the Soviet Union in 1991.

Decolonization

While it is true that most colonies became independent states only after World War II, the process had begun in the aftermath of World War I. The sense of betrayal after World War I, combined with the clear recognition of the vulnerability of the colonial powers, had fueled nationalist-inspired independence movements throughout Asia and Africa. By the time World War II broke out, some nationalist leaders, especially in Asia, began to break with their colonial masters by siding with Japan and their call of "Asia for Asians."[9]

The independence of the largest of all colonies, India, was on the agenda by the end of World War II, and after the war Britain quickly arranged the terms of its departure and the independence of the subcontinent. The tragedy of Indian independence, though, is the massive violence that attended the process. Where Gandhi and the Congress Party had intended to create a multiethnic, multireligious state, one part of India's Muslim leadership in the 1930s had begun agitating for the creation of a separate Muslim state to be called Pakistan. Hindu nationalists too wanted an India for Hindus, and it was an ultranationalist Hindu who assassinated fellow-Hindu Gandhi for proposing a single, multiethnic state with protections for Hindus, Muslims, and other ethnic and religious groups. By 1947, independence meant the partition of the colony into the states of predominantly Hindu India, and predominantly Muslim Pakistan (the latter in two parts, east and west). The state of Kashmir, which had a predominantly Muslim population but had been ruled by a Hindu prince, was divided and remains a source of tension and conflict between Pakistan and India.[10]

With the withdrawal of the British, and fears of Hindus and Muslims of each other fanned by nationalists on each side, Hindus in what was to become Pakistan fled toward India, and Muslims in India streamed toward Pakistan. In the course of this huge movement of people during "partition," as it came to be called, millions lost their property and homes, and hundreds of thousands were killed. Not surprisingly, India and Pakistan have ever since been wary, and twice warring, neighbors, in addition to having numerous border skirmishes, struggling over control of Kashmir, and (since 1998) aiming nuclear weapons at each other.

Indian independence and partition points to two significant aspects of the postwar decolonization of Asia and Africa. First, European colonialists assumed that independence meant the independence of territorial states. Some parts of their colonial holdings certainly had had historical experience with states (especially in Asia and the Middle East), but much of Africa did not. The borders that Europeans drew were often quite arbitrary and did not take into consideration the peoples living there. Thus just as the lines dividing India from Pakistan wrought havoc for the tens of millions of Muslims and Hindus inconveniently on the wrong side, so too did line drawing in Africa and the Middle East create states with people of common languages and cultures across two (or more) borders. Important examples are the Kurds who now inhabit northern Iraq, western Iran, and eastern Turkey, and Hutus and Tutsis in Rwanda and Congo.

Much of Asia and the Middle East was decolonized by 1950, and most of Africa was composed of independent states by 1960. Smaller island territories in the Caribbean and Pacific attained independence in the 1960s. This spurt of decolonization created a host of newly independent states, boosting membership in the United Nations from fifty-one at its creation in 1945, to 127 by 1970.

Asian Revolutions

The global scale of World War II created the conditions not only for decolonization, but also for revolutions, mostly led by communist or other leftist parties. In China, the Communist Party had been formed in 1921 in the aftermath of the Versailles Peace Conference and the Bolshevik Revolution in Russia. Rural poverty in China provided a vast reservoir of support for the communists, who delivered on rent and interest reduction promises and then targeted the landlords whose exploitation of the peasantry deepened rural misery. When Japan invaded China in 1937, the communists formed a "united front" with the ruling Guomindang party to resist Japan. The Japanese invasion forced the Guomindang to retreat to China's far southwest, while the communists organized guerrilla warfare behind Japanese lines, strengthening their military skills and expanding the territory they controlled. When Japan surrendered to the United States in 1945, civil war between the communists and their Guomindang foes led to communist victory and the establishment in 1949 of the People's Republic of China. The Chinese communists were determined to create a strong China that would never again be threatened by foreign powers. That resolve was tested in 1950 when communist China fought the United States to a draw in the Korean War (1950–1953).

In French Indochina at the end of Word War II, the Viet Minh under the leadership of Ho Chi Minh declared independence from France after having fought an anti-Japanese guerrilla war there and building up not just vast popular support but also a formidable military. The French, though, were not ready to give up their Asian colony (just as they wanted to retain their Algerian colony), and so sought to reestablish their power in Vietnam. In the war that followed, Ho Chi Minh's forces defeated the French forces in 1954. The United States then became involved, at first diplomatically and then militarily. Rather than national elections and unification, which had been promised for 1956, the United States decided to support a client regime in the south, and Vietnam remained divided between North and South Vietnam. When the U.S.-supported southern regime had difficulty governing itself and maintaining popular support against the northern and the southern Viet Minh guerrilla fighters, the United States sent first advisors, and then in the mid-1960s large numbers of combat troops, to support the south. After a decade of war, the United States and South Vietnam were defeated, and in 1975 Vietnam was reunited under communist leadership.

Violence was also necessary to shake French control of Algeria, which finally became independent in 1960. The other colonial power to resist granting independence to its colonies was Portugal, which held on to Angola on the west coast of Africa until forced by armed rebels to give up control in 1975. The age of empire,[11] spawned by the European industrial revolution and military superiority, was over. In the decades after the Second World War, Asians, Africans, and Latin Americans were determined to use their newfound independence to improve the lot of their peoples by industrializing.

Development and Underdevelopment

There is no mystery as to why colonies had not industrialized: with the exception of Japan, policies of the home country mostly forbade it.[12] China had some modern industry, but much of it was owned by foreigners and limited to pockets of coastal cities. For the first half of the twentieth century, China remained rural and in the grip of landlords. The Chinese communist victory in 1949 changed all that by eliminating the landlord class, nationalizing foreign-owned businesses, and having the military power to back up their actions.

Post–World War II decolonization and revolution brought to power regimes committed to explicit policies of "development." Moreover, since most of those former colonies (to say nothing of China) had bitter experiences with the capitalist West, the models they chose for the most part were strongly influenced by socialist, communist, or other statist ideas. In the postwar world, much of the underdeveloped world was beginning to move toward some form of state-driven industrialization. That was a problem for the United States, which had a different global vision, one centered on private ownership of property and capital, and on the principles of international free trade.

The Cold War World, 1947–1991

Even before the end of World War II, the United States actively planned to reconstitute the world on the basis of capitalist principles emphasizing free trade to prevent the world from sliding back into the autarkic (and then warring) blocs of the Great Depression, and to ensure sufficient global demand to fuel the United States economy. Abandoning its prewar "isolationism," the United States also took the lead in setting up the United Nations to resolve international conflict and creating new institutions to manage the postwar global economy, in particular the World Bank and the International Monetary Fund. A strong Soviet Union, the Chinese revolution, and the influence of socialism in the former colonies threatened both that free market vision and the global reach of the United States.

That, coupled with the Soviet occupation of much of eastern Europe at the end of World War II and the creation of "satellite" states there as well as Soviet support for communist North Korea and Vietnam and the growing power of communists in China, prompted U.S. decision makers to revive the German and Japanese economies, the workshops of Europe and Asia combating Soviet influence everywhere. This "reverse course" with respect to Germany and Japan and the policy of "containment" toward the Soviet Union was in place by 1947. The United States would not seek to go to war to roll back the Bolshevik Revolution (in today's language, to seek "regime change"), but to "contain" its power and influence in the world.

The Cold War was on, and would last until 1991, defining much of the post–World War II world. As part of its containment policy, the United States would go to war in Korea (1950–1953), confronting not just North Korean but Chinese communist troops as well, get involved in Vietnam and then war there (1956–1975), use covert operations to overthrow democratically elected, left-leaning governments in Latin America, support authoritarian regimes there and in the Middle East, and prop up undemocratic but anti-communist regimes throughout the world.

The Cold War had other consequences as well. The United States began the post–World War II era as the only nuclear power, but in 1949 the Soviets detonated their first atomic bomb and the nuclear arms race was on in earnest, leading not just to fleets of warplanes equipped to drop nuclear bombs, but more ominously to intercontinental ballistic missiles (ICBMs) capable of reaching their targets just minutes after launch. There was (and still is) no defense against these weapons of mass destruction other than the surety of a massive retaliation once missile launches had been detected. By the 1960s with each side having thousands of ICBMs and nuclear warheads, a nuclear attack could have ended not just human civilization, but quite possibly humans as a species.[13] As it was, although there were numerous threats of nuclear attack, the world came to "the brink" just once in the early 1960s, when the Soviet Union moved missiles to Cuba shortly after Fidel Castro came to power.

The Cold War also militarized much of the world and led, for the first time, to the full-time military mobilization of many states, in particular the United States and USSR and their respective allies. Unlike the periods following previous wars, the United States and its allies, as well as the Soviet Union and its allies, were fully mobilized and ready to fight wars on several fronts, in Europe as well as Asia. The U.S. government thus devoted about one-third of its annual expenditures to the military, while the Soviet Union spent an even greater percentage (perhaps half) on its military. The size and vitality of the competing economies thus became a crucial element in the ability of the two superpowers to build and maintain their military arsenals during the Cold War years. More than anything else, the Cold War was a battle of economies. Hence as the U.S. economy developed beyond the "smokestack" industries into advanced computer technologies in the 1980s, the gap between the productivity of the U.S. and Soviet economies grew.[14]

Consumerism versus Productionism

As mentioned above, the Soviet Union had a planned economy in which the central state made the decisions and choices about the allocation of resources.

To that extent, its economy was quite immune from the ups and downs inherent in a capitalist free market economy. That explains a lot about how and why the Soviet Union had been able to industrialize rapidly during the Great Depression when the capitalist economies were shrinking disastrously. After World War II, the Soviet Union also gained access to the resources and productive capacity of the East European countries it dominated.

What kept the Soviet bloc economies growing was the state plan. Although it is arguable whether state-run economies have anything to do with "true" communism, it is true that the communist leaders of the Soviet Union were influenced by Marxist views of human beings. Karl Marx had argued that human beings naturally were productive beings, that their essence was to labor and to enjoy the fruits of their labor. The problem with the capitalist system was not that people had to work, but that they worked for wages and were "alienated" from the product of their labor, which the capitalist expropriated and sold. In the socialist future, Marx envisioned that people would continue to work, but would find self-realization in their labor because it would be theirs, not the capitalist's.

In the Soviet system, people certainly worked, but the fiction was that because the state represented the interests of the working people, work on behalf of the state was work on their own behalf. The Soviet model was a "productionist" one: the more that was produced, the better. The Soviet state plans thus called for significant industry and factories, but most of that industrial production was destined to create additional industry or to support the military. Production, especially of and for heavy industry (e.g., coal, iron, steel, electricity), became its own end. Managers were valued and rewarded on the basis of how much they produced, and measures of production sometimes became skewed so that it didn't matter so much whether the coal that was produced actually reached a power plant but that it had been put on a railroad car. Some railroad managers thus shipped the same coal back and forth to increase the production ratings of their unit. The state plan called for very little investment in consumer goods, although the state did make a commitment to providing minimal housing (in huge apartment blocks), health care, and education.

The Soviets also harnessed science to their system, and invested heavily in scientific education and development of new technology, especially with regard to military applications and space exploration. Thus the Soviets beat the United States to space by launching *Sputnik* in 1957 and sent the first man into earth orbit shortly thereafter, thus spurring the "space race" with the U.S. and President Kennedy's 1960 pledge to put an American on the moon by the end of the decade, a goal reached in 1969.

The Chinese communists after their 1949 victory initially followed the Soviet model of development, and China's first Five Year Plan (1953–1957) achieved annual growth rates of 18 percent and succeeded in establishing foundations for a heavy industry base for the Chinese economy. But China's leader, Mao Zedong, who was wary of the unintended results of the Soviet model, especially the creation of privileged urban elites that began to appear like a new ruling class, sought to find a more egalitarian way to develop. He believed he found a new model based upon the large-scale rural collective (communes) and the full employment of labor through rural industrialization, and in 1958 called for a "Great Leap Forward," proclaiming that China would surpass the industrial output of Great Britain within fifteen years.

That experiment was to turn into a disaster, in part because of three years of bad weather (drought in the north and floods in the south), but mostly because communist leaders became obsessed with reports of higher and higher figures for agricultural production, even when such reports had no basis in reality. The Chinese state thus carted grain out of the villages in the mistaken belief that adequate supplies remained for people to eat. The ensuing three-year famine (1959–1962)—made worse by the natural disasters—killed as many as twenty million people, destroyed the faith of other leaders in Mao's abilities, and raised questions in the minds of Soviet leaders about China's path. When Soviet leader Nikita Khrushchev refused to share nuclear weapon technology with China and Mao publicly criticized the Soviet Union, the Soviets withdrew their advisors and a split in the communist world became apparent for the first time to the Western world. Tensions between the Soviets and the Chinese continued to mount during the 1960s, leading to armed border clashes along the Amur River in 1969.

Despite the differences between the Soviet Union and China over the proper road to socialism and the way to combat the capitalist world, they did share a commitment to increasing economic production. The productionist biases of the Soviet and Chinese models of communism had horrific environmental consequences. In the Soviet Union, the formerly crystal-clear Lake Baikal in Siberia was clouded by industrial pollution; the Aral Sea dried up as nearby cotton fields received all its water; the air around most cities was among the foulest on earth; and in 1986 the nuclear power plant at Chernobyl exploded. Stinking heaps of industrial waste polluted land, air, and water. In China, the "war on nature"[15] led to steel complexes spewing pollutants that covered nearby vegetation with gray soot, rivers ran black with industrial poisons, residents of Beijing bicycled to work in the winter with masks to keep charcoal dust from their lungs, and so much water continues to be taken from the Yellow River for irrigation that it seldom empties into the sea. Perversely, the last twenty years of accelerated growth on the basis of market reform and private enterprise in China, far from improving the situation, has exacerbated it: seven of the world's ten most polluted cities are in China, and the near-term outlook is for environmental degradation to intensify.

Consumerism

As both the acknowledged leader of the postwar capitalist world and its economic powerhouse, the United States was determined not to allow the post–World War II world economy to slide into the overproduction and economic decline that plagued the world after World War I. Not only were reforms of the international trading system necessary to lower tariffs and increase global demand for America's industrial products, but changes to the domestic economy too were needed.

Like the rest of the industrialized world, much early industrialization had provided products to create additional factories and industries. To that extent, industry created more industry, which drew workers into ever-larger cities. Cities and their populations certainly provided the labor for factories, but they also created demand for consumption. Until the post–World War II era, that urban consumer demand mostly had been for the necessities of life— housing, food, and clothing. But a series of post–World War II developments in the United States soon spurred the growth of whole new sectors of the economy to provide consumer goods.[16]

Indeed, the United States had already pioneered the mass production of goods sold primarily to consumers, not to other businesses or factories. Prior to World War I, Henry Ford had invented the assembly line for automobiles, but he also recognized that workers would have to be paid adequate wages to be able to purchase the Model Ts his factories produced if the economy was to be sustainable. The Great Depression and then World War II dampened consumer demand for cars, but the end of the war and the need to convert factories from wartime to peacetime production provided an opportunity for American auto manufacturers. Starting in the late 1940s, U.S. auto production soared, and soon nearly every American family owned a car. But once everyone had a car, demand would slacken, and industrial production of autos would grind to a halt.

To keep demand for cars up, new demand had to be created, and that was done by two means: planned obsolescence and advertising. In the 1950s, cars became obsolete not necessarily because they fell apart, but because the styles changed. And as styles changed, consumers were enticed to want to buy that new car by slick and powerful advertising. Many families became convinced of the need to buy a new car every three years, if they had the resources, or to want to if they didn't.

Easier credit helped the automobile to become a consumer commodity. Credit first became available for purchasing houses. Prior to World War II, mortgages were relatively short (from three to five years) and purchasers had to come up with half of the purchase price before banks would lend the money. That limited the number of people who could afford houses to about 40 percent of the population in 1940. After World War II, changes in banking rules encouraged banks to lower the down payment requirement and to extend the mortgage to twenty years. Two new federal agencies—the Veterans Administration and the Federal Housing Administration—made mortgages even more available by guaranteeing the loan. In a further expansion, credit soon came dispensed via "cards" issued first by department stores to customers, and by the 1960s by firms simply organizing and selling credit (Diners Club, American Express, MasterCard, Visa).

The car and cheap housing combined to create vast swaths of suburbs around cities, the archetype being Los Angeles. With cars there making the commute possible, the dismantling of the "Red Car" trolley system, and the construction of "freeways," Los Angeles–area suburbanites could get to work in the city in the morning and be home by dinner. The postwar building boom created new suburbs where cow pastures or orchards had flourished, and extended new housing tracts around small farming towns.

One other development made the post–World War II consumer revolution possible. Electricity, which had first begun powering factories and lighting cities in the late nineteenth century, extended to urban households in the early twentieth century. Then the various public works projects of the 1930s electrified most of rural America by 1940. When small electrical motors began running all sorts of household products such as refrigerators and washing and sewing machines, whole new industries flourished. With outlets in every house and increasing leisure time, televisions flooded American living rooms, and most households came to have a telephone as well.[17]

The mass consumption culture thus was created in the United States in the 1930s to the 1950s, and came to represent a growing portion of the U.S. economy. By the late twentieth century, two-thirds of the domestic economy was devoted to producing consumer goods; only one-third provided producer goods. That was a reversal of the proportions at the beginning of the century. The postwar growth of the U.S. economy, the engine of the world economy through much of the twentieth century, was largely powered by the consumer revolution. Americans came to equate consumer purchases with "freedom," and to condemn the Soviet Union for its absence. Indeed, one critic argued that in the 1950s the U.S. government required only two things of its citizens: consumption and anti-communism.[18] Among its consequences was the fact that the consumer revolution liberated women from onerous daily tasks, making possible both their greater participation in the worlds of work and politics, and demands for equal treatment.

The consumer society was premised on cheap and available energy—gas to run the car culture and electricity to keep the lights burning and motors running at home. If the nineteenth century had been the age of coal, iron, and the railroad, the twentieth century was the age of oil, steel, and the automobile. Like coal, oil is distributed unevenly around the world, and the United States was fortunate to have significant fields in Texas and southern California. Mexico, Venezuela, Nigeria, and Russia also have deposits, but by far the world's greatest concentration of oil is in the vicinity of the Persian Gulf, notably Saudi Arabia, followed by Iraq and Iran. The automobile created the oil industry, and because U.S. consumption soon exceeded the capacity of its domestic wells, a global transport and financial system arose to move it around the world. By the early 1970s, the United States was importing about half of the oil it needed for domestic consumption. That focused U.S. attention on the Middle East, but it also had deeper consequences: a technological "lock in" to a particular kind of global economy dependent on burning oil. The world is not only dependent on oil and natural gas for energy, but also on the particular social, economic, political, cultural, and military complexes that have arisen to control it.

In the 1950s, the consumer society spread to Britain and Canada, and in the 1960s to France, Italy, other West European societies, Japan, and pockets in Latin American cities, and with it the automobile and even greater demand for oil. By the 1970s, demand for consumer items such as refrigerators and TVs, if not the whole consumer society, spread to communist East Germany and Czechoslovakia as well.

Like the productionism of the Soviet and Chinese models, the consumerism of the West had significant environmental consequences. Not only did refining oil and burning gasoline pollute the air in virtually all major cities in the United States, Europe, and Japan, but extracting the oil and moving it around the world in tankers left spills on land and sea. Making cars also requires huge amounts of energy, creates nearly thirty tons of waste for every ton of car made, and uses charcoal burned from the Amazon rain forest, contributing directly to global warming and deforestation.[19]

Third World Developmentalism

Decolonization and revolution after World War II created several score of new states, especially in Asia and Africa, but some in Latin America as well. Despite the friendliness of these new states to broadly statist and collectivist approaches associated with the Soviet model of socialism, many failed to emulate the Soviet Union, particularly following the Korean and Vietnam Wars, which showed graphically what could happen when the Cold War turned hot. As India's leader Nehru put it, when elephants fight, the grass gets trampled. So in the early 1950s leaders of several of these states, in particular Indonesia, Egypt, Yugoslavia, and India, started a "nonaligned" movement to keep out of the Cold War alliance systems that the United States and the USSR were putting together. In 1949, the United States had created NATO (the North Atlantic Treaty Organization, essentially western Europe and the United States) to confront the Soviets in Europe; the Soviet Union then responded with the Warsaw Pact, creating an economic and security bloc dominated by the Soviet Union. To "contain" the Soviet Union to its south in the Middle East, the United States got the conservative leaders of Iran, Turkey, and Iraq to form CENTO (the Central Treaty Organization); Pakistan, Thailand, and the Philippines constituted the Southeast Asia Treaty Organization (SEATO). In response to these moves by the superpowers, "the nonaligned states" held their first conference in 1955 at Bandung in Indonesia. All those countries plus Latin American states soon became lumped together as "the third world," in contrast to the "first world" of the industrialized capitalist world and the "second world" of the communist states.

Although there were many differences among third world states, they did share some common issues and problems, three of which stand out. First, their economies had been controlled either by their colonial masters or a regional hegemon (e.g., the United States in the case of Latin America), which had kept them largely rural and suppliers of food and raw materials. Even after gaining political independence, their economies remained "dependent." To break that dependency became a goal of "development." Second, because little industrial development and in some instances limited urbanization had occurred, third world states were predominantly peasant societies. Even today with more than twenty years of rapid industrial development behind them, the world's two most populous countries—India and China—remain overwhelmingly rural societies. And third, decolonization and revolution set the stage for the massive post–World War II population explosion in third world countries.

Peasant societies typically have both high birthrates and high death rates (especially for infants). In the biological old regime, infectious disease and limited food supplies carried off as many as half of all children born. Ensuring adequate numbers of children to work the farms and provide brides for other families thus required many births—four to seven live births was not uncommon. Those high birthrates continued after World War II, but the death rates dropped precipitously because the newly independent states, with support from WHO (World Health Organization, a UN organization), made modern drugs (e.g., antibiotics and immunizations) available to rural people. Infant mortality rates fell sharply (by as much as half) and populations exploded, in many countries doubling within thirty years. Increased food supplies sustained those growing populations. As a result, where in 1950 the population of the world was about 2.5 billion, by 1970 it was 4 billion and by 2000 it was 6 billion; most of those additional billions were born and live in third world countries.

That is a compelling fact about the world in the late twentieth century. Consider Mexico and China as examples. With vastly different social, economic, and political systems, the population of each nearly doubled from 1950 to 1980: in Mexico the population increased 125 percent from 29 to 71 million, and in China from about 500 million to 900 million. In each country, the economy would have to have doubled in size as well *just to maintain the 1950 standard of living*. To *improve* the standard of living of its people during that time, each country would have to have an economy that is growing *faster* than the rate of population growth. Just maintaining the growth in the food supply at about 3 percent per year to match the population growth was treading water. No wonder "development" became the catchword for the leaders of nearly all third world countries, or that those countries would come to be called "developing nations."

With growing populations, development first and foremost meant improving agriculture to increase the food supply. On the one hand, new land could be brought under the plow, but much of it was marginal, ecologically fragile land or forested land. Either way, trying to meet food demands by increasing the land under cultivation created environmental problems caused by deforestation and siltation. So to increase food production largely meant improving agricultural yields, and the quickest way to do that is to irrigate and apply synthetic fertilizer. As we saw at the beginning of this chapter, the industrial process for making ammonia-based fertilizer was invented at the beginning of the twentieth century, and served to increase agricultural yields in Europe and the United States in the first half of the century. In the second half, its use spread to the developing world, at least to those areas with farmers well off enough to buy the artificial fertilizer. The combination of synthetic fertilizer with irrigation and the development of new high-yielding seeds in the 1960s came to be known as "the green revolution."

But even successfully implementing a green revolution would keep a third world country agricultural and poor—ever since the Great Depression of the

1930s, food and raw material prices relative to manufactured goods prices have been falling. To put it another way, an agricultural country would have to export increasing amounts of its products simply to buy the same amount of manufactured goods *all the while the population is increasing*. In other words, because of population increases and the relative price weakness of agricultural products, most people in most of the third world got poorer in the second half of the twentieth century. The way out—for some countries at least—was industrialization.

Even in England in the decades around 1800 where industrialization began, a strong, well-organized, and efficient state with capable leaders pursued policies that nurtured industry.[20] Additional examples of strong, interventionist states include Japan and Germany in the late nineteenth century, Soviet Russia under Stalin in the 1930s, and China since 1949. In East Asia, some smaller states too have vigorously pursued industrial policies in the late twentieth century, and all of them have had strong states to direct the process: South Korea, Taiwan, Singapore, and Hong Kong, the "four tigers" of Asia.[21] In Latin America, Brazil, Mexico, and Chile have established significant industrial sectors while maintaining large and poor rural sectors.

In part, those industrializing countries had strong states that took the lead in promoting industrialization, keeping in check demands both of labor for unions and higher wages and of traditionalist religious leaders who felt their visions of the world threatened by the new ways of social organization represented by cities and factories. In addition, from the 1970s on, structural changes in the world economy also provided opportunities that these states could benefit from. In particular, in a world of international trade and competition, improvements in global transportation and communications made it possible for first world manufacturers to relocate plants to lower-wage parts of the world, especially in Asia and Latin America. After the collapse of the Soviet Union in 1991, the former "eastern bloc" also attracted factories from western Europe. Powered largely by the consumer demands in the wealthy countries, Nike shoes manufactured in Vietnam, T-shirts in Thailand, telephones, and a thousand other products from Asia and Latin America filled container ships heading for the ports of Long Beach, New Orleans, or New York and the nearest Wal-Mart.

One part of the third world whose economy relied almost exclusively on the export of a single raw material—oil—succeeded in significantly raising its international market price. Oil-producing countries (mostly in the Middle East, but including Nigeria in Africa and Mexico and Venezuela in Latin America) formed the Organization of Petroleum Exporting Countries, but OPEC had had little success in shoring up the price of oil; in 1970, oil sold for about $2.50 per barrel. But in 1973, in the midst of the second Arab-Israeli war, OPEC announced an embargo on its oil exports to the United States, the main supporter of Israel, and in its aftermath was able to pump up the price of oil to $40 per barrel by 1980. Dollars flowed into the oil-producing Arab sheikdoms, creating fabulously wealthy (if unindustrialized) societies.

Migration

Not only did capital start moving around the world, so too did labor. The world has seen several waves of migration, sometimes sparked by foreign invasions (as with the Mongols in the fourteenth century), or more recently with the rural-to-urban movements in the early stages of industrialization. Some of the largest migrations came from the Old World to the New. Until the nineteenth century, most of that migration was the forced relocation of African slaves to sugar and cotton plantations. But by the middle of the nineteenth century, increasing numbers of eastern and southern Europeans migrated to the United States and Latin America looking for work in factories or farms. From 1690 to 1913, twenty-three million people migrated from the Old World to the Americas. The great westward movement across the United States was accompanied after the Civil War by the migration of freed black Americans from the rural South to industrial northern cities. Around the turn of the twentieth century, Chinese and Japanese migrated to the Americas as well, sparking a racist backlash and exclusion laws. After World War II, much migration in the Americas has been from south to north; by the end of the twentieth century, laborers of Mexican heritage in the United States were sending back some $8 billion a year to relatives in Mexico. Today, one of the largest mass migrations of all history is underway in China where in the past decade up to one hundred million have moved from the countryside to cities, and in the next five years an estimated seventy-five million more will crowd into China's cities.[22]

The (Continuing) Gap

Despite the industrialization of some parts of the former third world, the luck of OPEC states, or the migration of millions of others to richer states, the gap between the richest and poorest parts of the world has not closed in the twentieth century; indeed, it has increased. In 1990, the per capita income of the wealthiest countries was $18,280, or fifty-five times that of the poorest nations. Seen another way, from 1960 to 1995, the ratio of the income of the richest states in the world to the poorest increased from 30:1 to 80:1.[23] What is perhaps even more shocking is that the poorest people constitute *one-half* of the world's population, or some three billion people.[24] Significant numbers of those are the rural poor in the world's two largest countries, China and India, with millions more in Southeast Asia and the Caribbean island nation of Haiti. But the largest proportions are in Africa. (See map 6.1.)

Africa's poverty can be traced to several factors, including slavery, colonialism, postcolonial indebtedness, and civil war. Decolonization left in its wake territorial states where none had existed. The new states constituted organizations that possessed the administrative and military power to extract and control resources, both in the form of taxes and raw materials. To fund "development," rulers of those new states sought loans from the World Bank, the International Monetary Fund, and the African Development Bank, but mostly those loans funded corruption. Controlling the state apparatus thus conferred wealth on leaders, and desire for those outside the government to control wealth by gaining control of the state, mostly by violent means, thereby creating successive military regimes, armed opposition movements, and civil war. Often the contending parties belonged to different ethnic or linguistic groups who had been thrown together into the same state when colonial rule ended. Chronic diseases, in particular malaria and AIDS, sap energies and the ability to work of hundreds of millions in sub-Saharan Africa.[25]

By the 1980s, much of sub-Saharan Africa was so poor that it held little attraction to foreign investors, so little capital flowed into Africa; even Africans sent capital out of Africa for investment elsewhere. As a result, many African states became dependent on even more loans to keep afloat. So now, many African states are burdened by such crushing levels of debt on top of everything else that they have been labeled "Heavily Indebted Poor Countries," or HIPCs. Of the world's forty HIPCs in 1999, thirty-four are in sub-Saharan Africa, four in Latin America, with one each in Asia and the Middle East.[26] The number of extremely poor people in Africa doubled from 1981 to 2001, and despite international goals to reduce African poverty, the poor there are expected to continue to increase to 340 million by 2015.[27]

Perversely, policies of the industrialized world conspire to keep poor nations poor. The United States, Japan, and the European Union all subsidize their farmers and keep high tariffs on exports of their agricultural imports to protect their agricultural sectors. Their farmers are rich and can afford synthetic fertilizer, advanced seeds, and irrigation, all of which increase their agricultural output. Farmers in poor countries are disadvantaged enough, but the high tariffs on agricultural products makes it almost impossible for them to compete in the international market: markets tend to work best for those with money. The demand for lowering rich country tariffs on agricultural products thus comes not from the industrialized world, but from the poor countries—to little response by the industrialized world.[28]

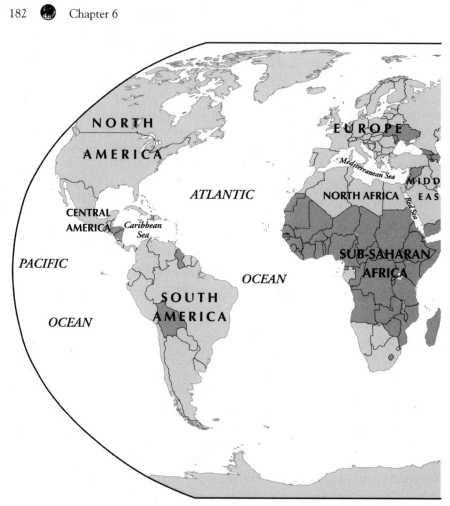

Map 6.1. The World's Poorest Countries by Region (defined as having a gross national income in 2001 of less than US$1,000, as indicated by darker shading)

Source: UNICEF, "The State of the World's Children, 2003" http://www.unicef.org/sowc03/tables/table6.html.

The End of the Cold War

The 1973 "oil shock" caused by the OPEC oil embargo, designed to raise world oil prices, compounded global economic troubles first signaled in 1971 when the United States abandoned the gold standard and allowed the value of the dollar to "float," which it did—down (intentionally, to devalue the dollar and make it possible to pay for oil imports). The U.S. economy was thrown into the horrors of an unexplainable "stag-flation," or economic stagnation *and* inflation, a combination that baffled economists. A stumbling U.S. economy drew the rest of the capitalist world economy down with it.

Crisis? Slump? Recession? Historian Eric Hobsbawm sees 1973 as the end of a post–World War II "golden age" and the beginning of "the crisis decades."[29] Whatever the 1970s might have been called, it was a stressful time for the capitalist world.

But it was worse in the Soviet bloc. Economic growth had been slowing steadily since the 1950s, and it was not possible to supply the needs of the military, industry, *and* consumers. So consumers suffered, with long lines and waits at grocery stores for basic foodstuffs. Equally, if not more importantly, the "productionist" biases of the system were leading to huge environmental problems that could no longer be avoided. By the 1970s, it was clear that reforms were in order, but getting the huge and unwieldy Soviet bureaucracy to change was difficult, if not impossible, because the Communist Party cadre who staffed the state ministries benefited from their positions. Attempts at reform in other East European countries had been met with Soviet tanks (Hungary in 1956; Czechoslovakia in 1968). Keeping their East European satellites in orbit was getting increasingly expensive for the Soviet Union.

In these crisis years for both the United States and the USSR, two political leaders played significant roles in reducing and then ending the Cold War: Ronald Reagan (elected U.S. president in 1980) and Mikhail Gorbachev (selected to lead the USSR in 1985). In part to lift the U.S. economy out of the deep recession he had forced by sharply raising interest rates in 1981–1982, President Reagan vastly increased military spending (and the U.S. deficit as well). Reagan hoped a renewed arms race would spend the Soviets into oblivion, and to a certain extent he was right. When Gorbachev came to power, he recognized the Soviet Union could not keep up with U.S. military spending and the threat of a U.S. space-based missile defense system, and so sought not just nuclear arms control, but arms reduction, through agreements with the United States. He hoped his program of "glasnost," or openness to ideas and culture from the West, would breathe some life into the stale Soviet system, while "perestroika," or readjustment, would reform party, state, and economy. The Cold War was coming to end, but so too was the Soviet system.

Simultaneously, communist power in East European states was being challenged, in part by labor leaders like Lech Walesa in Poland and in part by the Roman Catholic and Eastern Orthodox churches. Deep economic distress, political corruption, and weakening control from Moscow emboldened East European citizens to make public demonstrations that the state police and armies suddenly refused to suppress. From August 1989 to the end of the year, "people's power" peacefully drove communist regimes from power throughout eastern Europe. Only in Romania was a Communist Party boss killed. The end of the Soviet Union too was at hand. As the nominally independent republics that constituted the Soviet Union became truly independent, the Soviet Union ceased to exist, rendering Gorbachev's position as head of that state irrelevant. In August 1991 some leaders of the Soviet military tried to use force to bring the "union" back together, but the leader of the Russian federation, Boris Yeltsin, stood up to them, the coup collapsed, and along with it the Soviet Union. By the end of 1991, the United States was the world's sole remaining superpower.

The immediate effect of the collapse of the Soviet Union was to increase the number of nation–states in the world. Mostly, the process was peaceful.

The former Soviet Union broke up into fifteen new states, the largest of which is Russia, which inherited much of the power, including nuclear power, of the former Soviet Union. In one case—Germany—the process yielded one fewer state when the former communist East Germany reunited with West Germany, which dominated the marriage. Czechoslovakia split into two states (the Czech Republic and Slovakia). In the former Yugoslavia, though, civil war, "ethnic cleansing," atrocities, and war crimes, and ultimately military intervention by NATO and U.S. forces, accompanied its breakup into six smaller states. In all, the number of territorial states increased to 191 members of the United Nations.

The End of History?
The Clash of Civilizations?

The demise of the Soviet Union and the end of the Cold War was greeted with relief, celebration, and caution: relief for those who had fretted that the Cold War might turn hot; celebration by those committed to the imminent global triumph of the values associated with capitalism and democracy; and caution by those wary of the intent and actions of a United States unburdened by the Soviet threat.

Indeed, the Soviet Union had been a defining feature of the twentieth century, from its origins in the wake of World War I as a challenger to capitalism, to its critical role in defeating Hitler in World War II, and then its contest with the United States for global leadership in the Cold War. With the Soviet Union gone and the Cold War ended, some believed that the causes of global conflict—and hence of "history"—had been eliminated for good, and that the future would consist of the largely uneventful and peaceful unfolding of democratic institutions and free market economies.[30]

To be sure, the end of the Soviet bloc meant the end of its form of "productionist" communism. Russia and most of the former Soviet and East European states have since legalized private ownership of property, established the rule of law to protect capital, welcomed foreign investment, and embraced free trade. In short, the part of the world open to capitalism greatly expanded in the 1990s, leading to a great capitalist expansion in the 1990s; as a result, "globalization" entered the consciousness of many in the world.

Market reforms in communist China too added fuel to the expansion of free market capitalism and the intensification of global integration in the 1990s. Under the leadership of the Chinese Communist Party, in the early 1980s China began dismantling its state-owned and controlled economy. That may seem strange, but concerned with spurring economic growth more than anything, China's leader Deng Xiaoping claimed he didn't care whether the cat was white or black, as long as it caught mice.

Beginning with the privatization of agriculture in the early 1980s and moving on to industry in the late 1980s and then opening China to foreign investment, by the early 1990s China's economy was basically capitalist, although the banking system and energy production remain state owned. Attracting foreign capital to build new factories, China's strategy has focused on producing consumer goods for the export market. In the 1990s, so much Chinese-made stuff flooded the world market, especially the United States, that China each month exports about $18 billion more than it imports. As a result, China has a huge accumulation of dollars (about $710 billion) with which it buys U.S. Treasury bonds and now American companies (IBM's personal computer division is the most notable). For the past twenty years, China's economy has been the fastest growing in the world, and at current rates is likely to surpass Germany, Japan, and the United States, by 2035.

Global Free Trade

Although not "the end of history" following the end of the Cold War, the 1990s did in fact see the global spread of markets and capitalism. Indeed, the two major challengers to that way of organizing the world—the Soviet communist model (and its Chinese variant) and the statist German Nazi or Japanese imperial models—have been destroyed, leaving the United States as the sole superpower. Under its auspices, the global economic order has become much more uniform and much more globally integrated. Paradoxically though, no state—no matter how powerful or rich, the United States included—can control the world economy.[31] To be sure, the United States retains a powerful voice in the World Bank and the IMF as well as in the WTO, and the leaders of the industrialized "G8" countries meet every July to coordinate global economic policy.

But the growth of the global market has rendered most governments quite powerless to control their own economic fate, placing all in ruthless competition, which thus far continues to be dominated by the rich, but not without challenges. Policies designed to ensure full employment or to control inflation (or deflation) have been shown to be useless in the face of international competition which puts downward pressure on wages and benefits. In this highly integrated global economic environment, states that refuse to allow greater corporate profits by insisting on large payments of social security, unemployment, or health insurance face the prospect of companies closing their factories and moving elsewhere to more favorable sites. As a result, the costs of industrial production around the world fall, as well as prices for most agricultural and raw materials, not because of the results of "comparative advantage" as predicted by those championing international free trade, but because of declining living standards, not just in the poor, developing world, but in rich countries like the United States as well.[32]

As the linchpin of this global system of states and economies, the United States is in a paradoxical position. On the one hand, it has the most powerful military on earth; on the other, while economically powerful, its share of world production is falling while that of others, in particular China, is rising. It cannot control the world economy, but it feels compelled to use its military power to channel global forces in ways that keep the international system well oiled (literally). Some see the United States as presiding over a new, global empire and "policing" the world for its interests.[33]

The Clash of Civilizations?
Some observers were not so sure that the end of the Cold War had banished conflict from the world, or that new forms of conflict would not emerge. One influential view was that the Cold War had merely served to cover up deeper "civilizational" differences that would emerge once again, in particular pitting "the West" against its historic challenger, Islamic and Chinese civilizations. These theoreticians advised the United States to gear up for a coming "clash of civilizations."[34]

Numerous events since the end of the Cold War seemed to lend credence to that view, especially with regard to the Muslim world. In 1991, Iraq under Saddam Hussein invaded neighboring Kuwait claiming that it was historically part of Iraq. The United States led a coalition of forces first condemning Iraq in the United Nations and then using military force in the first Gulf War of 1991 to push Saddam's forces out of Kuwait. With U.S. forces then stationed in Saudi Arabia as a check on Iraq, Muslims who in the 1980s had fought against Soviet influence in the region turned their ire on the United States, attacking U.S. interests in Saudi Arabia (the Khobar Towers bombing in 1996), U.S. embassies in Kenya and Tanzania in 1998, and the U.S. destroyer *Cole* in Yemen in 2000. The Islamic group that carried out many of these attacks, al Qaeda under the leadership of Osama bin Laden, on September 11, 2001, then launched attacks on the World Trade Center and the Pentagon in which 3,000 U.S. citizens were killed.

The 9/11 attacks, Osama bin Laden's videotaped statement about it, the U.S.-built coalition against global terrorism,[35] and the subsequent military action in Afghanistan and Iraq, all raise the question of whether or not the dynamics of the modern world have changed. The basic problem with both bin

Laden's vision of a revived Islamic empire, and the idea of "the clash of civilizations," is that they ignore the processes and forces that brought the modern world into being. While the gap between the richest and poorest in the world may well fuel resentment in the third world (among Palestinians, Afghans, or Pakistanis, for instance) against the United States, Europe, and Japan, there is little reason to think that bin Laden's dream of an Islamic empire approximating its eighth-century scope has any possibility of being erected over a framework of nation–states. Such an archaic vision of the future has little possibility of coming to fruition in a world of national interests, even in Arabic-speaking lands where most people profess one version or another of Islam. Palestinian hopes for the future, for instance, are rooted in their nationalism and prospects for a sovereign state, not a transnational Islamic empire. Neither is there any evidence that "civilizations" are actors on the global stage (even if they can be demonstrated to exist in the modern world). In fact, the September 11 attacks are best construed not as attacks on Western civilization, but on symbols of the building blocks of the modern world: global capitalism represented by the World Trade Centers, and the nation–state represented by the Pentagon (or more pointedly, by the White House, if it in fact was a target).

To that extent, what appears to be a conflict between "the West" and radical Islam is mostly an accident of history. The United States is engaged in the Islamic world not because of some civilizational crusade against Islam, but because of an accident of geography: most of the world's supply of oil is to be found in the Persian Gulf region, the home of Islam. The United States would be involved in the Middle East regardless of who ruled the region or their religious beliefs. That the Persian Gulf is both the historic home of Islam and the depository of most of the world's supply of oil is coincidental.

Energy, Oil, and War

Human societies require energy. For most of our history on earth, humans have relied on their own and animal muscles, transforming calories from vegetable and animal matter into movement. The great fifteenth-century maritime explorations of Zheng He, Vasco da Gama, and Christopher Columbus began the age of sail, with humans capturing power generated by wind. The Industrial Revolution greatly expanded the sources of energy by tapping coal, and in the twentieth century other fossil fuels, in particular oil, have increased energy output and the mobility of energy-generating machines such as automobiles and airplanes. Each of those ways of generating and using energy gives rise to technologies, social and economic relationships, and political interests that lock societies into those particular regimes.

Societies which can mobilize sources of energy for industry, consumption, and armies are strong and powerful, and use that power to ensure flows of energy from other parts of the world to themselves. Such power, like the deposits of coal, oil, and natural gas, is distributed unevenly in the world, accentuating global differences in wealth and poverty: today, the consumer societies, with about 20 percent of the world's population, use about two-thirds of all the energy produced, nearly all of which comes from fossil fuels.

Additionally, the rapid development of China and India, including the advent of high-consuming "middle classes," has increased their demand for, and consumption of, oil, leading one analyst to see a "frenzied search" and "intensifying global struggle for energy" leading to competition and potential conflict among China, India, the United States, and Japan. Increased global demand for limited supplies of oil certainly has led to rapid increases in the price of oil; whether it will lead to increased production or armed conflict remains to be seen, although the United States has begun talking about "having a strategic plan for dealing with the problem."[36] Whether "strategic" means simply "long-term" or "military" remains to be seen. But the global quest for oil certainly is neither the "end of history" nor can it be understood as the "clash of civilizations."

The Great Departure[37]

The dependence of the modern world on fossil fuels is one reason a leading historian has argued that the twentieth century represents a major break with the past and the beginning of a vast, uncontrolled, and unprecedented experiment—a gamble that the fossil-fuel-consuming, twentieth-century way of organizing the globe will not undermine the ecological bases for life on earth.[38] Twentieth-century American consumerism, Soviet productionism, and third world developmentalism, phenomena that have reverberated globally and shaped all societies in varying degrees, have placed a premium on industrialized economic growth, collectively creating an "anthroposphere" of such size and power as to rival, replace, and rechannel the natural processes of the biosphere. By the end of the twentieth century, humans already were taking 40 percent of the product of the natural process of photosynthesis.[39]

In very rough terms, the size of the global economy at the beginning of the Industrial Revolution in 1800 was three times larger than it had been three hundred years earlier in 1500. Since then, economic growth has accelerated, tripling from 1800 to 1900. During the twentieth century, the world economy has become fourteen times as large as it was in 1900, with most of that growth coming since the end of World War II.

Economic growth is a rough indicator of our species' relationship with the environment because virtually anything that counts as "economic" results from a transformation of nature. Mining, manufacturing, and farming, all are processes that change some part of nature into something usable or consumable by humans. The more economic development we have, the more we change nature. After World War II, consumerism, productionism, and developmentalism combined to push even more economic growth. The pursuit of economic development has dramatically altered not only global power relations but also the environment and global ecological processes. According to the Millennium Ecosystem Assessment, "over the past fifty years, humans have changed ecosystems more rapidly and extensively than in any comparable period of time in human history, largely to meet growing demands for food, fresh water, timber, fiber, and fuel. This has resulted in a substantial and largely irreversible loss in the diversity of life on earth."[40]

Nitrogen fertilizer, first manufactured in 1913 as a result of the Haber-Bosch process, now puts as much nitrogen into the environment as all global natural processes. By 1950, 3.6 million tons (Mt) of nitrogen fertilizer were used, mostly in advanced industrial countries. By 1980, that had increased to 60 million tons, and by 2000, to 80 million tons, with partial diversification to more countries beyond the industrial core. Significantly, 70 percent of that use is in just three countries: China (25 Mt), the United States (11 Mt), and India (10 Mt). By contrast, almost no synthetic nitrogen fertilizer is used in sub-Saharan Africa, the poorest place on earth.[41] There and elsewhere, increasingly poor farmers with no money for artificial fertilizer, irrigation, or high-yielding seeds remain trapped within the biological old regime, and increasingly use up natural resources to sustain their lives, further impoverishing their environment. Poor rural populations burn forests, grasses, or anything else for cooking, heating, and lighting—survival—that further impoverishes both their environment and them. It's not just industry that transforms the global environment, but rural poverty too.

Some suggest that new technologies such as biotechnology, computers, and the Internet might foster the needed economic growth that will break the grip of poverty, touting for example the liberating effects of the $100 computer, while reducing impact on the environment. Manufacturing computer chips or manipulating genes uses very little raw material compared, say, to locomotives or ships. But without electricity, the computer and biotechnology worlds could not exist. Indeed, the world's energy use in the twentieth century parallels the century's economic and population explosions with sixteen times as much energy being used in 1990 as in 1900. One analyst calculates that humans used more energy in the twentieth century than in all the 10,000 years from the agricultural revolution to the Industrial Revolution. Coal and steam fired early industry, but the twentieth century is the oil era, fueling both the spread of the automobile and power plants for electricity. Much electricity is generated by coal, and the combination of burning oil, gas, and coal—all nonrenewable "fossil fuels"—has led to global warming and the poisoning of air and water.

Global warming is caused by the release of "greenhouse gases" into the atmosphere (air pollution), notably carbon dioxide from burning coal and gas, but also sulfur dioxide. Methane from irrigated rice paddies and animal herds too contributes to global warming. The effects of rising average global temperatures to date have been felt mostly in polar or cold regions with melting glaciers and thawing permafrost. A greater danger, though, is that it is not known how much more global temperatures will rise and whether the rise at some point will have a sudden, unexpected, and catastrophic consequence. Rising ocean levels are already causing problems in Alaska, low-lying Pacific Islands, and Bangladesh, and threatening coastal areas everywhere. But rising ocean temperatures might precipitate even greater changes in ocean currents, depriving Europe, for example, of the warming effects of the Gulf Stream/ North American current.

Human activity in pursuit of economic growth and development has affected other natural processes as well. Besides disrupting the nitrogen cycle and global climate, humans have ripped up vast swaths of the earth's surface for the coal, copper, gold, bauxite, and other natural resources that lie beneath. Acid rain sterilizes lakes in the eastern United States, northeast China, and Japan. Lakes and oceans fill with nitrogen fertilizer runoff and bloom with algae, sucking oxygen from the water and creating dead zones. Additionally, expanding consumption of beef has increased the global cattle population to two billion eating, drinking, defecating, and gas-emitting animals that also contribute to global warming.

Logging and farmland expansion denude vast rain forests in Africa, Asia, and Latin America, altering local climates and driving thousands of species to extinction. To be sure, people have been burning or cutting down trees since the end of the last Ice Age and the beginning of agriculture 10,000 years ago. Advanced biological old-regime economies in China and England, for instance, had effectively deforested their lands by 1800. The pace quickened in the nineteenth century with the felling of North American, Russian, and Baltic forests, before slowing with war and the Great Depression in the first half of the twentieth century. But the fifty years after the end of World War

II have seen the most ferocious attacks on forests in human history: *half* of all deforestation in human history has occurred in the last half century, prompting historian Michael Williams to call it "The Great Onslaught."[42] Nearly all of that recent deforestation has been in the tropical zones of Africa, Asia, and Latin America, where most of the world's poor live. With the loss of thousands of animal and plant species, natural ecosystems are being radically simplified and hence less diverse and resilient.

Will it be our fate to poison our world with the unwanted pollutants of the industrial world? Will "island earth" go the way of the Easter Islanders who used up their natural resources, saw their population decline and descend into warring, cannibalistic groups huddling in cold, dark caves?[43] If the world we live in is contingent upon what has happened in the past and the choices that people made, then so too is the future contingent upon choices and actions we make today. To be sure, the two major problems the world faces are daunting: on the one hand, providing a decent standard of living for a rapidly growing world population; and on the other halting and then reversing the degradation of the environment caused by twentieth-century models of industrial development. Is the modern world, structured as it is, capable of addressing these global problems? Maybe.[44]

The fundamental problem is the prevailing view of the relationship of global economic growth to the environment. Economic activity, which is essential for humans to exist, has always been dependent upon and hence part of natural processes. The major difference between the twentieth century and all preceding human history is that the human impact on the environment was so small or so local that modern economic theorists (beginning in the eighteenth century) developed models of how the world works that do not account for the uses or services to humans of the natural environment. In the twentieth century, and to this very day, advocates of global free trade, developmentalism, consumerism, and (until recently) productionism assume that the global economic system is separate from the global ecological system.[45] That may turn out to be a colossal mistake. The biosphere and the anthroposphere became inextricably linked during the twentieth century, with human activity increasingly driving biospheric changes in directions that can neither be known nor predicted. Albert Einstein once famously said that God does not play dice with the universe; apparently the same cannot be said about humans and the earth.

Conclusion

The twentieth century thus marks a major departure from the past in regard to the relationship of human beings to the global environment, and, relatedly, in terms of the number of humans on the planet. Neither of those were intended outcomes of the modern world, and we may well wonder whether the constituent elements of that system—sovereign territorial states linked globally by free markets to sustain industrial growth—are capable of addressing the global issues that they raise for all of us. Perhaps a world government would be able to focus adequately on these global issues, but given the jealously guarded system of sovereign states, that seems unlikely.

The twentieth century also marks a departure in the shift of the locus of global wealth and power from the West European core to the United States. Some have argued that the twentieth century thus was the American Century. To be sure, the United States had the largest and most productive economy at the beginning of the century, although few understood it at the time. But it took the profound thirty-year crisis of two world wars and the Great Depression to prepare the United States to step up to the leadership position in the capitalist world system. And when it finally did after World War II, challenging it was the Soviet Union, which like the United States had devoted massive resources to defeating Nazi Germany. Indeed, one could make the claim that the twentieth century was as much a Soviet Century as an American one, for without the Soviet Union, there is little about the course of the twentieth century that would have been the same.[46]

Moreover, labeling the twentieth century an American Century obscures the rise of East Asia over the past forty years. Japan's economic resurgence after World War II; the Chinese communist revolution, which led first to a powerful military and now an industrial economy; the industrialization of the "Four Tigers"—Taiwan, South Korea, Singapore, and Hong Kong (and the democratization of the first three); coupled with changes in India and Southeast Asia, have shifted the global center of both economic production and population back toward Asia. After the United States, Japan already has the second largest economy in the world, and China is projected to surpass both by 2035.

Indeed, the rise of China's political, military, and economic power constitutes a challenge to U.S. interests and influence in Asia, and there seems to be little doubt that China intends to assert its historic weight in East Asia. That may make Japan, Korea, and Vietnam uneasy and prompt them to seek close ties to the United States, bringing rising tensions between the United States and China. But in contrast to the Cold War between the Soviet Union and the United States, where there was little trade between the two, each year China sells $100 billion worth of manufactured goods to the United States, making it a major trade partner. And while the United States sells much less to China, it does invest, and vast, cheap Chinese imports help to hold down the cost of living in the United States.

The world may well be witnessing the beginning of an "Asian Century," although whether it will be one with Chinese or Indian characteristics remains to be seen. China is following the tried-and-true method of a strong state driving rapid economic growth for global strategic purposes and has little interest or desire in taking its citizens' views of the process into account. In India, on the other hand, a democratic state has opened its economy to global forces, and because it is democratic, the Indian government does listen to the voices of its rural population. As a result, there are now more well-to-do among India's 650,000 villages, and less pressure to migrate to the cities. So far, India's economic growth has been slower than China's, but its democratic institutions may make change deeper, better supported, and more widespread than is the case in China where an authoritarian system suppresses the voices of the rural poor.

To the extent that the twenty-first century witnesses the "rise of Asia," world history may well revert to the previous pattern of the dominance of Asia from 1400 to 1800. But will it be the same Asia, appearing pentimento-like through the layers obscured by European and American dominance of the last two centuries? No. For just as the re-creation of an Islamic caliphate is not possible, so too will the world not see Asian empires based on productive agricultures. The world has so changed that the secrets of wealth and power are unlocked by powerful states directing industrial economies. Whether China, India, and the rest of the developing world will be able to pursue the oil-dependent, car and consumer culture of the United States, though, is open to question given the increasing scarcity of raw materials, in particular oil, to sustain that economic model.

In the long run, then, the question of who will "own" the twenty-first century may well shrink in importance as our changed relationship to the earth's environment rises in significance. For it was not just the industrialization of the capitalist world that contributed to that "Great Departure," but so did the productionism of the communist model, the developmentalism of India and China, and the rural impoverishment of much of the third world. Intentionally or not, we are all exhausting the earth.[47]

Notes

1. This argument is developed in John M. Hobson, *The Eastern Origins of Western Civilization* (Cambridge: Cambridge University Press, 2004), chap 10.

2. Vaclav Smil calls this period "the Age of Synergy." See *Creating the Twentieth Century: Technical Innovations of 1867–1914 and Their Lasting Impact* (Oxford: Oxford University Press, 2005).

3. Eric Hobsbawm, *The Age of Extremes: A History of the World, 1914–1991* (New York: Pantheon), 12.

4. Unless otherwise noted, this extraordinary story of the importance of nitrogen and its synthesis as ammonia is based upon Vaclav Smil, *Enriching the Earth: Fritz Haber, Carl Bosch, and the Transformation of World Food Production* (Cambridge, Mass.: The MIT Press, 2001).

5. In 1995, Timothy McVeigh blew up the Murrah Federal Office Building in Oklahoma City with a bomb composed of nitrogen fertilizer and kerosene.

6. If, as demographers predict, the world's population will peak at about nine billion around the year 2050, the twentieth century will have seen the largest population increase ever, making it unique in world history. See William McNeill, "Demography and Urbanization," in Michael Howard and Wm. Roger Louis, eds., *The Oxford History of the Twentieth Century* (New York: Oxford University Press, 1998), 10–21. The reason demographers expect that population will stabilize is because as societies urbanize and industrialize, their populations experience a "demographic transition" where families become smaller with children about the number (2.1) needed to replace their parents.

7. For the first three years, World War I "was fought predominantly with agrarian resources." C. A. Bayly, *The Birth of the Modern World 1780–1914* (Oxford: Blackwell, 2004), 455.

8. Hobsbawm, *The Age of Extremes*, 97–98.

9. Japan's "Greater East Asia Co-Prosperity Sphere" would have driven Europeans and Americans from Asia, and replaced them with Japan as the industrialized core of a system that still had the rest of Asia providing food and raw materials to them.

10. At the time of partition in 1947, Pakistan was divided into two parts, east and west. In 1971, following decades of neglect by west Pakistan, where the government was located, rebellion in the east resulted in the creation of the new country of Bangladesh.

11. The phrase is from Eric Hobsbawm, *The Age of Empire, 1875–1914* (New York: Pantheon, 1987).

12. Japan fostered industrial development in its colonies in Korea and Manchuria, in part because of the ready accessibility of coal, iron ore, and petroleum there, and in part because those colonies were physically close and relatively easier to administer directly. Taiwan, though, taken from China in 1895, was designed to be a rice- and sugar-producing agricultural colony.

13. The concept of the "nuclear winter" and human extinction is explored in Jonathan Schell, *The Fate of the Earth* (New York: Knopf, 1982).

14. As Paul Kennedy makes clear in *The Rise and Fall of the Great Powers: Economic Change and Military Conflict from 1500 to 2000* (New York: Random House, 1987), that relationship between economic productivity and military power has been true for the past five hundred years.

15. The term is from Judith Shapiro, *Mao's War on Nature: Politics and the Environment in Revolutionary China* (New York: Cambridge University Press, 2001).

16. Much of the following is based on David Reynolds, *One World Divisible: A Global History since 1945* (New York: Norton, 2000), chap. 5.

17. See Smil, *Creating the Twentieth Century*, chap. 2 "The Age of Electricity."

18. Herbert Marcuse, *One-Dimensional Man* (Boston: Beacon, 1964).

19. For an extended discussion of autos, oil, and the environment, see J. R. McNeill, *Something New under the Sun: An Environmental History of the Twentieth-Century World* (New York: Norton, 2000), esp. chap. 7.

20. See Hobson, *The Eastern Origins of Western Civilization*, chap. 11.

21. The late twentieth-century "rise of East Asia" is as much a regional phenomenon involving China and Japan as specific to any one of those states. See Giovanni Arrighi, Mark Selden, and Takeshi Hamashita, eds., *The Resurgence of East Asia: 500, 150 and 50 Year Perspectives* (New York: Routledge, 2003), especially the introduction and chap. 7.

22. *International Herald Tribune*, October 19, 2005: 1, 10.

23. Peter Jay, *The Wealth of Man* (New York: Public Affairs, 2000), 246–247.

24. Hobsbawm, *The Age of Extremes*, 363.

25. In 2001 in much of sub-Saharan Africa, 50 percent or more of children did not get a primary school education; 100 or more infants per 1000 died; and half of the population subsisted on less than $1 per day. Those statistics mark life for millions in India, Pakistan, Southeast Asia, and China as well. What that means for daily life is illustrated by a recent story from rural China where hundreds of millions lack health insurance or access to government-supported clinics. Unable to pay the 25–60 cents to a rural clinic for care, people suffer at home and die: "Every year hundreds of millions of rural Chinese . . . face the clash between health and poverty, knowing that if they treat their illnesses they will lack the money needed for marriage, education and, sometimes, food." For the story, see "Wealth Grows, but Health Care Withers in China," *New York Times*, January 14, 2006: A1, A7.

26. See http://www.worldbank/hipc.

27. In 2001, the international community adopted the "Millennium Development Goals," one of which is to halve the number of extremely poor people (defined as those making less than US$1 per day) by 2015. The World Bank is skeptical about sub-Saharan Africa achieving those goals. See http://ddp-ext.worldbank.org/ext/MDG/regions.do.

28. See "Promises, Promises," a *New York Times* editorial, August 22, 2005: A16.

29. Hobsbawm, *The Age of Extremes*.

30. Francis Fukuyama, *The End of History and the Last Man* (New York: Free Press, 1992).

31. This point about the modern world system was first made most powerfully and elegantly by Immanuel Wallerstein in his groundbreaking work, *The Modern World-System: Capitalist Agriculture and the Origins of the European World-Economy in the Sixteenth Century* (New York: Academic Press, 1974).

32. See Herman E. Daly, "The Perils of Free Trade," *Scientific American* (November 1993): 50–57.

33. Michael Hardt and Antonio Negri, *Empire* (Cambridge, Mass.: Harvard University Press, 2000).

34. Samuel Huntington, *The Clash of Civilizations and the Remaking of the Twentieth-Century World Order* (New York: Norton, 2000).

35. But as Jamal Nassar warns, the label "terrorist" is very slippery: it is applied by states to those who attack them, while to the dispossessed seeking their own sovereignty they may well be seen as freedom fighters. Nassar examines the questions of how and why the

latest round in the "war on terror" has become intertwined with the processes of global-ization and radicalized Islam in *Globalization and Terrorism: The Migration of Dreams and Nightmares* (Lanham, Md.: Rowman & Littlefield, 2005).

36. U.S. Secretary of State Condoleezza Rice, quoted in Michael T. Klare, "The Inten-sifying Global Struggle for Energy," *JapanFocus*, May 8, 2005 (http://japanfocus.org/article .asp?id=275).

37. This phrase follows in the tradition of Karl Polanyi's *Great Transformation: The Po-litical and Economic Origins of Our Time* (Boston: Beacon Press, 1957) and Kenneth Pomer-anz's *Great Divergence: China, Europe, and the Making of the Modern World Economy* (Princeton: Princeton University Press, 2000).

38. Most of this section is based on McNeill, *Something New under the Sun.*

39. Daly, "The Perils of Free Trade," 56.

40. Millennium Ecosystem Assessment, *Ecosystems and Human Well-Being: Synthesis* (Washington, D.C.: Island Press, 2005), 1.

41. Smil, *Enriching the Earth*, chap. 7.

42. Michael Williams, *Deforesting the Earth: From Prehistory to Global Crisis* (Chicago: The University of Chicago Press, 2003), 420.

43. The Easter Island warning is cited in Clive Ponting, *A Green History of the World: The Environment and the Collapse of Great Civilizations* (New York: Penguin, 1993) and David Christian, *The Maps of Time: An Introduction to Big History* (Berkeley: University of California Press, 2004). Jared Diamond explores the fate of civilizations in *Collapse: How Societies Choose to Fail or Succeed* (New York: Viking, 2005).

44. These are very complicated questions, and the only thing we know for sure about the future is that it cannot be predicted. Nonetheless, social and natural scientists have modeled four different scenarios to try to examine likely stresses and outcomes. For a dis-cussion, see Bert de Vries and Johan Goudsblom, eds., *Mappae Mundi: Humans and Their Habitats in a Long-Term Socio-Ecological Perspective: Myths, Maps, and Models*, second up-dated printing (Amsterdam: Amsterdam University Press, 2003), chap. 8.

45. See Herman E. Daly and John B. Cobb Jr., *For the Common Good: Redirecting the Economy toward Community, the Environment, and a Sustainable Future*, 2d ed. (Boston: Beacon, 1994), esp. chap. 11.

46. This argument is made by Hobsbawm in *The Age of Extremes.*

47. This phrase was first used by Peter Purdue with respect to late imperial China; see *Exhausting the Earth: State and Peasant in Hunan, 1500–1850* (Cambridge, Mass.: Harvard University Press, 1987.

CONCLUSION

Changes and Continuities

This brief inquiry into the history of the modern world has attempted to synthesize the results of recent historical research into a global narrative. Unlike most world histories, which either chart the rise and fall of various high civilizations without exploring what connected them, or use Eurocentric glue to hold the pieces together, I have attempted to develop a global storyline that shows how the modern world came to be while criticizing Eurocentric explanations. At times that may have seemed a paradoxical task, since I began by defining the modern world as industrial capitalism coupled with the system of nation–states and divided by a gap between the "haves" and the "have-nots," all of which highlight European or Western strengths and achievements.

What emerges as central to understanding the emergence of the modern world is a global and ecological point of view which is essential for understanding what happened in and to the various parts of the world. In fact, *interactions* among various parts of the world account for most of the story of the making of the modern world, not the cultural achievements of any one part. Indeed, those achievements are not understandable *except* in a global context. The whole—in this case the world and its modern history—thus is greater than the sum of its parts.

However influential Europeans and Americans may have been in the making of this modern world, they did not make it themselves, and the West certainly did not "rise" over other parts of the world because of cultural (or racial) superiority. As this book has shown, Western superiority or preeminence has hardly been evident throughout much of human history over the past millennium, and the final decades of the twentieth century have witnessed the resurgence of Asia as a powerful challenge to European and American hegemony. Moreover, the history of the twentieth century demonstrates the roles that Asians, Africans, and Latin Americans have played in shaping their own histories through revolutions, independence movements, and economic development.

A strong strain of post–World War II American political thought, reinforced by scholars who paint a picture of American "exceptionalism" in world history, sees the United States as having attained a uniquely special place atop the global hierarchy. This dominant position, which actually materialized only in the specific circumstances of the thirty-year crisis of 1914–1945 and particularly since the end of the Cold War in the 1990s, is held by these proponents to be the end result of 2,000-plus years of Western development starting with Greek democracy. The United States is, in this view, not merely the inheritor of the mantle of democracy and freedom from the British, but its highest fulfillment. Such a view is the latest incarnation of a Eurocentrism that is not only blind to the actual ebbs and flows of world history, but now also informs the thinking of some American policymakers who attempt to impose those values on the rest of the world, by force if necessary.

The Story Summarized

In this book's narrative, until very recently (about 1800 or so) nearly all of the world's inhabitants lived within the constraints of the biological old regime. Within that world, agrarian empires proved to be successful states, developing high standards of living for their people, high cultural achievements, and substantial governmental power. The most highly developed states of the Old World—in China, India, western Europe, Japan, possibly parts of Southeast Asia—were broadly comparable, with well-developed market systems, institutional arrangements enabling people to squeeze the most from economies rooted in agriculture, and productive industries, albeit ones still largely dependent on capturing annual flows of energy from the sun.

The ability of one part of the world—in this case western Europeans, led by the British—to escape from the limitations of the biological old regime by tapping stored sources of energy (coal and then oil) was contingent and came about as a result of a global conjuncture. The first contingency was China deciding in the early 1400s to abandon its naval domination of the Indian Ocean, the crossroads where the wealth of Asia was traded for raw materials (including silver and gold) from the less developed parts of the world, and to remonetize its economy using silver, creating a new, global demand for silver that would soon be met by New World supplies. For four centuries (from 1400 to 1800), the commercial and industrial prowess of China and India, both made possible by highly productive agricultures, enabled Asians to dominate the world economy and to attract the attention, and resources, of those elsewhere in the world who wished to gain access to the riches of Asia. The demand for silver in Asian economies thus set into motion several other world-changing processes.

The second significant contingency in our story thus was the discovery of the New World and its stores of silver, the subsequent decimation of the native population by diseases carried by the conquerors, and the construction of an African slave-based plantation economy subordinate to European interests. Third, the failure of the Spanish in the sixteenth century to impose an empire upon the rest of Europe led to a system of competing European states locked in almost constant warfare, thus promoting rapid military innovation.

In the eighteenth century, a vast conjuncture of forces enabled Britain—a small island off the western-most edge of Eurasia—to begin breaking away from the pack. Wars between France and Britain, culminating in the Seven Years' War (1756–1763), paved the way for Britain's dominance in Europe, North America, and India. Almost simultaneously, Mughal power in India began to crumble, largely for domestic reasons, providing an opening for British adventurers to gain a colonial toehold. China, though, was still too powerful for the British, and so could define the terms of British participation in their East Asian world until the combination of opium from Britain's colony in India and their steam-powered gunboats led to China's defeat in the Opium War (1839–1842). Coupled with internal difficulties of their own, the Opium War inaugurated a century of Western and Japanese aggression against China.

In retrospect, the tipping of the scales against China would not have happened had Britain not begun to industrialize and to apply the fruits of industry to its military. Moreover, industrialization there was contingent upon Britain having a peculiar kind of periphery in the New World, one that had the need for Britain's manufactured goods, especially cotton textiles, to clothe African slaves. Britain also had the good fortune to be sitting on conveniently located coal deposits after it had deforested a good bit of the island to heat London. Thus, where Asia and Latin America by 1800 remained hemmed in by the limits imposed by the biological old regime, Britain first, then other European countries (fearing the consequences of losing ground to Britain), began to escape by applying sources of stored energy (first coal and then oil) to the production process.

The resulting transformations changed economic dynamics, resulting in the boom and bust of the business cycle, growing divisions between new social classes and between the people and the state, growing competition among European states for colonies that would be captive markets and guaranteed sources of raw materials, and the scrambles for control of Africa and for concessions in China. Unfortunately for those parts of the world working within the constraints of the biological old regime, the most powerful el Niño conditions in five hundred years developed in the last quarter of the nineteenth century, killing tens of millions in drought-induced famines, and driving much of Asia, Africa, and Latin America further into conditions we now call the third world.

As historian R. Bin Wong argued in *China Transformed*, in the nineteenth century two distinct ways of organizing human societies came to confront each other. One—agrarian empires with highly productive agricultural economies—had been the most successful for nearly a thousand years, as China and India demonstrated. Other peoples too (e.g., Aztecs and Incas in the Americas) had found ways to maximize the benefits of the biological old regime, but because their energy sources ultimately were based on tapping annual solar flows, the power of those states, the size of their populations, and the productivity of their economies were limited. The other, newer way—nation–states with economies harnessing energy from fossil fuels to dramatically increase industrial output and military power—developed first in western Europe during the nineteenth century. That new political economy gave Europeans the power to dominate 85 percent of the world by 1900.

Dominance was not achieved because Europeans had a superior culture than others, despite attempts to contrast the "civilized" heirs of ancient Greece with the "barbarians" of Asia and Africa. The idea of cultural superiority is nonsense. Rather, "the rise of the West," if we must use that term, has more to do with the Great Dying, sugar, African slavery, pilfered silver, opium, guns, and war.

With those advantages, at the beginning of the twentieth century Europeans ruled or controlled much of Asia, Africa, and Latin America. They were not so much interested in changing those agrarian regimes as tapping them for the natural resources that could not be manufactured but were necessary for modern industry. The lifting of third world countries from the limitations imposed by the biological old regime thus needed to await Asians, Africans, and Latin Americans creating and ruling their own states. How and why that happened through anti-imperialist independence movements and social revolution— that is, movements centered not in Europe but in Asia, Africa, and Latin America—is an integral part of the story of the twentieth century.

Indeed, much about the modern world changed in the twentieth century. Two world wars and the Great Depression destroyed the empires and power of European and Japanese states, opening the way for the rise of the United States and the Soviet Union, and the Cold War between them. Simultaneously, the independence of the former colonies coupled with revolution in China gave those countries a stake in industrial development, leading to a massive increase in humanity's productive power in the second half of the twentieth century. That explosion in economic activity enlarged the size of the human footprint on the earth, in many cases exceeding natural biospheric processes and casting a dark shadow over the future of development. That is the "Great Departure" from past patterns. Not so with globalization.

Globalization

Anti-globalization protests over the past decade against the World Bank, the International Monetary Fund, the World Trade Organization, and the meetings of the G8 leaders (such as that which opens this book), may make it appear as if globalization is a recent phenomenon. But if globalization is understood as the process by which markets, politics, values, and environmental change are integrated across the globe, then globalization has a long history. Even prior to the Portuguese circumnavigation of the globe in 1521, Asians had created such dynamic economies that goods and ideas flowed around the Indian Ocean, linking China, Japan, and the "spice islands" with India, the Middle East, East Africa, and even northern Europe. Before that, in the thirteenth century the Mongols had created the largest land-based empire the world had ever seen. Among its consequences was enabling the plague to travel across Eurasia from China to Europe, with great devastation to human populations. And "dar al-Islam," or "the abode of Islam," was a cultural and linguistic ecumene that by the thirteenth century stretched from Spain and Tunis in the west to Aceh in what is now Indonesia in the east.

Despite the size and significance of those Asian worlds, they did not encompass the entire globe. So, if the birth of globalization has a date, it is not 1492, but 1571 when Spain established its colony of Manila in the Philippine Islands. Even though the globe had been circumnavigated earlier, and people, plants, and pathogens had begun their travels around the world on those wooden sailing ships, there was not yet the regular exchange of commodities around the world. Manila made that possible for the first time, with New World silver traveling not just across the Atlantic, but loaded onto Spanish galleons in Acapulco and heading west across the Pacific. From 1571 on, global flows of silver found their way to Asia, and Asian goods streamed around the world to Europe and the Americas. Driving that first wave of globalization was the voracious appetite of China for silver.

The second wave of globalization began in the nineteenth century. First the British and then other West European states, the United States, and

Japan, harnessed the fruits of industrialization to military power, and turned that new power to colonizing Asians and Africans. Imperialists established colonies, semicolonies, and dependencies to provide secure markets for their industrial products and sources of supply for industrial raw materials such as rubber, gold, oil, and bauxite, among others. Even greater amounts of goods and ideas flowed around the world during the second globalization, including nationalism, which energized Asian dreams of independence from European colonial domination.

This second wave of globalization, often called the "New Imperialism" of the nineteenth century, did not lead immediately to a new phase of globalization, but rather to its breakdown. The First World War and then the Great Depression divided the world into more or less autonomous "autarkic" zones of imperial powers. These powers were trying to resolve the crisis of the depression on their own terms, yet came into increasing conflict with each other, leading to the Second World War. The United States and the Soviet Union emerged from that war as global "superpowers," each with its own vision for structuring the world, leading to a third wave of globalization in a polarized world. Both the United States and the USSR created institutions designed to further their global objectives of creating, respectively, a capitalist or a socialist world. They shared, however, participation in the institution—the United Nations—founded at the end of World War II to prevent conflicts between states from escalating into global conflagrations. Decolonization created nearly a hundred new nation–states, so that by the 1970s nearly every human being on earth lived within the boundaries of states that claimed to rule over them, if not their active allegiance.

The fourth and latest wave of globalization began with the demise of the Soviet Union in 1991, and has proceeded since then largely under U.S. auspices. With the Soviet Union and European socialism gone and China abandoning the socialist model, the goals pursued by the United States—global free trade, privatization of state-owned enterprises (e.g., land and factories) in all states, and more open ("transparent") political systems—have more closely integrated the former socialist world and the third world into the rhythms and needs of the global capitalist world. In this latest round, globalization means the expansion—led by the United States—of capitalism into every nook and cranny of the world. Many observers see the United States, while powerful, in decline and perhaps China and/or India best poised to reap the fruits of the current wave.

If there is to be a fifth wave, it will probably be generated in Asia, just as the first was. If present trends continue, within thirty years China will have the largest (though not the richest) economy on earth, surpassing in size the United States, Japan, and Germany. India is rapidly developing as well, and the successes of the "four tigers" of East Asia (South Korea, Taiwan, Hong Kong, and Singapore) have been touted for twenty years. The combination of China, Japan, and Southeast Asia, already a fairly well-defined economic unit with massive demands for raw materials (including oil) and exceptionally productive industries, with India could reorient the economic weight of the world back to Asia, just as it had been in the period from 1400 to 1800.

Into the Future

In the 1950s, a Chinese communist leader was asked what he thought of the French Revolution of 1789. "It's too soon to tell," Premier Zhou Enlai replied. What he meant was that processes set in motion by that event were still working themselves out, so its history was not yet complete. That being the case, Zhou thought it premature to pass judgment.

Similarly, we were born into the modern world—a world with about six hundred years of history, but one that has not yet run its course. To that extent we are all insiders with insiders' advantages, but also the disadvantage of not being able to see ourselves and our times as clearly as someone two hundred or three hundred years in the future might be able to. Nonetheless, a long-term historical perspective does enable us to draw some meaningful conclusions about the past and present and to make educated forecasts for the future.

Agrarian empires and the limitations of the biological old regime are gone, probably forever. To be sure, the world still depends on agriculture to feed its human population, but agricultural yields have been dramatically increased by the liberal application of chemical fertilizers produced in factories using electricity generated from fossil fuels. The population of the earth thus continues to climb. Having reached the one billion mark in the early 1820s, the world's population doubled to two billion over the next one hundred years, and then doubled to four billion by the 1970s. It has reached over six billion today, and is projected to climb to nine billion by 2050.

The chances are fairly high that most of the additional three billion people will belong to the world's poor as population stabilizes or declines throughout the middle income and richer societies. The poor, the disenfranchised, and the oppressed have little stake in the way the modern world works, and provide a deep reservoir of support for opponents of the new world order. Globalization and the modern world thus have their enemies. From the time the Tupi Amerindians ran into the Brazilian forests to avoid being enslaved to work Portuguese sugar plantations, people have resisted the new forces infringing on their world. That Osama bin Laden and al Qaeda find support among vast numbers of poor Muslims throughout the world who see them as "freedom fighters" should not surprise us, nor that some clearly identify the face of the fourth wave of globalization—the United States—as their foe.

Paradoxically, although the United States has defined al Qaeda as "terrorists," or nonstate actors who have attacked a state, the U.S. "war on terror" is waged through the system of sovereign states. The United States attacked Afghanistan in 2002 not because its Taliban leaders were terrorists (the United States had earlier supported the Taliban as the best hope for ousting a pro-Russian regime), but because the Taliban refused to control the actions of those within its borders—al Qaeda—and turn them over to the United States for prosecution. Similarly, the United States cannot send troops into Pakistan to search for bin Laden and the remnants of al Qaeda because Pakistan is a sovereign state and its leader, President Pervez Musharaf, is wary of what will happen to his regime should bin Laden be captured on Pakistani soil.

The nation–state and the state system, even as mediated through the United Nations, thus appear to remain the framework through which much global business is and will continue to be conducted in the foreseeable future. And that business, for the most part, consists of extending and protecting the capitalist global order economically, financially, and militarily.

As we have seen in this book, the biological old regime placed limits on human societies and the size of human populations. The Industrial Revolution and the use of fossil fuels have relieved those limits, ushering in a period of unprecedented economic and population growth. But does the new regime—the world that we now live in—also have ecological limits? Mostly, we act as if there are none; fossil fuel use continues to climb both with the population and the rapid industrialization of China and India, probably with rather dire, but as yet unknown, environmental consequences.

Global warming surely is but one of many emerging signs that we are pressing the limits, just as such signs appeared in the biological old regime. Nineteenth-century Chinese, faced with limited land for agriculture and raw materials for industry, lavished more and more labor on small plots of land to grow food. Similarly, we now could try to keep squeezing more and more drops out of declining oil and natural gas deposits. There is no guarantee that a new round of innovation comparable to the Industrial Revolution will loosen the energy constraints that are beginning to limit further extension or elaboration of the mass consumption/automobile/fossil fuel economy that has been constructed over the past century. Perhaps reflection on the historically contingent nature of the world we live in will enable us to make the choices—and take actions—that will ensure a sustainable future for all humanity.

Index

accidents, historical, 10, 12, 111
Acheh, 45, 50, 63
Aden, 34, 49, 50
Africa, 55–57; decolonization of, 168; empires in, 57, 71; European imperialism in, 142–44; European view of, 3; as Islamic world, 55; political situations, 56; Portuguese trade with, 61; poverty in, 2, 181, 196n25; trade goods from, 50, 55, 56
agency, 11
agricultural revolution, 22, 24–25, 95, 117–18. See also biological old regime
agricultural surplus, 25, 26, 132
agricultural yields; nitrogen and, 157; population growth and, 159
agriculture, 38–39, 117–18; cash crops, 128, 130; effect on ecosystems, 29; global poverty and, 181; industrialization of, 132; labor-intensive, 107; main crops, 22; productivity, 7, 97, 103, 200. See also food production
al Qaeda, 187–88, 206
Alexandria, 34, 53
Algeria, independence of, 169
Angola, independence of, 169
anthroposphere, 189, 192
America. See United States
Americas, 70; conquest by Spanish, 74–82; empires in, 71–74; population

of, 71–72, 77. See also Aztecs; colonies; Inca; New World
ammonia, synthesis of, 158; fertilizer and, 158–59. See also synthetic fertilizer
Appleby, Joyce, 10
Arabic, 47, 49, 52, 53. See also languages
armies, 27. See also military power; war
Arrow War, 128
Asia, 4; agricultural productivity of, 7, 97, 103, 156; comparability with Europe, 5, 6; decolonization of, 168; as economic engine, 10–11, 80; European view of, 3; goods from, 11, 12, 16, 112; industrial superiority of, 6, 7; population, 7, 80–81, 123–24; poverty in, 2; silver and (see silver); societal variation in, 6
Aurangzeb, 71, 99
Austria, 71, 79
Austria-Hungary, World War I and, 160
automobiles, 174–75, 200
Aztecs (Mexica), 3, 24, 40n5, 44, 72; empire of, 72–73

Baghdad, 26, 33, 44; Mongol destruction of, 54; trade route location, 34
Balkans, 141
Barbados, 83
Battle of Chaldiran, 70
Battle of Obdurman, 143
Battle of Plassey, 99

Battuta, Ibn, 52–53, 55
Beijing, 45, 69
Bengal, 51, 99, 129
Bey, Osman, 54
bin Laden, Osama, ix, 187–88, 206
biological old regime, 22, 22–32, 126,
    135, 200; constraints of, 101–2, 104–5,
    106, 206; evading constraints of, 110,
    118, 136, 202; nitrogen and, 157;
    stresses on, 148
biosphere, 192
Black Death, 21, 32, 36–38, 58;
    population decline and, 23, 37–38, 39.
    See also disease
Bolshevik Revolution, 161–62. See also
    Lenin, V. I.; Russia
books, 53
boom-and-bust cycle, 136
Braudel, Fernand, 18n23, 124–25
Brazil, 82, 148
Britain, 68, 91–92, 141; Chinese trade
    with, 112–17; coal resources, 96,
    108–12, 126; colonial policies, 128,
    130, 147, 149; colonization of Africa,
    142–43; colonization of India, 129;
    competitive advantages, 88, 89–90,
    101; debt, 86–87; decolonization of
    India and, 167–68; export markets, 99,
    107–8; French conflicts with, 98, 108;
    imports, 81; military power, 131; New
    World periphery advantage, 100–101,
    107; opium trading by (see opium);
    preeminence in Europe, 92; textile
    industry in, 96, 98–101, 108, 118, 129;
    World War I and, 160–61; World War
    II and, 165. See also Industrial
    Revolution
Bruges, 34
Bukhara, 34
Byzantine empire, 79

Cabral, Alvares, 62
Caffa, 34, 37
Cairo, 26, 34, 44, 56
Calicut, 34, 45, 49, 50, 62
Cambay, 34, 49
cannon, 58–60. See also military power

capital, 158; accumulation of, 86–87, 88,
    102; crisis of, 165; permanent, 98;
    private, 132; state-provided, 134
capitalism: cultural values necessary for, 4,
    5; as European phenomenon, 4, 18n23;
    global, 127–30, 137, 161; industrial,
    13, 155, 158, 159; marketplace, 7; as
    progress, 3; resistance to, 139. See also
    consumerism, Great Depression
Catherine the Great, 69
CENTO (Central Treaty Organization),
    177
Champagne (France), 33
Charles V (Spain), 79, 80
Chernobyl, 173
childbearing, 14
children in workforce, 110, 127, 138. See
    also labor
Chile, 158
China, 24, 43–48, 50; agricultural
    productivity, 103–4; biological old
    regime limits on, 106; British trade
    with, 112–17; city size, 26; climate
    change and, 40n4; comparability with
    Europe, 57, 123; corruption in, 71;
    economic output, 2; environmental
    problems of, 173; European
    imperialism in, 144–45; European view
    of, 4; expansion after 1500, 68, 69;
    exports, 81; family size, 14, 102–4, 106;
    GDP share, 123–24; Han empire, 32;
    industry in, 119n1; maritime and naval
    ventures, 45–48, 62; markets in, 103,
    105–7, 125; market reforms of, 185;
    military power, 144–45; monetary
    system, 12, 16–17, 79–82, 127, 200
    (see also silver); oil consumption of,
    189; opium in, 114–15 (see also
    opium); peasant revolts in, 32; People's
    Republic of, 168–69, 173–74; plague
    in, 32, 36, 38; planned economy of,
    173–74; political goals, 45, 47–48;
    population and population growth, 24,
    104, 123–24, 178; Portuguese trade
    with, 63; role in world history, 16;
    twentieth-century rise of, 194; rural
    poverty in, 178, 196n25; succession in

1400s, 43–44; technological advantage of, 63; textiles from, 38, 81, 107 (*see also* textiles); tigers in, 28; trade concessions, 117, 144, 145, 157; trade control by, 92; trade goods, 50; trade needs, 51, 114; trade restrictions, 113; trade routes, 49; trade with the United States, 186

Churchill, Winston, 143

cities, 25; in Latin America, 92n5; maintenance of, 105; population concentration in, 137–38; relationship to countryside, 22, 24; size, 26; state building and, 88, 94n27; trading, 49

citizenry, 140

city–states, 72, 84, 86. See also Genoa; Venice

civilizations, 22, 24; agriculturally based, 27; centers of, 50; characteristics defining, 25; clash of, ix, 185, 187–88; comparability of, 156; fall of, 27

climate and climate change, 12, 23, 37, 136, 191; in China, 40n4; as resource limit, 64. See also environment

Clive, Robert, 99

coal, 95, 101; accident of deposition, 12, 111, 126, 157. See also Britain; Industrial Revolution

coffee, 148

Colbert, Jean-Baptiste, 88

Cold War, 156, 166, 167, 170–71, 177, 193, 202; end of, 182–84

Cologne (Germany), 26

colonialism, 6; end of, 169

colonies: advantage from, 100–101, 107; Asian lack of, 118; British, 98–101; competition for, 131, 137; French, 91–92; independence movements in, 162; Industrial Revolution role of, 111; land available in, 111; as markets, 101; New World, 96 (*see also* New World); trade restrictions on, 100

colonization, 35; avoiding, 134; exploitation after, 77, 82

Columbus, Christopher, 5, 11, 33, 43, 44; Portuguese rejection of, 62; reasons for voyage, 79–80

commodities, 16

communication, 140–41

Compagnie des Indies, 98, 112

comparative advantage, 130

competition, open, 18n23, 137

competitive advantage, 88, 89–90, 97, 101

Confucius, 65n2

conjuncture, 10, 12–13, 96, 200, 201; Black Death and, 36–38; Industrial Revolution and, 102; structural change and, 21; twentieth century and, 155, 156

Constantinople, 26, 34, 44; conquest of, 54, 59, 79

consumer society, 174–76

consumer tastes, 64, 119n5

consumerism, 171, 174–76

contingency, 10–11, 18n18, 151, 200–201; United States rise as, xiii–xiv, 193

core, 22, 35

corporations, 98

Cortéz, Hernan, 74–75

cotton, 16, 38, 50; in China, 106–7; export to Africa, 55; Indian (*see* Indian textiles); from New World, 100, 108, 111, 132; textiles, 96–101 (*see also* textiles)

countries, 1. See also nation–states; state system (European)

credit, 175

Crimean War, 142

Crompton, Samuel, 109

Cuban Missile Crisis, 171

culture, 6; exchanges of, 36; universal applicability of European, 8

Curtin, Philip D., 16n4

Cuzco, 44, 78

da Gama, Vasco, 5, 11, 33, 43, 44; Portuguese commission of, 62; reasons for voyage, 79–80

dar al-Islam, 53, 203. See also Islamic world

Darwin, Charles, 150

Davis, Mike, 149

decolonization, 167–68. See also colonies; colonization; empires

deforestation, 108, 110–11, 147–48, 191–92
Delhi sultanate, 52
democracy, 3, 7, 87
Deng Xiaoping, 186
depression, 136
determinism, 11–12, 18n18; geographical, 40n4
development, 169–70, 178–79; critique of, 192
developmentalism, 176–80. *See also* third world
Dias, Bartolomeu, 61
Dickens, Charles, 108, 138
disasters, natural, 30, 157
disease, 3, 11, 156; in Africa, 142–43; epidemic, 30, 32, 76–77; paths of transmission, 36, 38, 76; smallpox, 75. *See also* Black Death
dominance, Western. *See* Western dominance; *see also* Eurocentrism; rise of the West
duties. *See* tariffs

East Asia, rise of, 193–94, 196n21, 205
East India Company (EIC), 98–99, 112; colonization by, 129; warships, 116
Easter Island, 192
economic change, 4
economic growth, 1, 106; and environmental change, 190; Cold War and, 171; environmental damage by, 191–92
economic output, 1
economy, 82–83; biological old regime, 102; industrial, 136; productivity of, 95
education, 138, 141
el Niño droughts, 125, 130, 148–49, 202
elites. *See* ruling elites
empires, 26, 33, 140; African, 57, 71; agrarian, 13; American, 71–74; Asian, 32, 68, 155 (*see also* China; India; Japan); Aztec (*see* Aztecs); British, 98–101, 131; commonalities of, 71; Eurasian, 68; European, 78–79; expansion of, 68–74; Holy Roman, 79; Incan (*see* Inca); Islamic (*see* Islamic

world); Mali, 44, 55; Mamluk, 33, 54; Mongol (*see* Mongols and Mongol empire); Mughal (*See* Mughal empire); Ottoman, 54, 59, 68, 70, 141; Roman, 32, 58; Safavid, 54, 68, 70; sixteenth-century, 67–68; Spanish (*see* Spain)
energy, 188–89; from colonies, 126; fuel, 38, 110–11; sources of, 11, 12, 95, 108–10; supplies, 29, 118, 157. *See also* biological old regime; coal; fossil fuels; oil
Engels, Friedrich, 4, 139
England. *See* Britain
environment, 22, 38; human-caused change in, 82, 83, 148, 156, 189–90; limits of, 11, 102; population limits and, 160–61; third world and, 146–49. *See also* biological old regime; climate and climate change
epistemology, 10
ethnic cleansing, 185
ethnocentrism, 8
eugenics, 150–51
Eurocentrism, 8–9, 16, 43, 199; avoiding, 14, 125, 155; re Industrial Revolution, 96
Europe, 24; armed trade by, 50, 57–63; as Christian empire, 54–55; comparability with Asia/China, 5, 6, 57–58, 123; end of global dominance by, 156; internal competition, 82, 83–84, 89; as minor trader, 43; peripheral position of, 82; political units in, 58–60 (*see also* state system [European]); societal variation in, 6; state formation in (*see* state system [European]); trade goods from, 60, 64; World War I and, 160–62; World War II and, 165–66
European superiority/exceptionalism, 3, 5, 6
expansionism as progress, 4

family size, 30, 137, 138; in China, 14, 102–4, 106
famine, 30–31, 150, 157; el Niño droughts and, 125, 148–49
Feng, Wang, 104

Ferdinand (Spain), 59, 87
fertilizer, global nitrogen cycle and, 190–91
feudalism, 6
Fez, 26, 44
First World War. See World War I
food, cost of, 97
food producers. See peasants
food production: Asian capacity for, 97; climate and, 23, 136; development and, 178–79; land available for, 29–30, 37, 39; land's capacity for, 29; in New World, 100; surpluses, 24, 70. See also agriculture; Green Revolution
fortifications, 60
fossil fuel, 188–89; global warming and, 191; globalization and, 186
France, 59, 84; British conflicts with, 98, 108; colonies and, 168–69; competitive advantages, 88, 89–90; exclusion from markets, 112; industrialization of, 131–32; peasant revolts in, 32; tariffs, 136; World War I and, 161
Franco-Prussian War, 142
Frank, Andre Gunder, x, xi
free trade, 7, 17n8; British endorsement of, 100–101, 115, 117, 130; global, 1; globalization and, 186–87; retreat from, 136, 163–65; as third world creation factor, 130, 131; U.S. endorsement of, 145, 186
French Revolution, 3, 32, 87, 140

Gandhi, Mohandas, 162
gap between rich and poor, 2, 123–51; ecological factors in, 146–49; emergence of, 124–26; Eurocentric explanations of, 125; as global defining characteristic, 9; intrasocietal, 126, 140; resentment of, 161; resistance to, 162; social Darwinism and, 150; theories re, 4–6; twentieth-century growth of, 180–81
GDP. See gross domestic production
Genoa, 1, 33, 37, 44, 56; trade route location, 34; trade wars of, 60–61
geography as resource limit, 64

Germany, 79, 86, 136; Chinese holdings, 145; industrialization of, 132–33, 179; unification of, 140–41, 142; World War I and, 159–61; World War II and, 165–66
Ghana, 55
global warming, 191, 206
globalization, 1, 22, 67, 156; ages of, 12; China and, 186–87; demise of Soviet Union and, 185, 204; enemies of, 206; free trade and, 186–87; origins of, 203; stages of, 203–205; United States and, 204
Glorious Revolution (England), 88, 101
gold, 55–56, 75, 78
Gorbachev, Mikhail, 184
governance, 4; bureaucracy, 69, 70, 86, 140; Incan, 73; weak, 149
Granada, 44, 59
Great Departure, the, 189–92
Great Depression, 163–65, 166, 174, 202
Greeks, ancient, 3, 6, 112
Green revolution, 178–79
gross domestic production (GDP), 123–24, 151n1
Group of Seven (G7), 1, 16n1, 186, 203
growth: economic, 1, 106; environmental/ecological limits on, 11, 102; population (see population growth); potential for, 96
Guangzhou, 45, 49, 63, 113
guano, 158. See also fertilizer; nitrogen cycle
Gujarat, 51
gunpowder, 54, 157–59
guns. See military power

Haber, Fritz, 158
Haber-Bosch process, 158, 190. See also fertilizer, gun powder, synthesis of ammonia
Henry of Avis (Henry the Navigator), 61, 62
Hinduism, 52; Indian independence and, 167–68
HIPC (Highly Indebted Poor Counties), 181

history, 11; American, 9; causes in, 13; diffusionist theory of, 5; geographic terminology for, 6–7; global view of, 7, 10, 15–16,200–203; as method, 17n15; scholarship in, 14–15; tools of, 157–58. *See also* narrative
Hitler, Adolf, 151, 165, 166
Ho Chi Minh, 169
Hobson, John M., 154n31
Holland (the Dutch), 86, 89, 98
Holy Roman Empire, 79
Hong Kong, 127, 128,
Hormuz, 34, 45, 47, 49, 50; Portuguese occupation of, 63
Hunt, Lynn, 10

IMF. *See* International Monetary Fund
imperialism, 142, 157; globalization and, 204
import substitution, 107, 128
Inca, 3, 24, 40n5; conquest by Spanish, 74, 75; empire of, 44, 73–74
India, 24, 45, 48–52; agricultural efficiency, 97; British colonization of, 49, 129; comparability with Europe, 123; competitive advantages, 97; deindustrialization of, 108, 129–30; GDP share, 123–24; historical economic output, 2; independence movement in, 162; independence of, 167–68; invasions of, 51–52; as market, 129; Mughal empire in (*see* Mughal empire); oil consumption in, 189; as opium source, 127, 128–29; plague in, 38; political situations, 51–52, 71, 129; population, 24; role in world history, 16, 194; technological advantage of, 63; textiles from (*see* Indian textiles); trade goods, 50; traders from, 49
Indian Ocean, 33; armed trading in, 62–63; Chinese trade through, 47–48, 64; European access to, 53, 62–63; trade history of, 49; trade through, 34, 43, 46–52
Indian textiles, 38, 51; deindustrialization and, 129; demand for, 96–98, 108;

import bans, 81, 100, 129; slavery and, 100
Indochina, 24
Indonesia, 24, 50, 53
industrial production, 135–36
Industrial Revolution, 14, 95–118; balance of power and, 92; Britain and, 201; causes of, 13; contingencies underlying, 15, 200–201; cost reduction by, 129; factors in, 96, 101–2, 107–12; in rise-of-the-West narrative, 3
industrialization, 13, 89, 102, 131–35, 155; contingencies underlying, 112; effects of, 135–39, 201, 202; major industrialized countries, 1; population growth and, 23; state's role in, 131, 179; war and, 117; working class, 108
industry, 88; circa 1400, 30; dependence on natural resources, 95; as global defining characteristic, 9; mechanization of, 110
industries, new twentieth-century, 155, 172, 174–76
infant/child mortality, 30. *See also* life expectancies
institutions, universal applicability of, 7
interactions, in the making of the modern world, 63, 199–200
International Monetary Fund (IMF), 2, 181, 186, 203
Internet, 42n28
iron/steel production, 101, 109, 110–11, 119n1, 133
Isabella (Spain), 59, 87
Islam, 11, 47, conflicts within, 70
Islamic world, 52–55; Abbasid, 54; Chinese relations with, 47; circa 1500, 44–45; empires of, 70, 161; expansion of, 49, 52, 64; oil in, 187–88; plague in, 38; trade goods, 50; trade route control by, 61; West Asia, 24
Istanbul, 44, 54. *See also* Constantinople
Italy, 79, 136, 142, 144. *See also* Genoa; Venice
Ivan IV (Ivan the Terrible), 69

Jacob, Margaret, 10
Jamaica, 83
Japan, 2, 24, 69; defeats Russia in 1905,
    157; Great Depression and, 164–65;
    imperialism of, 145, 155, 156, 164–65,
    195n9; 195n12; industrialization, 131,
    134–35, 179; natural resources, 134;
    peasant revolts, 31–32; tariffs, 134,
    135, 136; trading partners, 63; U.S.
    Occupation of, 166; workforce
    composition, 138; World War II and,
    165–66
Java, 69, 98
Jedda (Jiddah), 34, 47

Kashmir, 167–68
Kilwa, 44, 49
Korea, 24, 69, 145
Korean War, 171
Koumbi-Saleh, 55
Kuhn, Thomas, 17n14

labor: allocation of, 105, 118; conflicts
    with management/owners, 138–39;
    cost of, 158; demand for, 112;
    discipline of workers, 138; sexual
    division of, 107; shortages, 77, 78, 100,
    111; worker revolts, 139, 140. See also
    slavery
labor unions, 135
land: availability for food production, 23,
    73, 104–5; necessities from, 104;
    saving, 110; shortages, 111, 118; use
    choices, 128
landowners, 26, 31, 86; Chinese, 144;
    church as, 41n18
languages, 71, 73, 132–33; in nation-
    building, 140–41
Latin America, 3; deforestation, 148;
    poverty in, 2. See also Aztecs; colonies;
    Inca; Spain
League of Nations, 163
Lebensraum, 29
Lee, James, 104
Lenin, V. I., 162
Leopold II (Belgium), 143
libraries, 53

life expectancies, 30, 123, 149
Lin Zexu, 115
loans, 86
Los Angeles, 175

Ma Huan, 47
Macao, 63
Macartney, George, 92, 113–14, 117
MAD (mutually assured destruction), 167
Madras, 45, 51, 99, 129
Malacca, 34, 45, 49; Dutch takeover, 98;
    Portuguese occupation, 63; trade goods
    through, 50
Mali empire, 44, 55
Malthus, Thomas, 3, 4, 5, 103
Mamluk empire, 33, 54
management, 138
Manchester (England), 99, 100, 101
market economies, 18n23, 102, 156;
    China, 105–7, 125
markets, free. See free trade
Martinique, 83
Marx, Karl, 4, 5, 139, 172
master narrative, 10, 18n16
material conditions circa 1400, 21, 22
Maxim, Hiram, 143
Maya, 72, 73
McCormick, Cyrus, 132
Mecca, 44, 47
Mediterranean Sea trade, 34; armed,
    60–61; Islamic domination of, 53
Menelik, King (Ethiopia), 144
mercantilism, 88–90, 98, 100–101
Mexico, 3, 72; population growth in, 178.
    See also Aztecs
Middle East, oil and, 179–80
migration, 29, 180
military power, 2, 13; British, 131;
    Chinese, 144–45; energy sources in,
    11; goods related to, 25; gunpowder
    weaponry, 54, 58–60, 63; guns, 125,
    132, 143, 150; innovation for, 156;
    Japanese, 135; for migration support,
    30; of nomads, 27; prerequisites for,
    135; Russia, 133; uses of, 31, 58;
    warships/gunboats, 116–17, 135, 157;
    weaponry sources, 89. See also war

Millennium Development Goals, 196n27
Millennium Ecosystem Assessment, 190
Ming dynasty, 43, 46, 69
Moctezuma II, 75
modernization, 4–5, 16n4; obstacles to, 6;
    opposition to, 161–62
Mogadishu, 44, 49
monetary systems, 46; Chinese (see
    China); gold and, 56; money shortages,
    88–89. See also silver
Mongols and Mongol empire, 33, 36, 37;
    Chinese campaigns against, 44;
    collapse of, 46, 48, 61; Islamic areas
    and, 54; location, 45; plague in, 37, 38,
    58; weaponry, 58–59
monopolies, 98, 131; EIC in Asia, 130;
    need for, 101; opium, 127
Moscow, 69
Mozambique, 44
Mughal empire, 54, 68, 70, 71; decline,
    92, 99, 112, 129, 156
Musa, Mansa, 55–56
Muscat, 34
Muslim nationalism, 167–68, 188
myths and mythology: Eurocentrism as,
    8–9; harm from, 15

Nanjing (China), 26, 45
Napoleon, 140
narrative, 9–16, 200–203; historical,
    17–18n16; Marxist, 18–19n25; non-
    Eurocentric, 15–16, 35. See also history
nation-states, 2, 7, 9, 155; development
    of, 13, 140; as global defining
    characteristic, 9, 159; modern, 141; as
    unit of historical analysis, 33
national debt, 86–87
nationalism, 140–42; anti-imperialism
    and, 162–63; differences in Europe and
    third world, 162–63
nations, 141; language and, 132–33
Native Americans, 11, 39; depopulation
    of, 76–77; resistance to invaders,
    75–76
NATO. See North Atlantic Treaty
    Organization
nature, 111

Nemesis, 116–17
New Imperialism, 137
New World: as British periphery,
    100–101, 107; economy, 82–83;
    exports, 100, 112 (see also cotton;
    silver); foods from, 76; as market, 99,
    112; natural resources of, 23, 64, 127.
    See also colonies; Latin America;
    United States
Newcomen, Thomas, 109
Niani, 55
nitrates, 157, 158
nitrogen cycle, 157, 190–91
nomads, 22, 26, 27–28; areas controlled
    by, 30; as raiders, 25, 68; threat from,
    71; Turkish, 54
North Atlantic Treaty Organization
    (NATO), 2, 177, 185

oil, 155; Middle East and, 188; war and,
    189
Olmecs, 72
OPEC. See Organization of Petroleum
    Exporting Countries
open trade. See free trade
opium, 114–15, 125, 137; Chinese
    demand for, 127, 130
Opium Wars, 115–17, 127, 144, 201
Organization of Petroleum Exporting
    Countries, 179–80
Ottoman empire, 54, 59, 68, 70, 141, 159,
    161

Pakistan, 167–68, 195n10
Palembang, 34
paradigms, 9, 17n14
parasites, macro- and micro-, 32. See also
    disease
Paris, 26, 44
Peace of Westphalia, 84
peasant revolts, 31–32
peasants, 22, 23, 32; production choices,
    106–7, 108, 128; rights of, 31; Russian,
    133
pentimento, 8, 135
periphery, 22, 35; New World as,
    100–101, 107

Perry, Matthew, 134
Persia, 70. *See also* Safavid empire
Peru, 73, 158
Peter the Great, 69
Philip II (Spain), 79, 80, 94n31
Philippines, 67, 80, 145
Pizarro, Francisco, 74, 75
plague. *See* Black Death; *see also* disease
planned economies, 172–74
planned obsolescence, 174–75
plantation system, 82, 100, 148
Poivre, Pierre, 103
Poland, 86
Polo, Marco, 33
polycentrism, 22, 35
Pomeranz, Kenneth, x, xi, 110
population, 22, 22–23; under biological old regime, 95; civilization and, 24; counts of, 25, 39; declines, 38; global, 205; twentieth-century increase in, 195n6
population density/concentrations, 24, 26, 28; in cities, 137–38
population growth, 37, 159; constraints on, 23, 38, 39; development and, 177–78; land and, 29–30, 103–4
Portugal, 89, 144; plantation system, 82; trade explorations by, 61–62; trade route control by, 62–63, 80
Potosí, 44, 78
poverty, 2, 14, 124; global indicators of, 180–81, 182–83. *See also* gap between rich and poor
power, 2, 60; balance of, 90, 92, 153n22; economic, 50–51; state, 101, 118; world structure of, 43. *See also* energy
priests, 25
production increases, 39, 105, 118
productionism, 171–74
profits, 98, 100, 130; from opium, 137
progress, 3
property rights, private, 102
protectionism, 97, 101, 136
Puri, 50

Qing dynasty, 69
quinine, 125, 142

racism, 142, 150, 151
railroads and railways, 109, 125, 140; American, 132; Chinese, 145; French, 131; Russian, 133–34
rationalism, 4
raw materials, 25
Reagan, Ronald, 184
rebellions, 71. *See also* peasant revolts
recession, 136
Red Sea, 63
religion: conflicts within, 70; as divisive force, 52; Mexican, 93n8; rulership claims based on, 87. *See also* Islam; Islamic world
rents, 26, 30, 31
resources: climatic and geographic constraints on, 64; management of, 125; mobilization of, 70; raw materials, 25, 38; wildlife, 28–29
revolts. *See* peasant revolts; *see also* rebellions
revolution, 25, 119n2
Ricardo, David, 3, 5, 130
rise of the West, 2, 3–8, 199–200; as inevitable, 10, 157; as master narrative, 9–10, 14–15, 151; timing of, 5–6; values inherent in, 7; voyages of discovery and, 43. *See also* Western dominance
rodents, 36–37
Roman empire, 32, 58
Romanov dynasty, 69
ruling elites, 22; food supply protection by, 25, 27; Incan empire, 73–74; indirect power assertions, 71; material support of, 26, 70; nation/state identification, 141; right to rule, 87; trade protection by, 35
Russia, 68–69, 141, 152n10; industrialization of, 131, 133–34; natural resources of, 133; peasant revolts in, 32; Revolution of 1917, 160–62; tariffs, 136; wars with Japan, 145. *See also* Soviet Union

Saddam Hussein, 187
Safavid empire, 54, 68, 70

Samarkand, 26, 34, 45
science, 111–12, 133, 150, 155, 157, 172
SEATO. *See* Southeast Asia Treaty
    Organization
Second World War. *See* World War II
Seminoles, 44, 75
September 11, 2001, ix, 187–88
Seven Years' War (French and Indian
    War), 84, 90–92, 99, 112, 156
silk, 38, 50, 105, 134–35
silver: Asian demand for, 10, 12, 16, 51,
    79–82, 127; Britain–China flow of,
    113–15, 120n33, 127, 130; in Chinese
    monetary system, 12, 46–47, 80, 200;
    New World sources of, 11, 12, 77–78,
    127; role in world economy, 80
Singapore, 159
slavery, 6, 56–57, 93–94n23; plantation
    system and, 82–83, 156; textiles' link
    to, 100, 108
slaves: African, 55, 56–57; as basis of
    wealth, 56; clothing needs, 100; as
    commodity, 16, 57; sources of, 11, 57
Slavs, 57
Smith, Adam, 3, 4, 5, 103, 130
social classes, 108, 140; conflicts, 139;
    middle class, 138; non-food-producing,
    25; working class, 108, 127, 137–38,
    140
social conventions, 64
social Darwinism, 150–51, 155
social science, 5
Song dynasty, 46
Southeast Asia Treaty Organization, 177
sovereign states. *See* state system
    (European); *see also* nation–states
Soviet Union, 202; anticolonial ideology
    of, 166–67; Cold War and, 170; as
    defining feature of twentieth century,
    193; end of, 167, 184–86;
    environmental problems in, 173; Great
    Depression and, 165; planned economy
    of, 171–74; reform of, 184; science in,
    172; World War II and, 165
Spain, 59, 62, 67, 84; conquests in
    Americas, 67, 74–76; empire-building
    attempts, 68, 79, 89, 112; resources

from Americas, 77–79; War of Spanish
    Succession, 90
specialization, 39, 105, 106, 107
Spencer, Herbert, 150
spices, 11, 60–61, 112
standards of living, 29, 97, 110; under
    biological old regime, 156; in
    eighteenth century, 123
state legitimacy, 140
state system (European), 59, 84–92, 112,
    131; development of, 67, 68, 168;
    results of, 140; terrorism and, 206; war
    as factor in, 68. *See also* nation–states
states, industrialization and, 131, 134–35,
    149; nationalism and, 139–42
steam engines, 101, 108–11, 117, 157. *See
    also* energy
steppe, 27, 37
subsistence levels, 31
sugar, 16, 82–83, 111; production method,
    100, 148
supply and demand, 16, 136
Swahili, 56
Sweden, 86
synthesis of ammonia, 190. *See also* Haber-
    Bosch process
synthetic fertilizer, 156, 157–59, 190

Taiping Rebellion, 144
Taiwan, 98, 145
Tang dynasty, 46, 49
tariffs, 89, 97–98, 100, 129; economic
    slumps and, 136; German, 133; lifting,
    131; limitation of Japanese, 134, 135,
    136; Russian, 134; United States, 132
taxes, 25, 26, 30; agricultural surplus as,
    31; church tithes, 41n18; from
    colonies, 99, 129; payment form, 46;
    for wars, 86
tea, 97, 113–14
technology, 111; agricultural, 29;
    exchanges of, 36; industrial, 125; trade
    advantage from, 63–64; twentieth-
    century, 158; of war, 6, 59, 75, 143,
    153n22
Tenochtitlán, 44, 72–73, 74, 78
terrorism, 196–97n35, 206

textiles, 30, 38, 50, 81–82; biological old regime limits and, 101; British (*see* Britain); Chinese production of, 38, 81, 107; cotton, 96–101; German, 133; Indian (*see* Indian textiles); Japanese, 134–35; mechanization of industry, 100, 109–10; slavery's link to, 100, 108; U.S., 132; workforce composition, 110

third world, 124, 151–52n4, 176–80, 202; competition for, 142; creation of, 126, 146, 149; India's status as, 130

Thirty Years' War, 79, 84

Thirty-Year Crisis, 156, 159–66. *See also* Great Depression, World War I, World War II

Thornton, John, 56

tigers, 28, 29

Tilly, Charles, 84

Timbuktu, 44, 55

Timur the Lame, 52

tobacco, 100

Toltecs, 72

trade: armed, 50, 57–63, 64, 80; economic engine of, 10, 50–51; embargoes, 81, 88; free (*see* free trade); government regulation of, 106 (*see also* tariffs); long-distance, 32; luxury items, 64, 97; market specialization, 39; necessity of, 25; pace of, 32, 38; protection of, 35, 46, 52; as regional link, 35–36, 64; restrictions on, 88, 97–98, 99, 113, 129 (*see also* tariffs); self-regulation of, 49–50; surpluses, 137; technological advantage in, 63–64; triangles, 83, 100, 121n37; war and, 98, 117

trade routes, 33; China–New World, 67; Europe–Asia direct, 61–62; Indian Ocean and, 43, 46–52; Mongol empire and, 61; Spanish access to, 80

trading companies, private, 98–99

trading networks in Old World, 21, 32, 33–36, 63–64; control of, 64; European regional, 37; subsystems, 33, 34

trading zones, 33, 34

transportation, 105, 106. *See also* railroads and railways

Treaty of Nanjing, 116–17

Treaty of Utrecht, 90

tribute systems, 69, 72–73, 74

Triple Entente, 160

Trocki, Carl, 130

truth, 9, 17–18n16

Tupi, 82, 206

twentieth century, 155–56, 193; as major break with the past, 189, 193; uniqueness of, 159, 193

United States, 155, 202: anticolonial ideology, 166–67; British trade with, 101; Chinese relations with, 159–60; Civil War, 132, 142, 143; Cold War and, 170–71; consumer society of, 174–76; exceptionalism of critiqued, 200; fertilizer use, 158, 190–91; Great Depression in, 163–64; industrialization of, 132; as linchpin of global economy, 187; Occupation of Japan, 166; opium trading by, 127–28; post–World War I "normalcy" and, 163; World War I and, 160–61; World War II and, 165–66; War of Independence, 91, 101, 112. *See also* New World

United Nations, 170, 185

values, 4, 7: universal applicability of, 7, 8

Venice, 33, 34, 37, 44, 56; trade wars of, 60–61

Vereenigde Oost-Indische Compagnie (VOC), 98, 112

Versailles Peace Conference and Treaty, 161

Viet Minh, 169

Vietnam (Annam), 45, 69, 153n22, 169

Vijayanagar (India), 26

war, 30, 36, 58, 59; causes of, 142; costs of, 86, 89; industrialization of, 117, 157; interstate, 68, 80, 84–86, 92, 112, 156; private armies, 99, 129, 144; technology of, 6, 59, 75, 143, 153n22; trade and, 98, 117. *See also* military power

War of Spanish Succession, 90
warriors, 25, 72
Washington, George, 91
Watt, James, 109
wealth, 1, 60; agriculturally based, 136; of
    American empires, 73, 74; of Asia, 4;
    definition of, 26; land as basis of, 56;
    rich–poor gap (*see* gap between rich
    and poor); sources of, 127; world
    structure of, 43
Weber, Max, 4, 5
Western dominance, 2, 146, 149–50, 155;
    Eurocentrism and, 8; as inevitable, 10.
    See also rise of the West
White Lotus Rebellion, 71
Whitney, Eli, 100
wildlife, 28–29
Williams, Michael, 153n27
Witte, Sergei, 133–34
wolves, 28, 29
women, 174, 176; household work, 107,
    138; in workforce, 110, 127, 138
Wong, R. Bin, 202

wool, 38, 64
work ethic, 4
workers. *See* labor; *see also* children; women
World Bank, 181, 183
World Health Organization, 178
world regions, interactions of, 15
world systems: circa 1400, 21–39; circa
    1760, 90–91; circa 1900, 145–46;
    conflict of, 68; connections among, 33,
    35, 38; controlling central force in, 35,
    42n28; polycentric, 22, 64; structures
    in, 21
World Trade Centers, September 11
    attack on, 187–88
World Trade Organization (WTO), 1,
    203; free trade and, 186
World War I, 156, 157, 159–61
World War II, 156, 165–66, 204
writing, 25, 73
WTO. *See* World Trade Organization

Zaytun, 34
Zheng He, 45, 46–48, 50, 52, 62, 64

About the Author

Robert B. Marks is Richard and Billie Deihl Professor of History at Whittier College and the author of *Tigers, Rice, Silk, and Silt: Environment and Economy in Late Imperial China* (Cambridge University Press, 1998). In 1996 he received the Aldo Leopold Award for the best article in the journal *Environmental History* and has published numerous other articles on China's environmental history. Holding his position at a college that focuses on undergraduate education, Marks regularly teaches a course for entering college students on the origins of the modern world, and in 2000 received Whittier College's Harry W. Nerhood Teaching Excellence Award.